IMAGES
of America

CAMDEN COUNTY

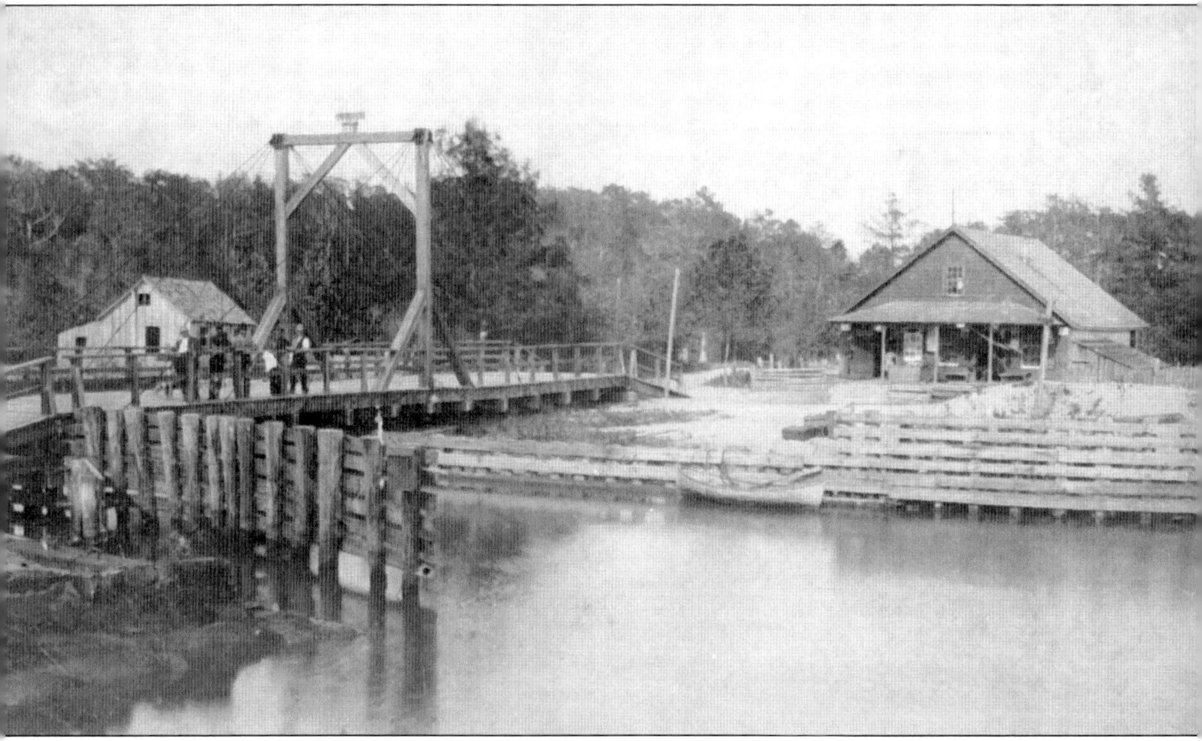

River Bridge was built across the Pasquotank River in the early 1800s north of Turner's Cut, and the D.S. Williams Store was on the eastern side, which was known as Joppa. The original bridge was destroyed by Union troops during the Civil War, and this photograph was taken from the west side at the end of Bingham Road shortly after the bridge had been rebuilt. (Courtesy of Joyce and Durward Medlin.)

On the Cover: In 1915, the Old Trap School was one of many neighborhood schools. In 1920, this school was replaced by a brick, two-story school building that only operated as a school until about 1930, when Old Trap students began to ride the bus to Shiloh. The goat cart was for transporting Elsie Leary, who had been crippled by an outbreak of polio, which devastated the community and crippled children. (Courtesy of Vernon Burgess Jr.)

IMAGES
of America

CAMDEN COUNTY

A. Burgess Jennings

ARCADIA
PUBLISHING

ISBN 978-1-4671-2209-2

Published by Arcadia Publishing
Charleston, South Carolina

Printed in the United States of America

Library of Congress Control Number: 2013957398

For all general information, please contact Arcadia Publishing:
Telephone 843-853-2070
Fax 843-853-0044
E-mail sales@arcadiapublishing.com
For customer service and orders:
Toll-Free 1-888-313-2665

Visit us on the Internet at www.arcadiapublishing.com

Dedicated to the people of Camden County.

CONTENTS

ACKNOWLEDGMENTS

Everyone knows or can well imagine all the many things my husband, Kevin Jennings, has done and put up with during the writing of this book. Public thanks are in order, although they are surely not adequate. Many individuals have been generous with sharing images and information, and they are Pamela Forbes Host Andrews, Martha Ann, Anna Cahoon Boyce, Betty Brock, Dewey Burgess, Portia Lee and Wilse Burgess, Vernon Burgess Jr., Annette Cuthrell, Joyce Mitchell Cuthrell, Beth and Charlie Forbes, Thelma Naomi Sawyer Forbes, Amy Forehand, Brian Forehand, Steven Forehand, Terry Forehand, Kitty Games, Sarah Forbes Hamilton, Eddie Harrison, Amelia Forbes Host, Miriam Jones James, Bob Jones, Thalia Jones, Sandra and Alex Leary, Linda Ann Mansfield, Joyce McQueen, Joyce and Durward Medlin, Tony Perry, and Anita Whitehurst. There have also been many who encouraged me and answered many questions when I tossed them out there into cyberspace. Several organizations have been very helpful, and I thank KaeLi Schurr, curator; Sarah Downing, assistant curator; Tama Creef, archivist; Stuart Parks II, archivist; and all of the staff at the Outer Banks History Center in Manteo, North Carolina, who were always helpful, pleasant, and efficient in providing me just what I was looking for and fulfilled my requests quickly and accurately. Donna Stewart, director of the Dismal Swamp Canal Welcome Center, went the extra mile to help me locate and obtain scans of rare photographs. Mary Ann Converse of Center Line Digital Printing helped me salvage an important image that I had inherited from Hugh Jones. Gordon Cameron of ICW Consulting set up my operating system and found solutions for my technical inadequacies. Merry Combs of Richmond Camera Shop helped me get some precious old negatives printed. The Family Research Society of Northeastern North Carolina, Inc. provided use of its research library and photograph archives. High-quality images were made available from the Library of Congress, the State Archives of North Carolina, the Wilson Library at the University of North Carolina at Chapel Hill, Camden County Sheriff's Office, and the Camden County Museum. Many good folks, including my hardworking acquisitions editor, Katie McAlpin-Owens, helped in small and big ways that came together to save this much Camden County history.

Introduction

Camden County, North Carolina, reaches like an arm out of the Great Dismal Swamp into the Albemarle Sound with its index finger, Camden Point, indicating the southeastern direction of its orientation. Camden County historian Alex Leary likes to say of Camden Point and its small fishing community, "It is not the end of the world . . . but they say you can see it from there." The county is presently populated by roughly 10,000 persons in 310.21 square miles, 240.56 of which are land and 69.66 of which are water areas. It is in the heart of a valuable estuarine system located in the North Carolina Coastal Plain between Currituck, Pasquotank, and Gates Counties and is bordered by the state of Virginia to the north. Camden County is the site of the southern terminus of the Great Dismal Swamp Canal, begun in 1793 and the oldest surviving artificial waterway in the United States, which runs along US Highway 17 up through Virginia and eventually connects to an inlet running into the Atlantic Ocean. The Dismal Swamp Canal Welcome Center is the only state welcome center known to welcome visitors traveling both by highway and by waterway. There, one can see a small locomotive, called a "loki," once used for lumbering and may access the Dismal Swamp State Park Visitor Center and exhibit hall by a hydraulic arm bridge that spans the Dismal Swamp Canal. One quick stop on Highway 17 just south of the state line can provide the traveler with a wealth of information, including maps, brochures, exhibits, images, and directions thoroughly covering the rich history and both bountiful and beautiful natural areas, the imagery of which this book attempts to capture and preserve.

The Albemarle Sound was once known as Rogues Harbor, where those who found themselves on the wrong side of British law could slip out of view of the agents of the lords proprietors. Pirates like Blue Booten could float up Arenuse Creek, trade with the natives, and smoke their clay tobacco pipes. Planters began to sail their periaugers into Raymond's Creek to clear land for farming and build modest houses. By 1727, Paul Palmer was in the area encouraging locals to establish Shiloh Baptist Church on Portohonk Creek, which became the oldest surviving Baptist church in the state of North Carolina, the charter of which is included within these pages. Four square miles of land on the southwest side of the North River were set aside in 1704 as a reservation for the Yawpim Indian tribe. A map drawn by Mosley in 1733 indicates the Yawpim Village at what became known as Indiantown and includes most of Sandy Hook, where more than one European sailor fell in love with and took a Yawpim, later spelled Yoepim, woman as his wife. The Yawpim had a peaceful relationship with European settlers, and some of them assimilated into European families. Indiantown became a port of entry, and the McKnight Shipyard was located on Indiantown Creek. A winding trip in a small boat from the landing at Indiantown or Crooked Creeks into the undeveloped wildlife refuge today is a trip back in time into the realm of the black bear. Except for the passing of the occasional aircraft, one could experience the swamp as it was thousands of years ago. Black bears and whitetail deer still come up out of the swamp to gorge on milky wheat, roasting ears, and soybeans on the edges of the farmers' fields.

Because of the width of the Pasquotank River, ferries became a necessity for transportation in Camden County. In 1740, a franchise was granted to Samuel Palmer to operate a ferry from

Arnoes Creek to Newbegun Creek on the southwestern side, but the distance was too wide, and his venture failed. Later, John Solley operated a successful one-mile ferry from Chantilly to Relfe's Point until 1777 when the northeast side of the county was formed into Camden County. Enoch Sawyer began to operate a ferry near the courthouse from his house at the Pecan Farm to the mouth of Knobb's Creek. It became known as Lamb's Ferry and remained in operation into the 20th century, until the building of the "floating road" to Elizabeth City in 1923, when it ceased operation. When Camden County was formed, it was named for Sir Charles Pratt, 1st Earl Camden, who opposed the Stamp Act and supported the American revolutionaries. Camden County boasts the oldest standing two-story brick home in North Carolina, which was built by Thomas or William Palin on land deeded to them by their grandfather Thomas Relfe. The house is listed in the National Register of Historic Places and a brick found in the north chimney of the third floor is dated 1746. There was a period loom removed from a weaving house that formerly stood behind Milford, the name by which the house is known. The house survived the plundering of Union troops on April 19, 1862, on their return to Chantilly, where they had scrambled out of the river up the muddy "Red Bank" in the dark of night and made a fatal wrong turn in the darkness. Although both sides claimed victory, the Union failed to achieve its objective of destroying the lock and sustained heavy casualties in the Battle of South Mills, also known as the Battle of Sawyer's Lane.

Gen. Isaac Gregory, born in 1737, made his home at Fairfield, which had been built in 1735 near Billet's Bridge in Camden County, on a 3,640-acre tract of land known as Danson's Grant. General Gregory led the North Carolina Militia and Continentals in the Battle of Camden in South Carolina on August 16, 1780, during the Revolutionary War, where he received a bayonet wound and had his horse shot from under him. He recovered and returned to action. A memorial to Gregory is located near his home and final resting place, Fairfield, on Palmer Road. Another distinguished resident of Fairfield was William B. Shepherd, who was elected to Congress while living there. On March 15, 1782, Thomas Sawyer and his mother, Margaret Sawyer sold to Commissioners Lemuel Sawyer, Isaac Gregory, Dempsey Burgess, Caleb Grandy, and Joseph Jones a one and one-quarter acre plot of ground for the purpose of building a courthouse, prison, and stocks for Camden County. The courthouse, which was constructed in 1782, was replaced in 1847 by the present Camden County Historic Courthouse. All these facts were documented by Jesse Pugh, who is considered the greatest Camden County historian of all time. Pugh collaborated with Billy Forehand, who continued collecting many notes and documents when copy machines were not in use. You will meet Jesse Pugh, Billy Forehand, and Brian Forehand, who inherited his father's interest in local history.

North of Fairfield and south of Milford at Sawyer's Creek is the Courthouse Township of Camden, where the restored Historic Camden County Courthouse presides over the county complex. The 1847 Greek Revival brick structure replaced a wooden structure built next to the tavern in 1782. The courthouse underwent extensive restoration beginning in 2002, and on April 21, 2007, it was rededicated with an all-day historic event. Commemorative bricks with names and dates pave the walkways of the courthouse, and engraved granite benches have been placed along the walkways. Bricks commemorating Civil War veterans are located at the front door under the portico. Just south of the courthouse in the county complex stands the Old Camden Jail, which was constructed in 1910 and now serves as the Camden County Museum. The second floor of the old jail contains the restored iron bull pen–styled cellblock and a narrow catwalk from which the prisoners could be guarded and managed. Alex Leary and the Old Camden Jail have been featured in *Our State* magazine and in several documentaries.

The images contained in this book have been organized into subjects and regions and span from prior to 1900 to 1950 with several exceptions. First, you will meet the people of Camden County, whether from their likeness or from images of their memorials, homes, or representations of their way of life. Some of the people are considered historically important on various levels, while others will show you how the families fit together, did their jobs, and lived their daily lives. Because the county is narrow in one direction and very long in the other, opposite ends of the county are spread far apart. Even the color and salinity of the waters surrounding the peninsula changes as it flows down to the fingertip of Camden Point. The tannin-laden coffee flowing out of the north changes to a brackish cola hue and then to the color of weak tea when it meets the Albemarle Sound in the south. No matter what color the water is, the boats are always in it. South Mills is centered at the drawbridge just north of the lock in the canal. Once the canal meets the river, landings dot the shore. The Pasquotank River tries to take a shortcut from the Pecan Farm to Chantilly, but it has not quite made the cut through the causeway just yet. The river becomes wide, and in the old days, long piers extended far out into the river so the steamers could dock. The communities both then and now fall naturally into the topography of where the land and water meet.

According to federal census records dating back to 1830, Camden County's population changed very little between 1830 and 1970 and was steady at around 5,500 residents. There were only small increases in population between 1970 and 1990. In the years between 1990 and 2000, Camden County had a huge and startling increase in population, which has nearly doubled since 1830. The staggering population increase has been attributed mostly to in-migration, which has caused concerns to the natural population that the county might be overtaken by development; it could stress natural and human resources that have been renewable since Colonial times and dilute the unique culture and disposition that has sustained its citizens since its formation. This concern to maintain a certain flavor and quality of life in the county led to a public referendum that made Camden County the first and only county in the state of North Carolina with powers of both a city and a county. Camden County achieved this status in June 2006, and became a unified government as of July 1, 2006. Many county residents have expressed great desire that this incredibly rich local heritage and culture be preserved for their offspring by all means possible, including a Camden County Museum. Research for this book uncovered a trove of information so voluminous that it could not possibly fit into one small book, yet much remains to still be discovered. The images and stories found within the pages of this book attempt to dig deeply and accurately to excavate, with full force of intrigue, the history of Camden County.

One

Citizens of Note and Plain Good Folks

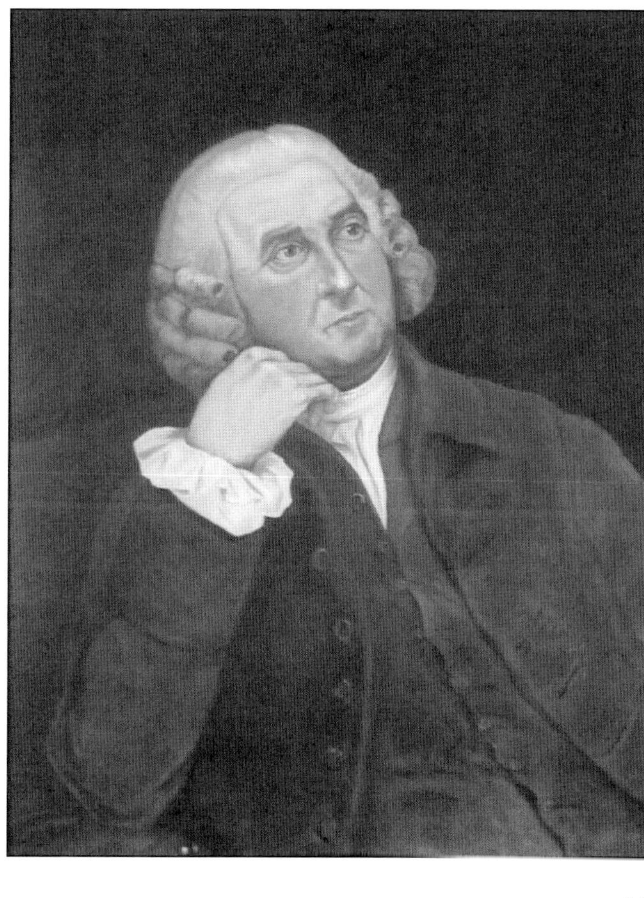

This portrait of Sir Charles Pratt, 1st Earl Camden, the man for whom Camden County was named, was painted by Camden County native Giles Williams in 1977 and now hangs at the front of the courtroom of the Historic Camden County Courthouse. In 1765, Pratt was named as lord chancellor in his native England, but he strongly defended the American colonies during the Revolution. (Courtesy of the Camden County Courthouse.)

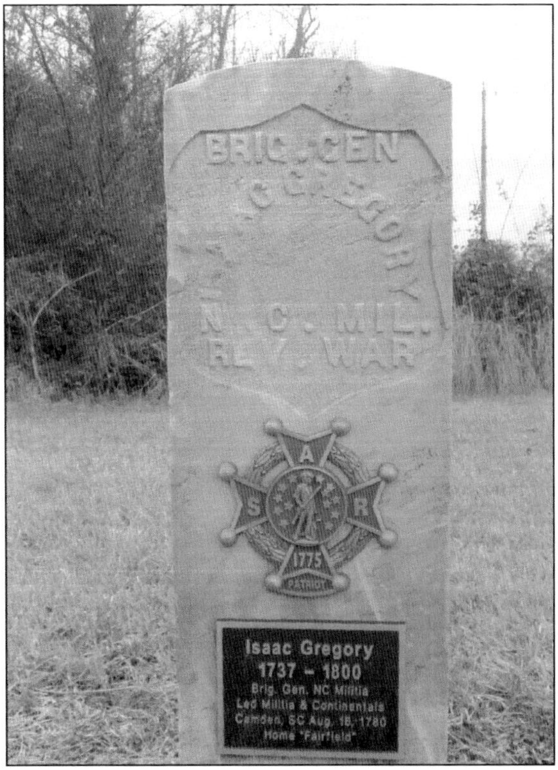

Gen. Isaac Gregory is arguably the most famous and important citizen ever to have made his home in Camden County. Gregory, who lived from 1737 until 1800, led the North Carolina Militia and Continentals in the Battle of Camden in South Carolina on August 16, 1780, during the Revolutionary War. This rededicated memorial to General Gregory is located near his home and final resting place, Fairfield, on Palmer Road. (Courtesy of the author.)

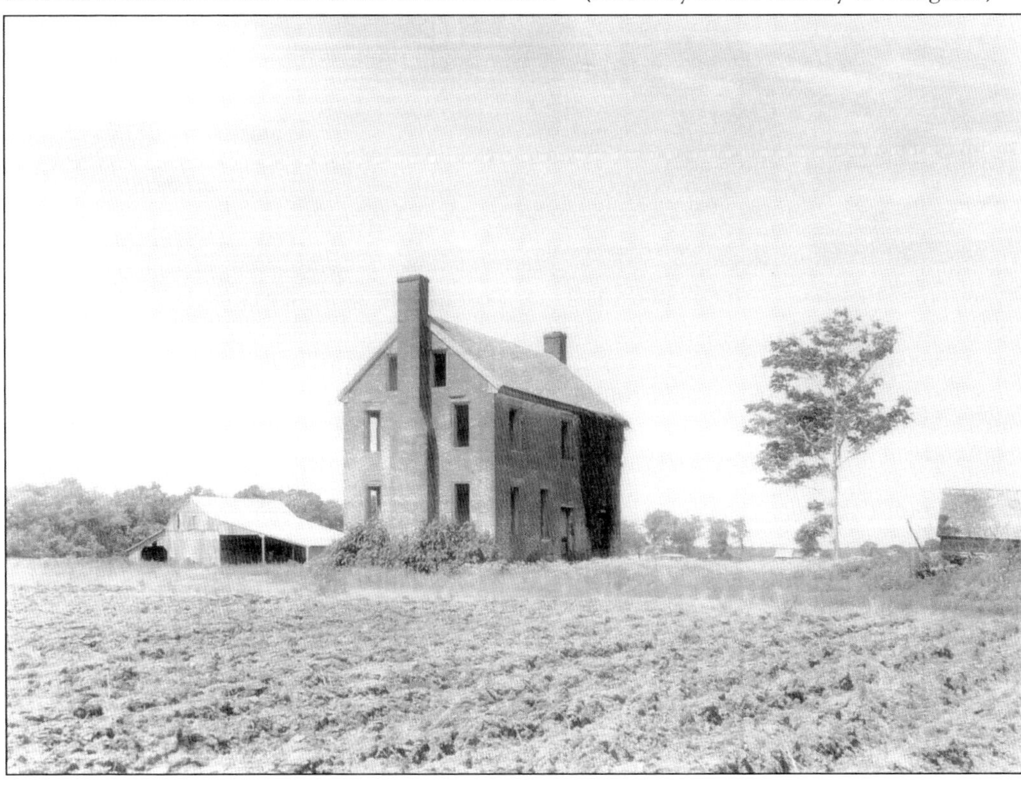

The Isaac Gregory home, Fairfield, was built in 1735 and was the residence of Gen. Isaac Gregory, who fought in the American Revolution. Gregory received a bayonet wound and had his horse shot from under him in the Battle of Camden in South Carolina. Another distinguished resident of Fairfield was William B. Shepherd, who was elected to Congress while living there. (Courtesy of the Library of Congress.)

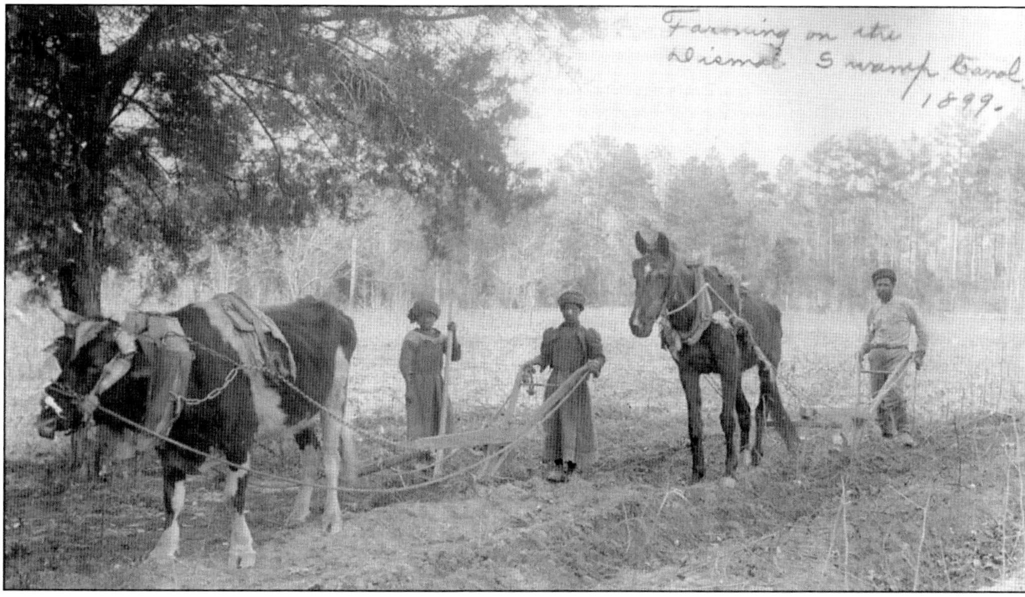

Born in 1786, Moses Grandy authored the only known account written by a former slave of maritime life in North Carolina. Grandy guided cargo vessels up and down the Dismal Swamp Canal and farmed and logged in the swamp. He earned and paid for his freedom twice, but his owner refused to set him free. With Quaker help, Grandy finally gained his freedom, escaped to the North, and eventually bought freedom for his wife. (Courtesy of the Outer Banks History Center, Cronk Cole Collection.)

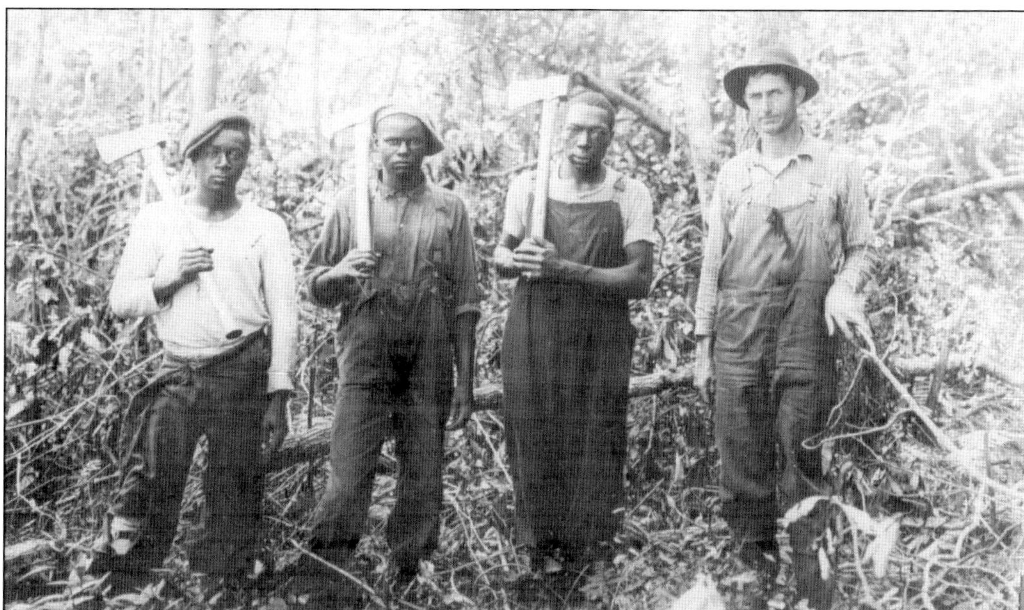

Sawmills were set up near mature timber, and logging took place in multiple locations in Camden County from Colonial times. Buck Island Logging Company was one company that supplied sawmills throughout Camden County with raw timber, which they processed into lumber and sold. This 1914 photograph shows one of many logging crews. The crewmen are, from left to right, unidentified, Wannamaker Boss, Peter Jones, and John Leary. (Courtesy of Alex Leary.)

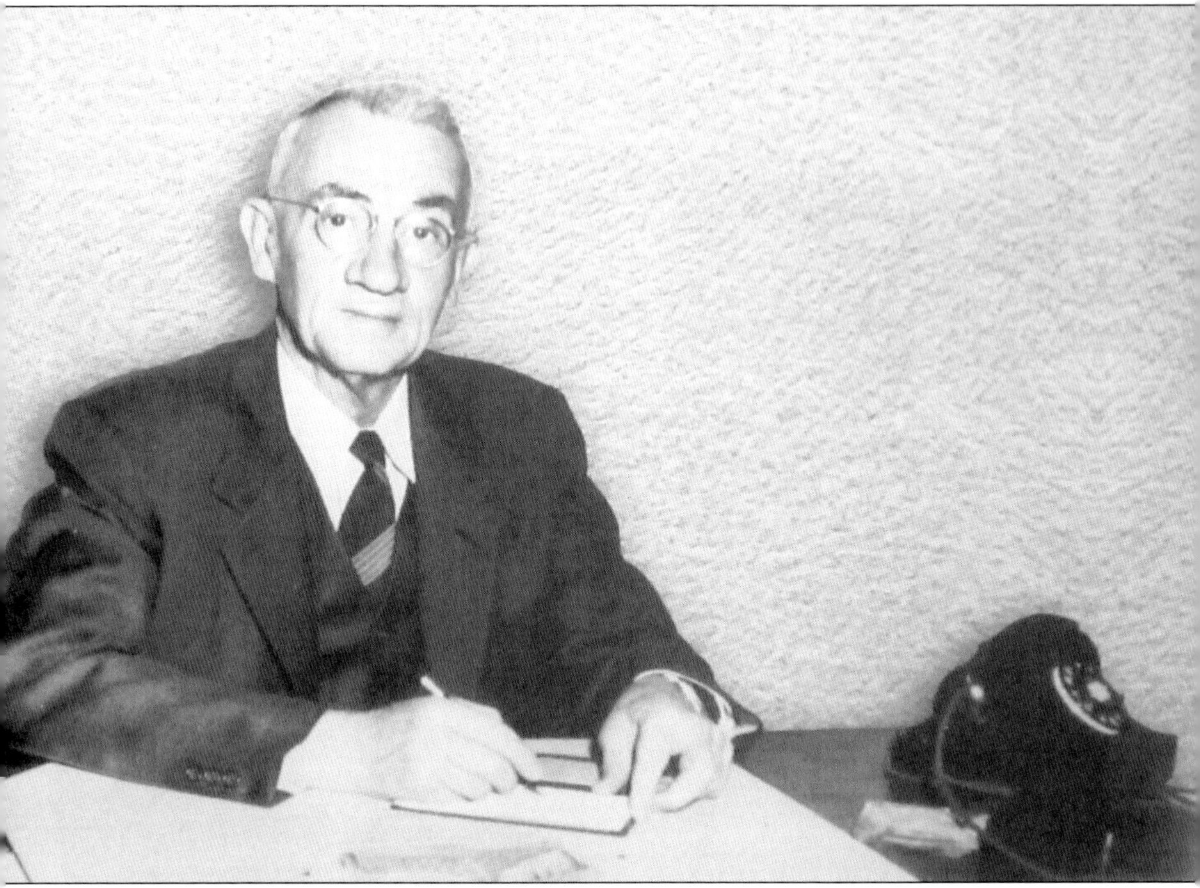

Born in Old Trap in 1891, Jesse Forbes Pugh wrote *Three Hundred Years Along the Pasquotank: A Biographical History of Camden County, North Carolina*, published in 1957, which still stands as the most comprehensive history of Camden County ever to exist. Pugh retired as superintendent of Camden County Schools and held a lifetime membership in the American Education Association. He was a member and Sunday school teacher at Wesley United Methodist Church at Old Trap and also a member of the Hall Lodge 53 AF & AM. Pugh did his graduate studies at the University of North Carolina and at Columbia University in New York City. He was remembered as a caring teacher and served the North Carolina public school system for 33 years. Pugh passed away on March 22, 1976, at the age of 84. (Courtesy of the Camden County Museum.)

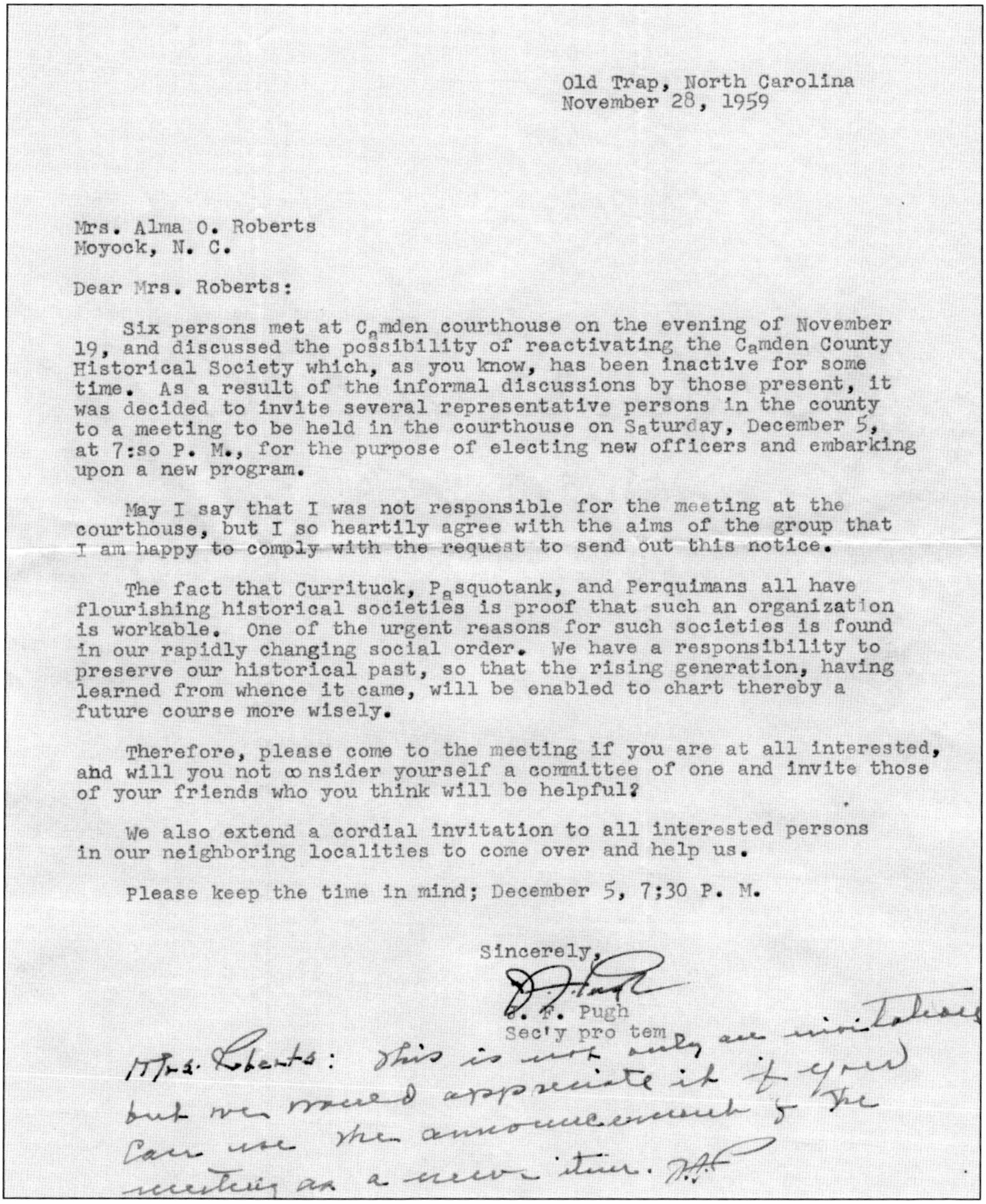

Old Trap, North Carolina
November 28, 1959

Mrs. Alma O. Roberts
Moyock, N. C.

Dear Mrs. Roberts:

Six persons met at Camden courthouse on the evening of November 19, and discussed the possibility of reactivating the Camden County Historical Society which, as you know, has been inactive for some time. As a result of the informal discussions by those present, it was decided to invite several representative persons in the county to a meeting to be held in the courthouse on Saturday, December 5, at 7:so P. M., for the purpose of electing new officers and embarking upon a new program.

May I say that I was not responsible for the meeting at the courthouse, but I so heartily agree with the aims of the group that I am happy to comply with the request to send out this notice.

The fact that Currituck, Pasquotank, and Perquimans all have flourishing historical societies is proof that such an organization is workable. One of the urgent reasons for such societies is found in our rapidly changing social order. We have a responsibility to preserve our historical past, so that the rising generation, having learned from whence it came, will be enabled to chart thereby a future course more wisely.

Therefore, please come to the meeting if you are at all interested, and will you not consider yourself a committee of one and invite those of your friends who you think will be helpful?

We also extend a cordial invitation to all interested persons in our neighboring localities to come over and help us.

Please keep the time in mind; December 5, 7;30 P. M.

Sincerely,
J. F. Pugh
J. F. Pugh
Sec'y pro tem

Mrs. Roberts: this is not only an invitation but we would appreciate it if you can use the announcement of the meeting as a news item. J.F.P.

Jesse Pugh undertook to reactivate the Camden County Historical Society. He wrote this letter to Alma O. Roberts, who was a charter member of the Currituck County Historical Society in the neighboring county in the hope of enlisting her help in reestablishing interest in historical preservation in Camden County. He extends a cordial invitation to all interested persons to attend a meeting intended to initiate a new program. Pugh also wrote *The Hotel in the Great Dismal Swamp, Historical Sketch of Camden County*, and a tour guide entitled *Journey Through Camden County*. It is doubtful that anyone has ever made or will make such a significant contribution to the preservation of the history of Camden County as Pugh. (Courtesy of the author.)

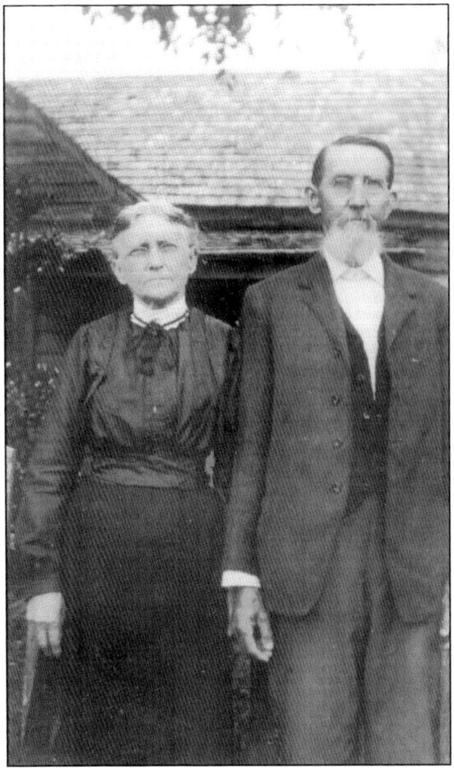

Pvt. Joseph Newton Spence, color corporal of the 8th North Carolina State Troops was wounded in the Battle of Plymouth and captured at Roanoke Island and held prisoner in February 1862. Spence was born on October 1, 1840, and died March 5, 1917. He is pictured here with his wife, Lucy Indiana Howell Spence, in front of their South Mills home, which was built in 1849. (Courtesy of Bob Jones.)

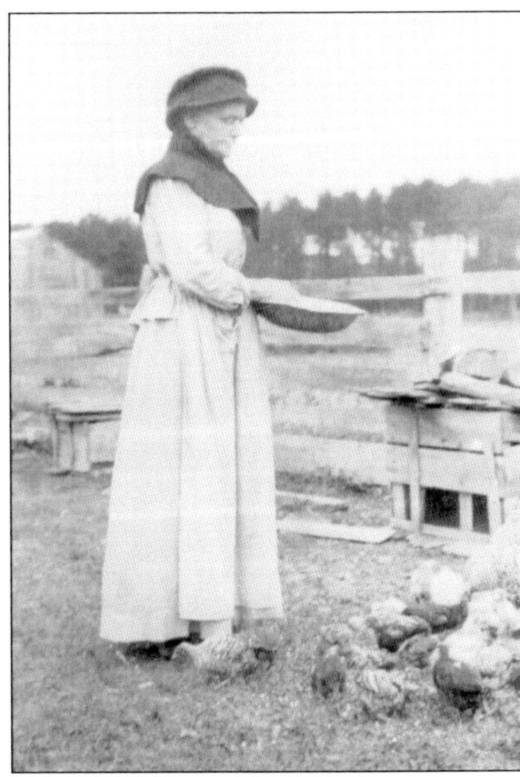

Lucy Indiana Howell Spence was born in 1850 and died in 1930. She was the wife of Joseph Newton Spence and the mother of Hersey Everett Spence and Sarah Elizabeth Spence Jones. She is pictured here feeding her chickens on Christmas Day 1926. Lucy is buried in the W.S. Jones Family Cemetery in South Mills along with her husband and daughter. (Courtesy of Bob Jones.)

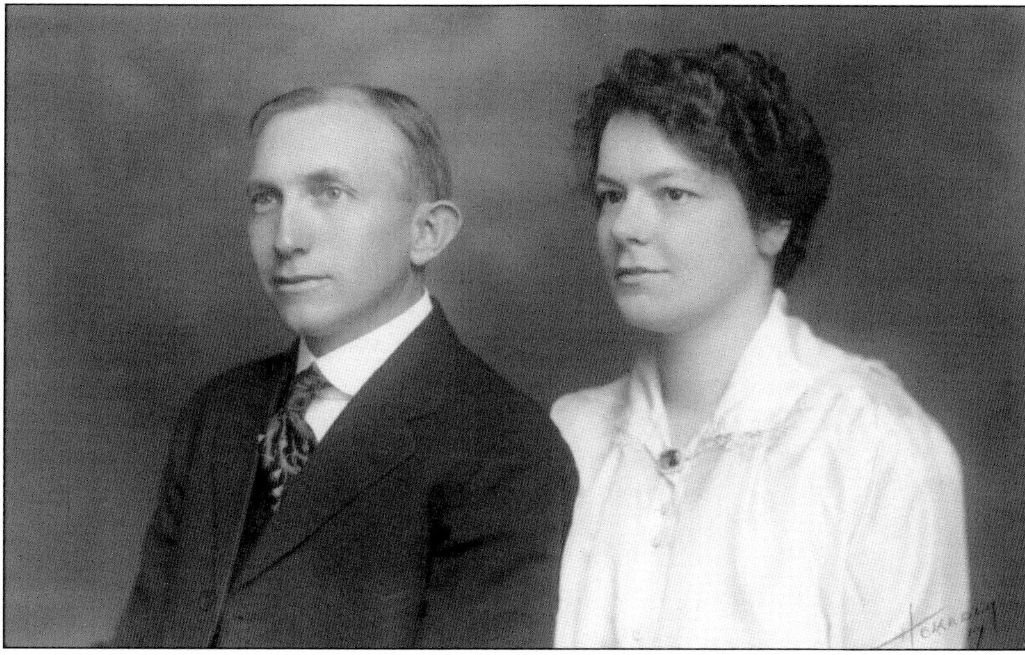

Hersey Everett Spence, born in South Mills on June 12, 1882, was the son of Lucy Indiana Howell Spence and Joseph Newton Spence. He was an author, teacher, and clergyman who, in 1957, wrote a careful history of McBride Methodist Church titled *McBride: A Mother in Methodism.* In October 1913, he married Bessie Octavia Whitted. They were both popular teachers at Duke University until their retirement in 1952. (Courtesy of Bob Jones.)

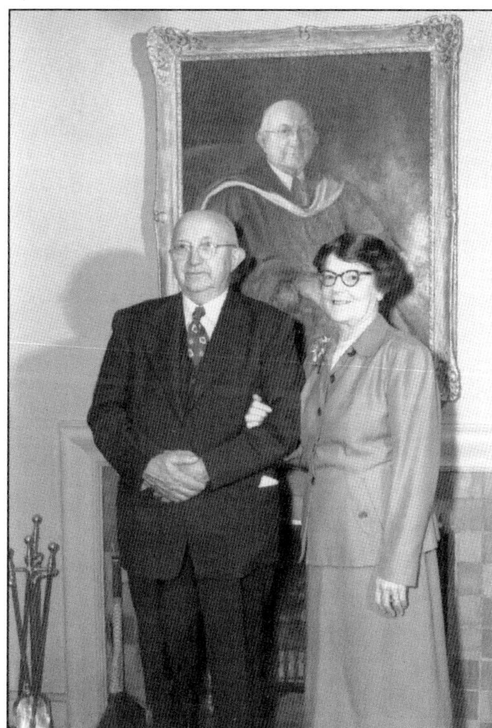

Dr. Hersey Everett Spence and Bessie Octavia Whitted served until 1952 as one of Duke University's best-known faculty couples. Dr. Spence was professor of religious education of Duke Divinity School. Bessie began in 1929 as assistant professor of Biblical literature in the Department of Religion at Duke University. The portrait of Dr. Spence, which hangs behind the couple, was painted by Irene Price of Winston-Salem, North Carolina. (Courtesy of Bob Jones.)

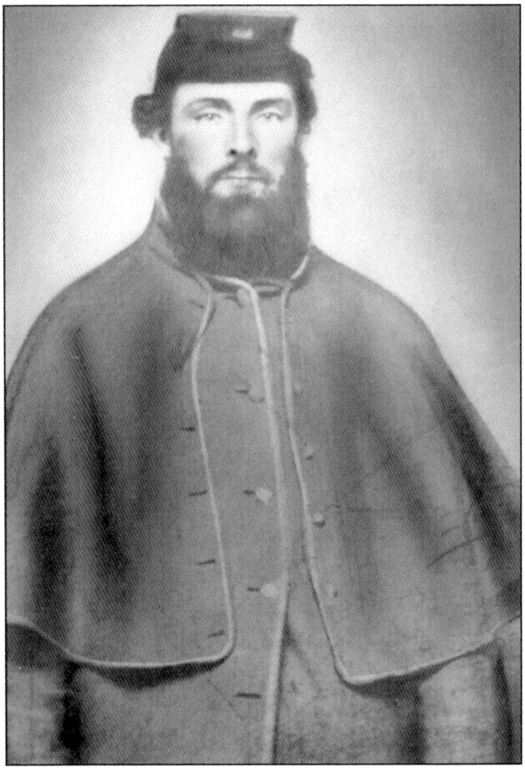

Lazarus Pierce was the patriarch of the Pierce family of Old Trap. Prior to the Civil War, Pierce left North Carolina and went to Iowa, where he found himself drafted into the Union army. Pierce served from December 10, 1861, to March 1862 in Company D of the 16th Regiment of the Iowa Infantry, organized at Davenport, Iowa. He left Iowa for St. Louis, Missouri, on March 20, 1862. (Courtesy of Thelma Naomi Sawyer Forbes.)

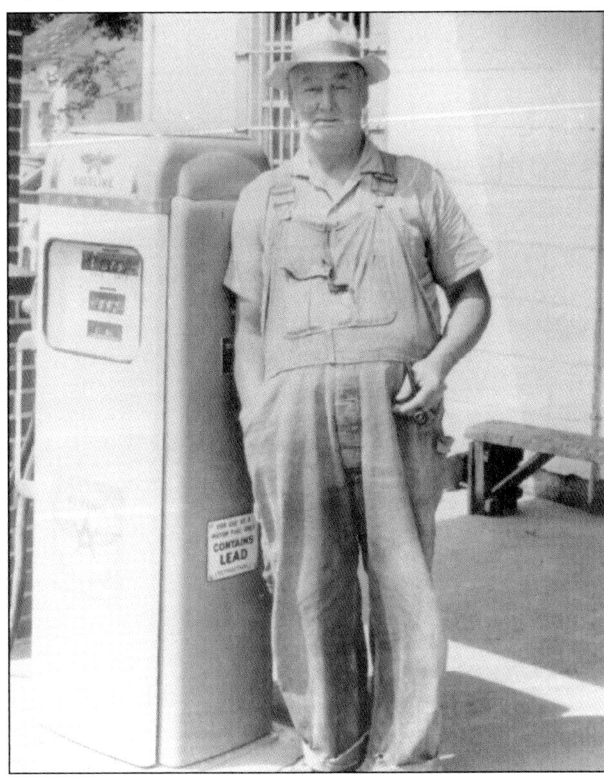

Howard Forbes Pierce, born in 1895, stands in front of one of several stores in Old Trap during the 1950s. Howard's father, Lazarus R. Pierce, was born in Iowa. The Pierce family descended from Lazarus is from the southern end of the county. The northern end of the county uses the alternate spelling of the surname and has an area known as Pearceville. (Courtesy of Thelma Naomi Sawyer Forbes.)

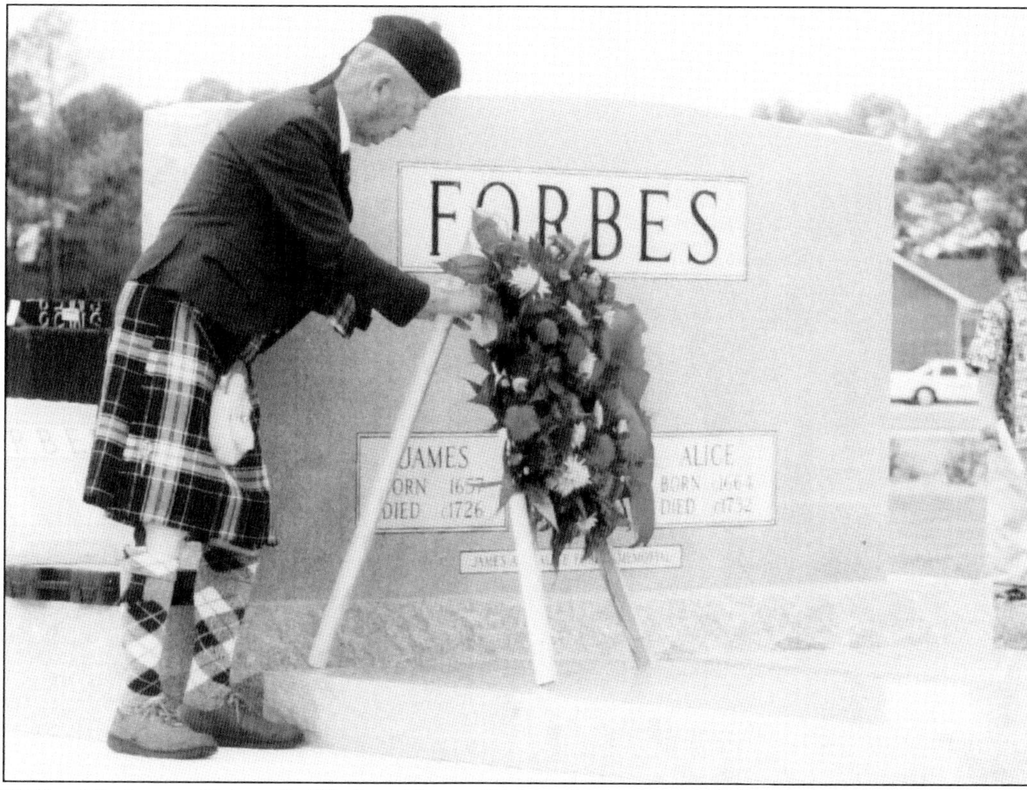

Willard Forbes and his wife, Thelma Naomi Sawyer Forbes, invited family and friends to a large reunion at their cabin in Old Trap annually for over 35 years. Forbes was generous in donating to the youth for their college educations and contributed a historical marker for the Old Trap High School. He persistently pursued erecting a monument on Pond Road for the Forbes family and is seen here dedicating that monument. (Courtesy of Thelma Naomi Sawyer Forbes.)

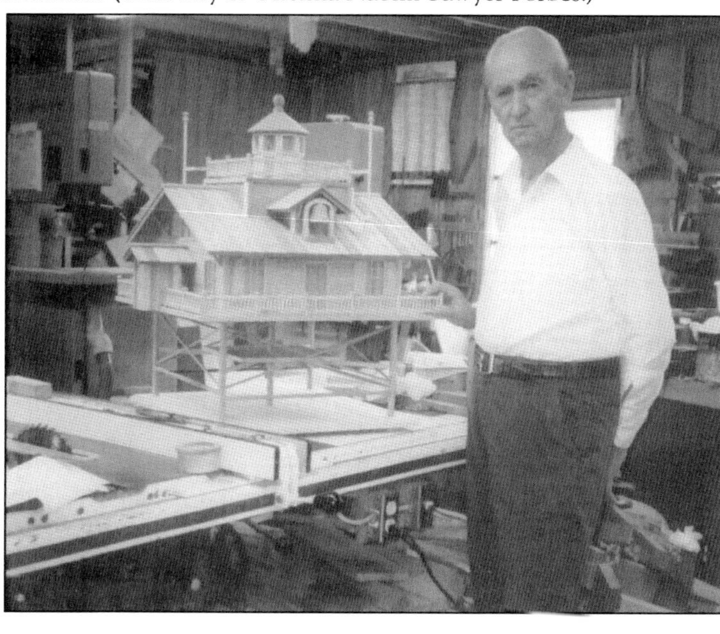

Willard Forbes was known for being an expert wood craftsman and taught others. He created models and paintings of the Wade Point Lighthouse, where he spent time as a child with his grandfather Joseph Mercer, who was the lighthouse keeper. Forbes is seen here in his shop, nearing completion of the construction of his model. (Courtesy of Thelma Naomi Sawyer Forbes.)

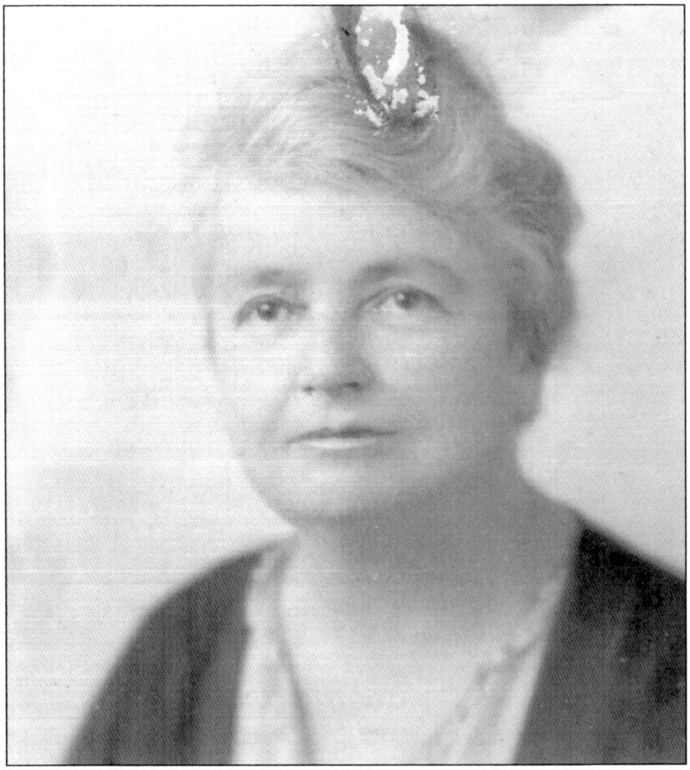

Lillie Grandy was prominent in civic affairs and was instrumental in the development of many community projects, especially those that supported education. She served on the faculty of Meredith College, was a strong influence in Camden County education, and donated the land on which Camden County's primary school was built. Grandy died in 1957 at the age of 87, and Grandy Primary School was named for her and her family. (Courtesy of Doris Dough Forehand.)

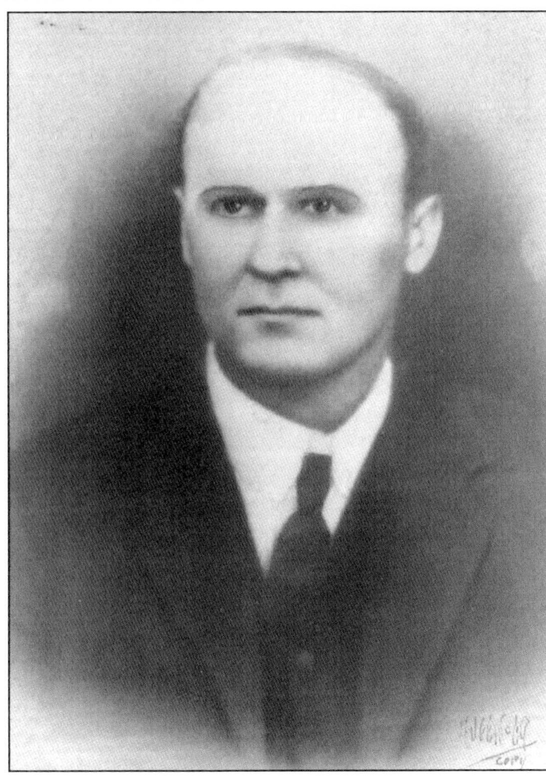

Daniel Edward Williams was born in South Mills in 1874 and married Mamie Webb in 1897. Williams continued in the family dry goods business as well as farming and lumbering. He became very successful in milling lumber and owned and operated related businesses in transportation, including that of tugboats and barges used to transport lumber. (Courtesy of Joyce and Durward Medlin.)

Robert Lee Forbes was born in Belcross in 1863 and married Lela Sanderlin, with whom he had two children. Forbes served as the clerk of court of Camden County from prior to 1899 until 1906, died on August 29, 1914, and was buried at Sleepy Hollow Farm near Sawyer's Creek Baptist Church. The portrait here shows Robert Lee Forbes Jr. at age 17. (Courtesy of Sarah Forbes Hamilton.)

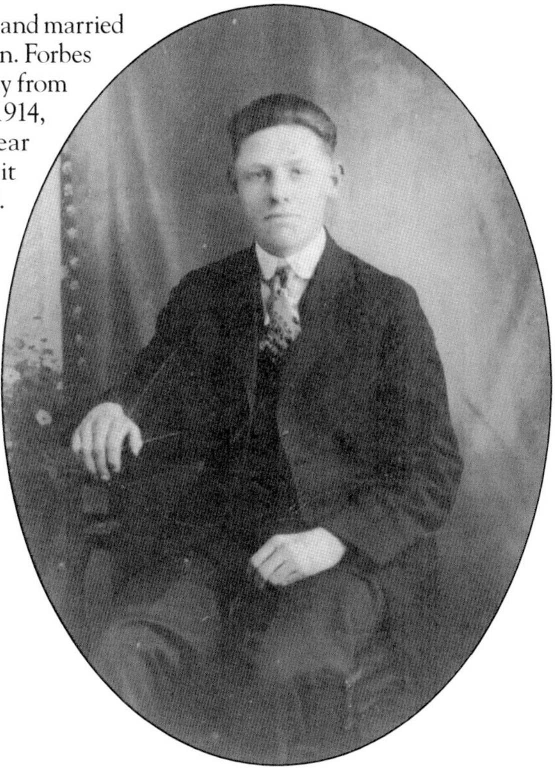

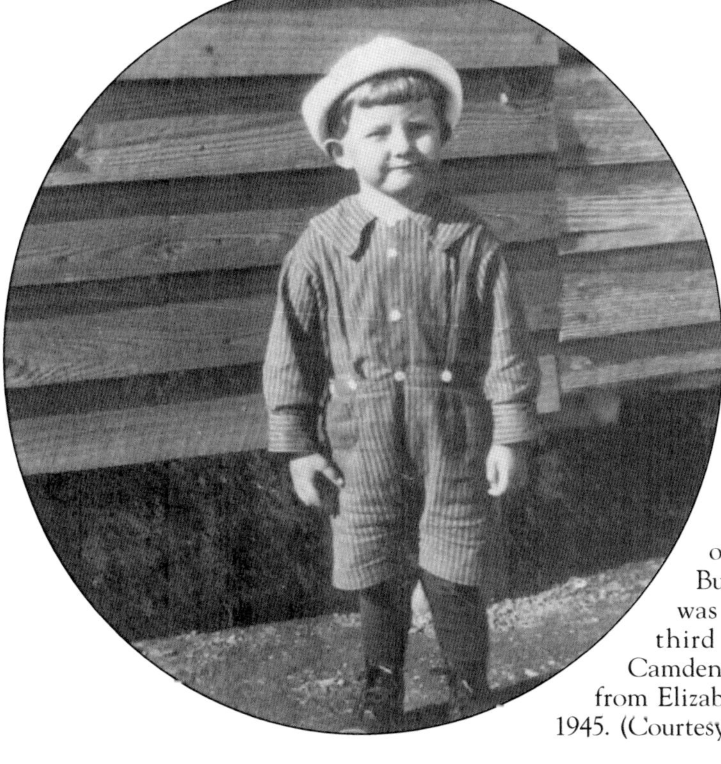

This photographic postcard is a good example of one made for stereoscopic viewers, which would create a three-dimensional image by a trick of binocular vision. Elroy Clifton Burgess, the son of Mary Blackburn Sanderlin Burgess and Ralph N. Burgess, was born in 1923 and attended third grade at Shiloh in 1932. Camden County students graduated from Elizabeth City High School after 1945. (Courtesy of Joyce Mitchell Cuthrell.)

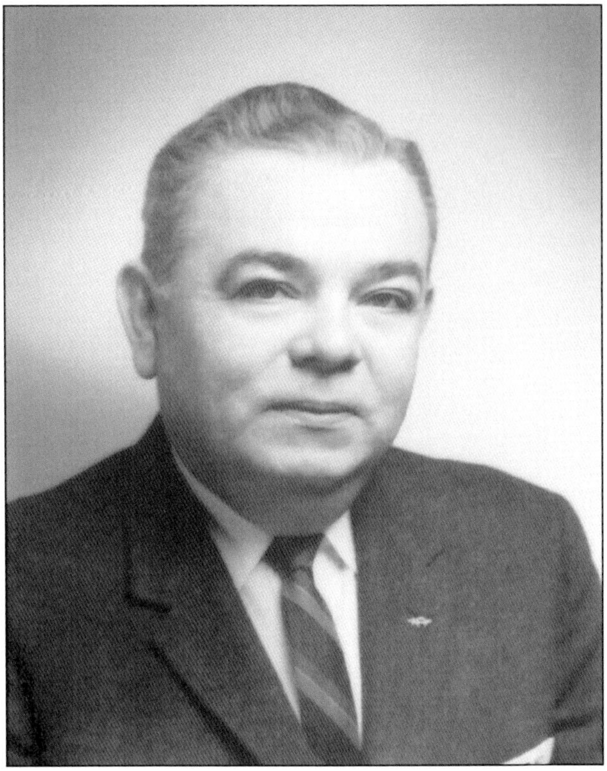

Sherman Everett Burgess was born in 1908 in Old Trap to Eva Belle Leary Burgess and Willie Henry Burgess. He earned his teaching credentials from Duke University and married Loraine Sawyer, the daughter of Florence Kight Sawyer and Alfred Sawyer. His brother Vernon managed the farm while Everett served as Camden County's representative to the North Carolina General Assembly in the late 1950s and early 1960s. (Courtesy of David Burgess.)

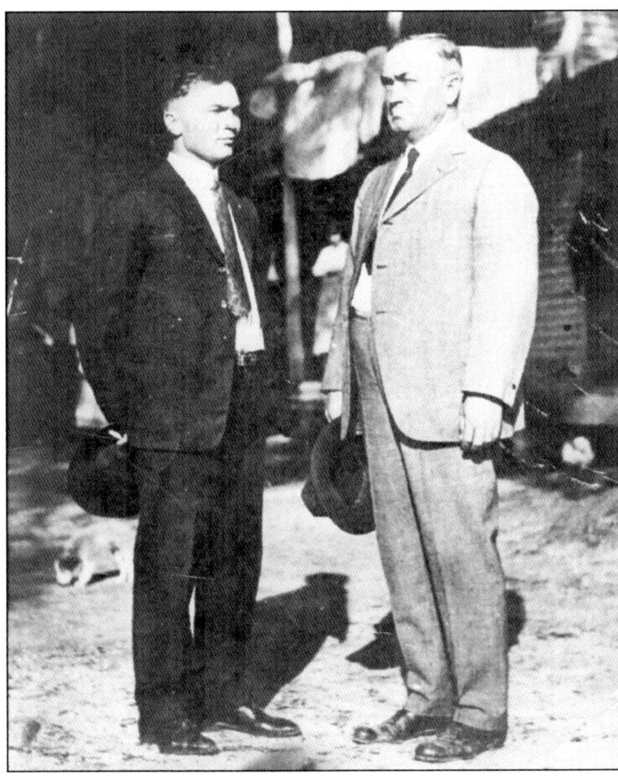

Marvin Chester Mitchell (left) was born in 1896. He was the son of Margaret Ann Mitchell, born in 1876, and Edmond Mitchell (right), born in 1869. Chester grew up in Old Trap and then moved his family to Manteo, where he became chief of police, and Doris Walker, his daughter, operated the popular Duchess of Dare Restaurant. (Courtesy of Joyce Mitchell Cuthrell.)

On the back of this photograph, Will Dough writes from France: "Dear Mother, This picture was taken after spending sixty days in the trenches, where it was almost impossible to stay above the ground. Have gained ten lbs. since this picture was taken weigh one hundred and fifty lbs. now and am enjoying life fine. Thinking about you. I went over the top six times without getting only two casualties—Will." (Courtesy of Doris Dough Forehand.)

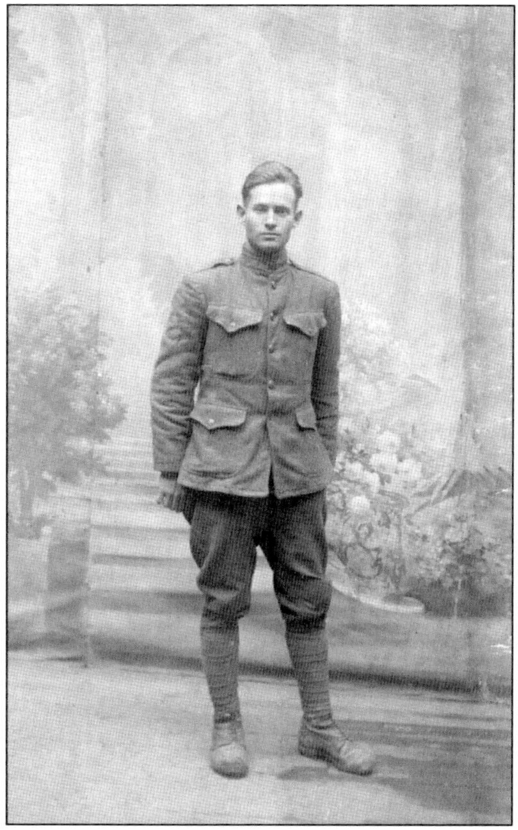

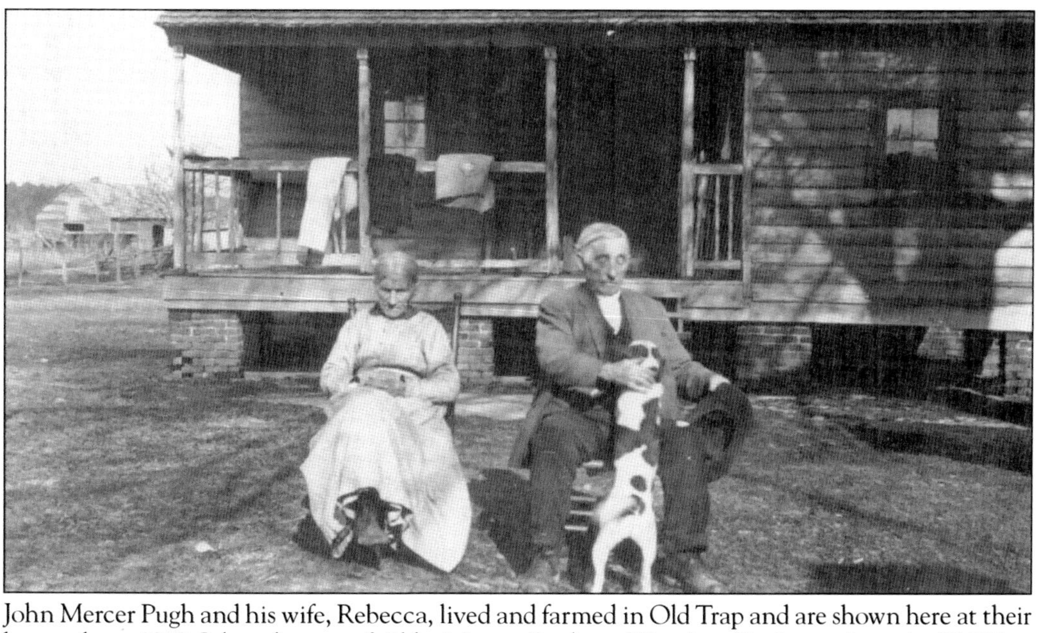

John Mercer Pugh and his wife, Rebecca, lived and farmed in Old Trap and are shown here at their home about 1910. John, the son of Abby Mercer Pugh and Stephen Pugh, was born in Old Trap in 1831 and Rebecca was born in 1834. She died in 1919, and John followed in 1920. (Courtesy of Joyce Mitchell Cuthrell.)

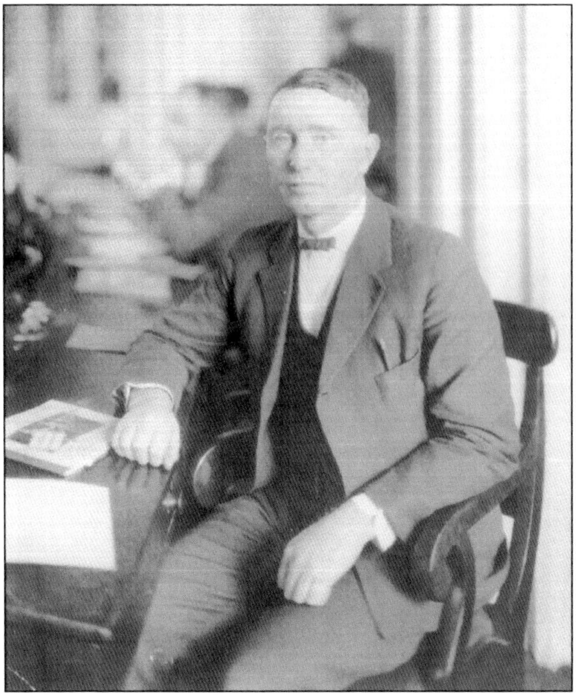

Curtis Lee Tarkington, born in Belcross in 1887, was elected in 1925 and 1927 as the Democratic representative from Camden County in the North Carolina House of Representatives. He worked in the post office in the general store owned by F.P. Wood until his death on December 3, 1937, after which his widow, Sally Clark Overton Tarkington, became postmistress until she retired. (Courtesy of Thalia Tarkington Jones.)

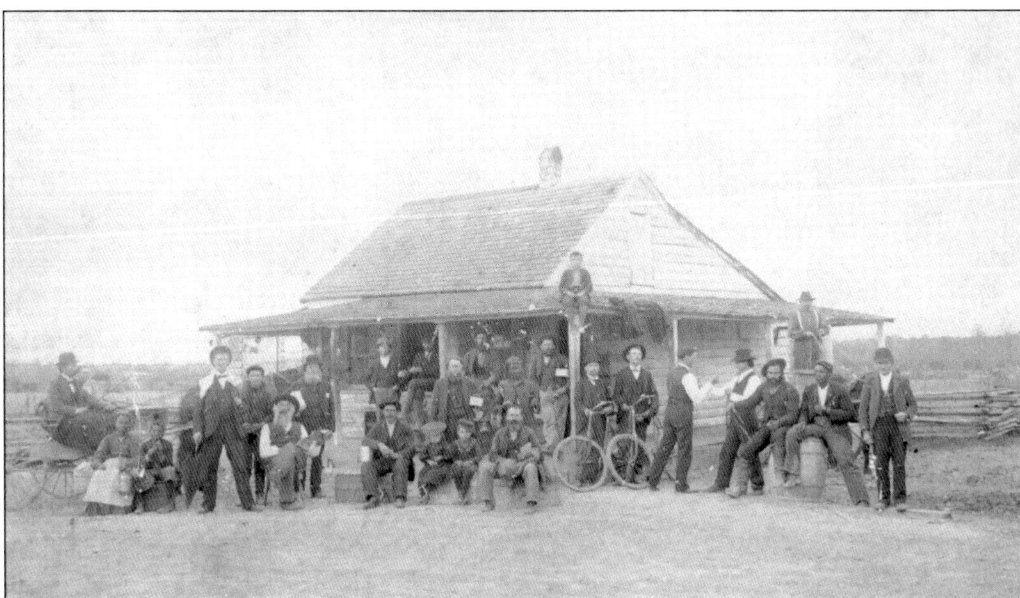

Pictured in front of the first Old Trap store in 1895 are from left to right, (first row, seated) Matilda Burfoot, Charlie Purser, Samuel Leary (bearded), Steven N. Pugh, Pearl Pugh, Jesse Pugh, and Peter T. Burgess; (second row) Edmond Mitchell and Nancy Jane Leary (in buggy), Joe Grandy Jones (standing), Willie Foster, Seth Needham, William Kight, Jordan Burfoot, John P. Forbes and Willie Jasper Burgess (with bicycles), Jabe Burfoot and John Morse (facing each other), Edgar Burgess and Abe Burfoot (on barrel), and Asa Kight (on right end); (third row, standing on porch) Jabez W. Burfoot, John Burgess, Wilse Burgess, George Burgess, and Griffin Burgess (standing on cart). Gideon Needham is sitting on the corner of the roof. (Courtesy of Alex Leary.)

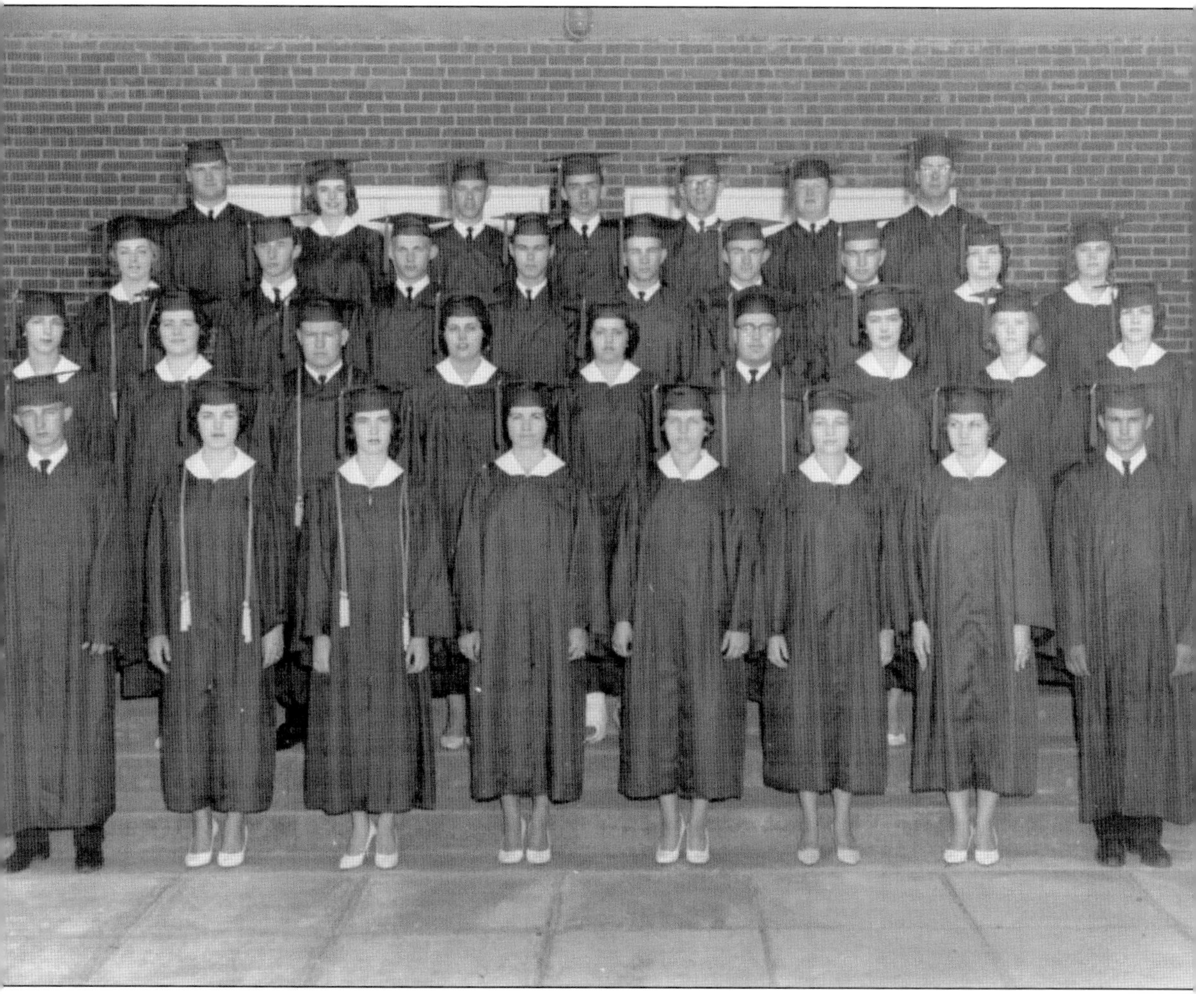

The members of the 1964 graduating class of Camden County High School are, from left to right, (first row) Marvin Trotman, Shirley Benton, Sandra Leary, Rita White, Janice Ferrell, Patricia Riggs, Jean Davenport, and Frank Bray; (second row) Mary Riffle, Joan Seymour, Grover Sawyer, Ella Cartwright, Janice Davis, Reginald Forbes, Sandra Cox, Janis Seymour, and JoAnne Walston; (third row) Diana Midgett, H.V. Leary, Don Gregory, Ben Benton, Terry Forehand, Hersey Smithson, Otis Brinkley, Janet Cartwright, and Delinda Etheridge; (fourth row) Tommy Baum, Charlayne Grimes, Terry Lee Wooten, Shelton Cartwright, Waverly Sawyer, Preston Colson, and Charles Glenn Forbes. (Courtesy of Anita Whitehurst.)

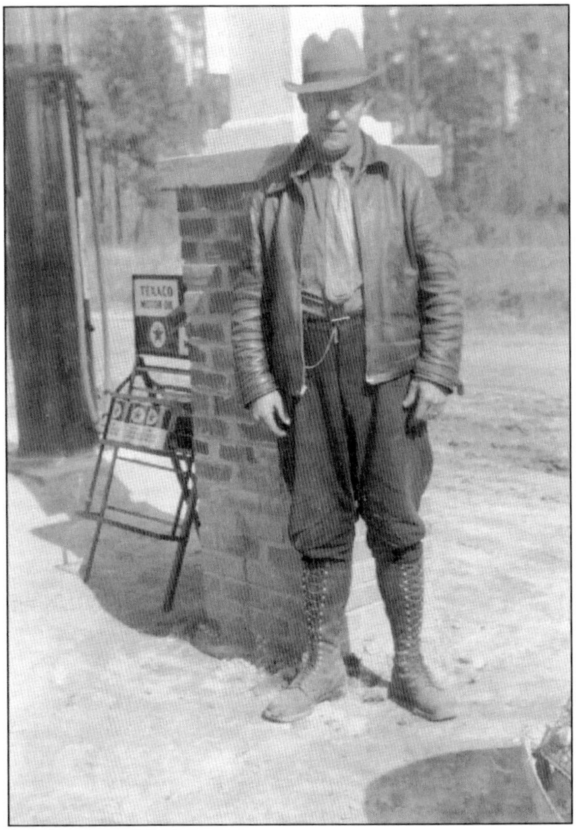

Caleb Staples Forehand, the son of Sarah Staples Forehand and Durant Walston Forehand, was born in Camden County in 1884. He married Lena Williams and made his living as a farmer and merchant. He is pictured here sometime in the early 1950s in front of the store, which was last operated by the Dough family and located on North Trotman Road at Indiantown. (Courtesy of Doris Dough Forehand.)

In 1966, John Joseph Walston was elected sheriff of Camden County. In this photograph are, from left to right, Sheriff John Joseph Walston, and his deputies James Cherry, Ambrose Staples, and Sam Jennings. Prior to being elected as sheriff, Walston served as a Camden County commissioner from 1950 until 1954 and as a member of the Camden County School Board from 1945 until 1947. (Courtesy of the Camden County Sheriff's Office.)

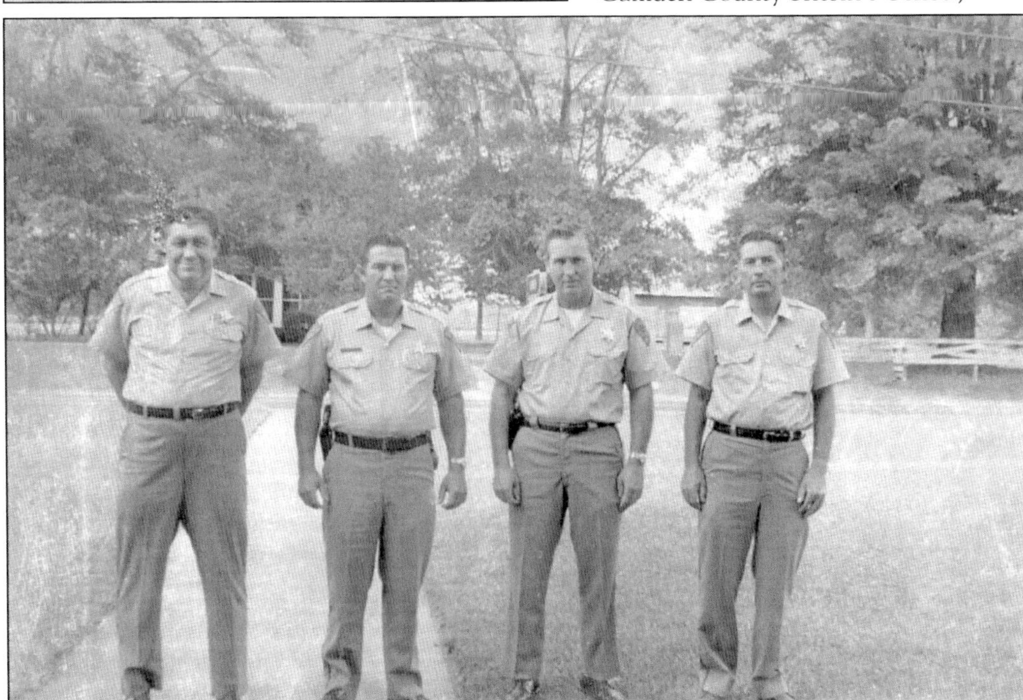

In 1965, William Alexander Jones applied for a loan from the Farmers Home Administration to build a municipal water system for the township of South Mills. An initial grant of $180,000 was awarded to serve 150 families. Jones is seen here opening the valves of the new system for the first time. (Courtesy of Thalia Jones.)

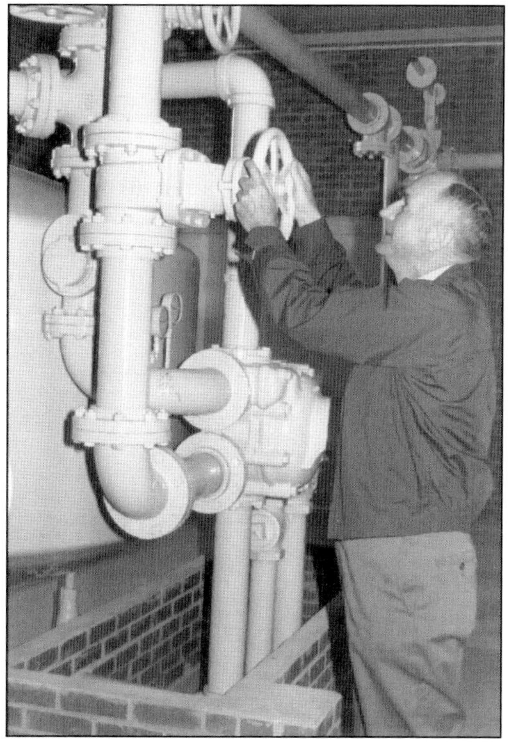

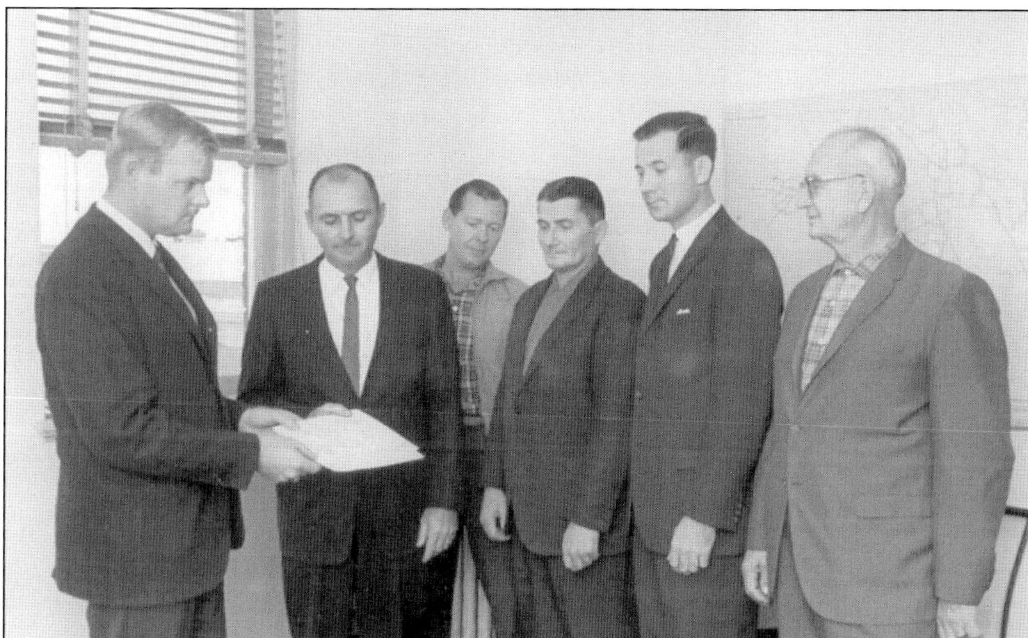

On November 26, 1965, South Mills received the first check for $50,000 from the Farmers Home Administration to implement its own municipal water supply. Shown looking over plans are, from left to right, Melvin E. Howell of the Farmers Home Administration; William A. Jones, president of the South Mills Water Association; W.H. Powell, director; R.E. Whitehurst, treasurer; E.B. Inge, secretary; and Durward P. Medlin, member. (Courtesy of Thalia Jones.)

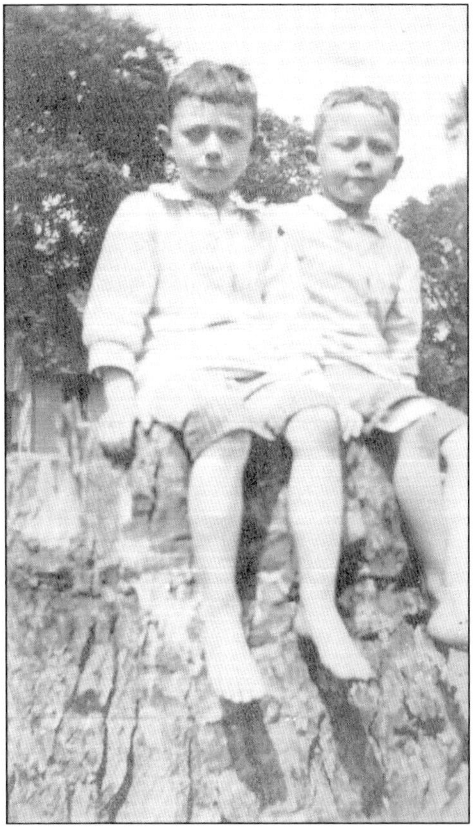

Claude Vernon and Frank Leslie Trafton were twins born to Fannie Sawyer Trafton and Samuel Luther Trafton on June 26, 1909. The story passed down is that the mother of the twins did not have enough milk to keep both boys fed, but the neighbor did. The women would walk down the lanes from their homes to the road with the babies every day to pick up the mail and let the children nurse. (Courtesy of Martha Ann.)

Seated on the Cherry porch in South Mills on December 25, 1901, from left to right, are (first row) J.G. Hughes, Annie Sawyer (seated up front), Dorothy Sawyer, Clara Sawyer, Walter McCoy, Lizzie Poole, Clara Bartlett, and John Taylor Spence; (second row) Jo McCoy, Sallie Sawyer, Lena Jacobs, and Mr. Tebedeau and Mrs. Tebedeau. The home was located where Ebenezer Church now stands. (Courtesy of Joyce and Durward Medlin.)

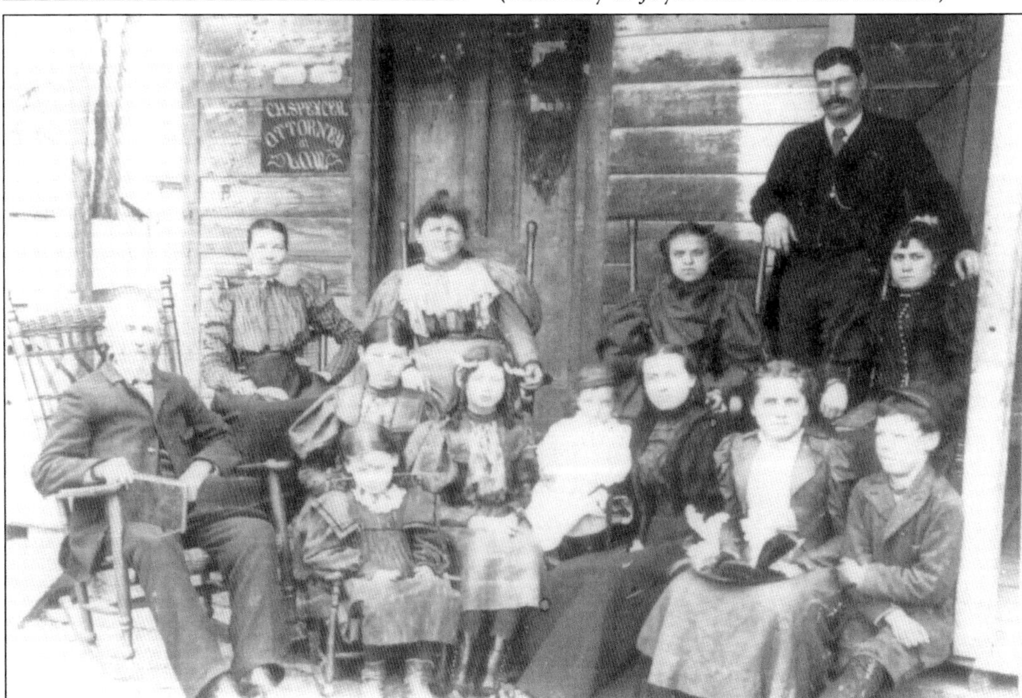

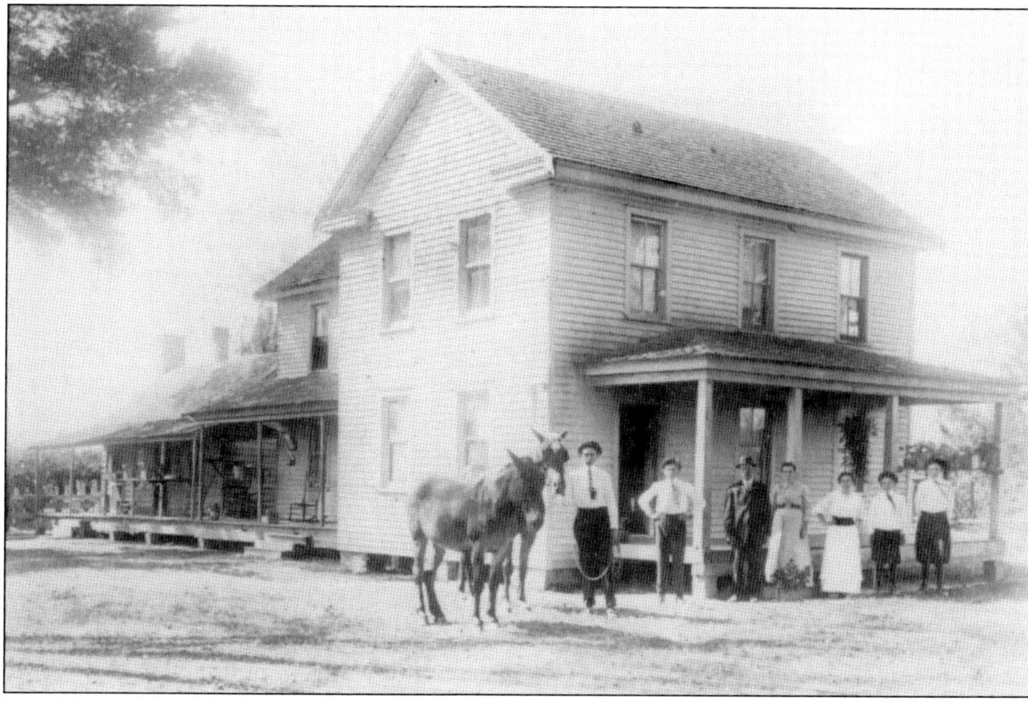

Members of the Cahoon family in front of their Riddle home in 1914, from left to right, are Dennis Cahoon, Herbert Cahoon, Edward D. Cahoon, Carlista Sawyer Owens Cahoon, Mart Jarvis, Clyde Cahoon, and Judson Cahoon. Judson married Bertha Mitchell Burgess, who became a local historian in the Old Trap area of Camden County and documented the names in this photograph. (Courtesy of Anna Cahoon Boyce.)

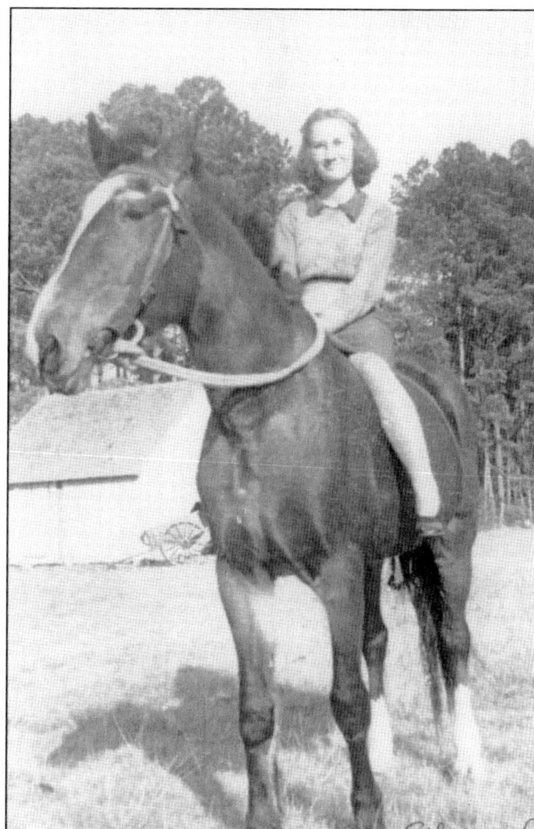

Etheleen Cahoon Davenport was the daughter of Bertha Mitchell Burgess Cahoon and Judson Cahoon and was born in Camden County on August 4, 1926. She wears her skirt and pumps on the family horse named Old Sally sometime in the 1940s. Etheleen married and moved to Perquimins County and died on March 14, 2002. (Courtesy of Portia Lee and Wilse Burgess.)

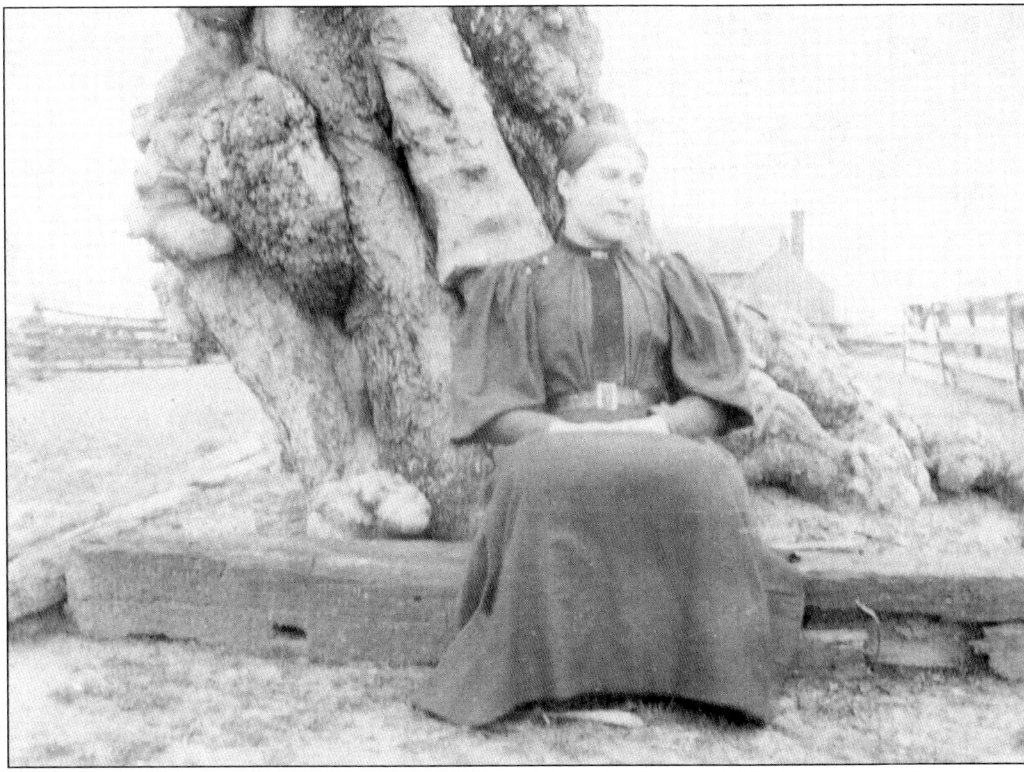

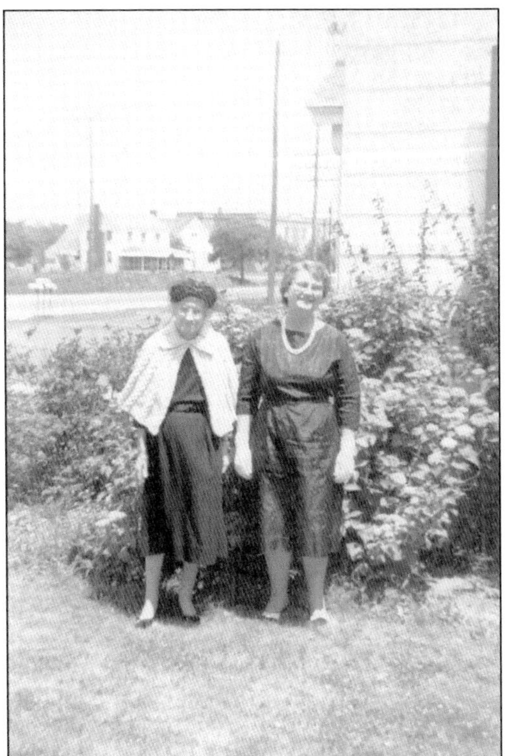

Marinda "Rennie" Forbes Bartlett, born in Shiloh on August 8, 1883, was the daughter of Henrietta Toxey Forbes and Sylvester Forbes. In 1932, she married Henry F. Bartlett. Rennie spent her entire life living in Shiloh and is pictured here with an ancient, gnarled tree. She died in 1966 at the age of 83. (Courtesy of Anita Whitehurst.)

Rennie Forbes is standing with her niece, Glennie Walston, who was the daughter of Bessie Forbes and Lancaster S. Walston. In this photograph taken in Shiloh prior to 1966, the Ralph Burgess home and Shiloh High School, which by this time had been converted to Toxey's Grocery Store, can be seen in the background. (Courtesy of Anita Whitehurst.)

Carlista Sawyer Owens Cahoon was born in Tyrell County, North Carolina, in 1861. In 1887, she married Edward D. Cahoon. In 1900, the census records that Carlista and Edward still living in Tyrell County near the Alligator River. This image shows Cahoon later in life feeding her chickens on the farm she and Edward had established in Riddle. (Courtesy of Anna Cahoon Boyce.)

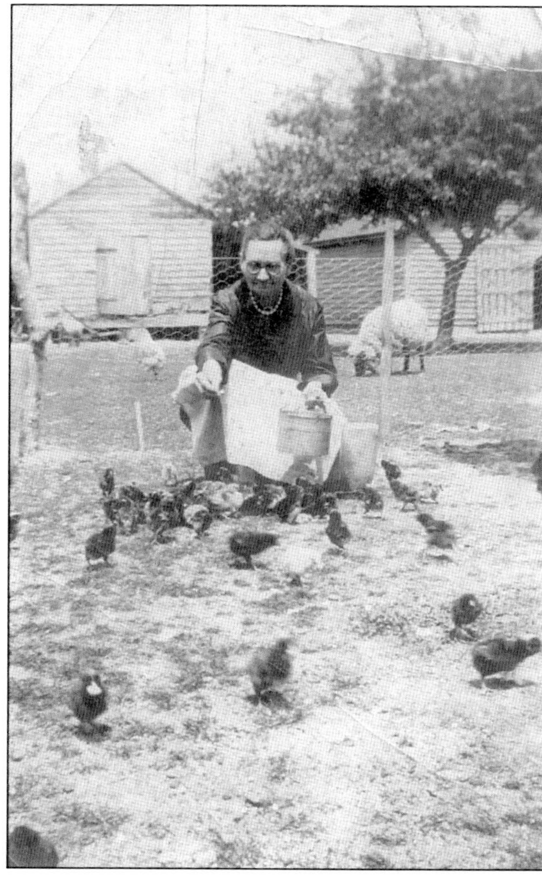

Edward D. Cahoon and Carlista Sawyer Owens Cahoon were both born around 1860 in Tyrell County, North Carolina. Sometime after 1900, they moved their family to the Riddle section of Camden County, where they established a farm. The grape arbor behind them is very typical of the local style of growing grapes in the era and would have produced a plentiful crop in September. (Courtesy of Anna Cahoon Boyce.)

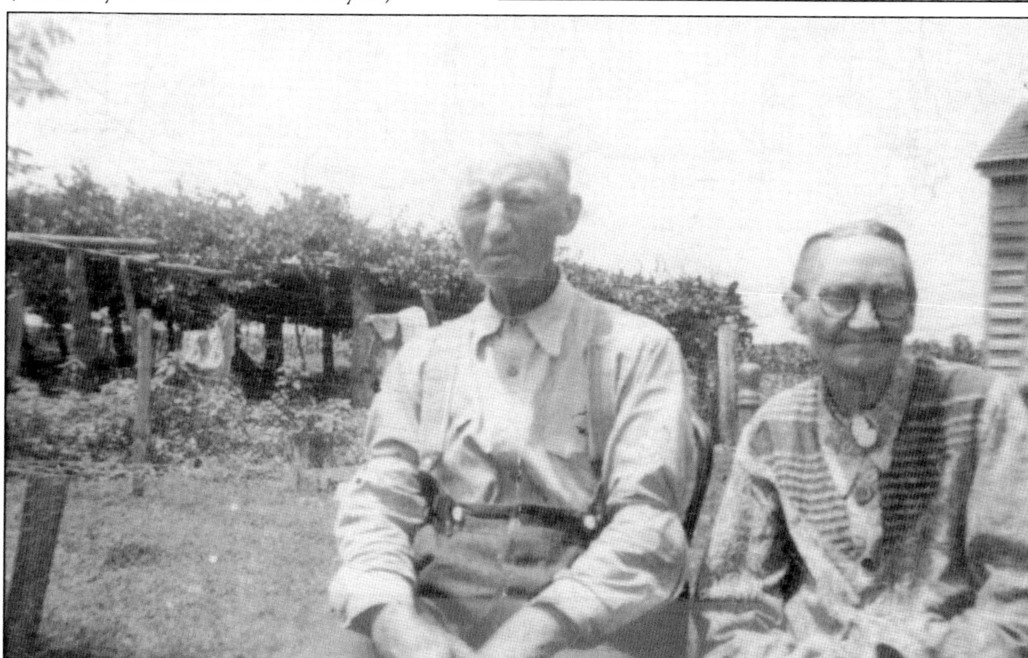

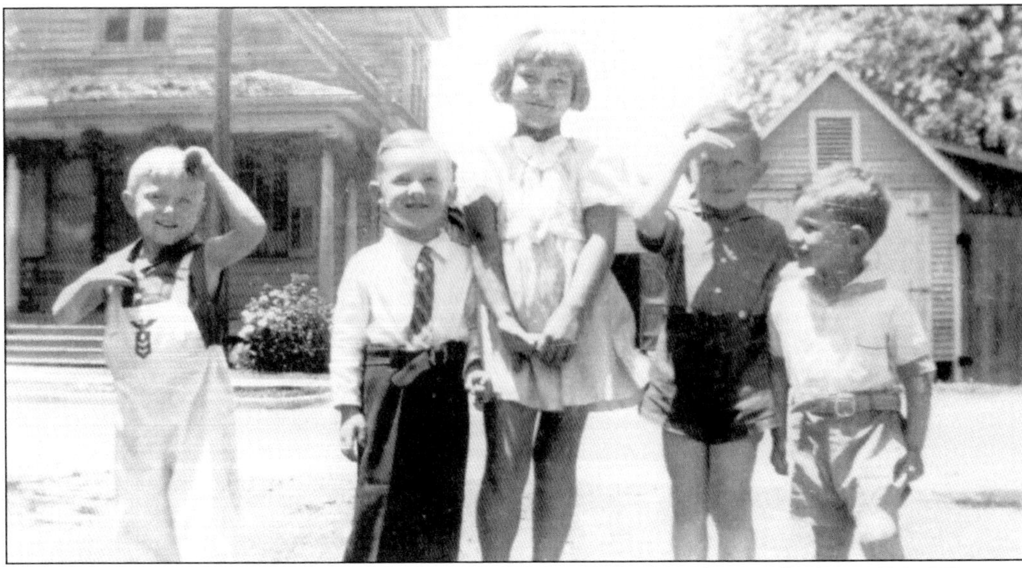

These Camden County cousins are having a nice afternoon together in the late 1930s. They are, from left to right, Charles Roland Jones, Vernon Burgess Jr., Marie Jones, Dewey Burgess, and Carl Burgess. Charles and Marie are the children of Roland Jones. Vernon is the son of Roland's sister, Mattie Jones Burgess. Dewey and Carl are the sons of Mary Jones Burgess, sister of Roland Jones and Mattie Jones Burgess. (Courtesy of Vernon Burgess Jr.)

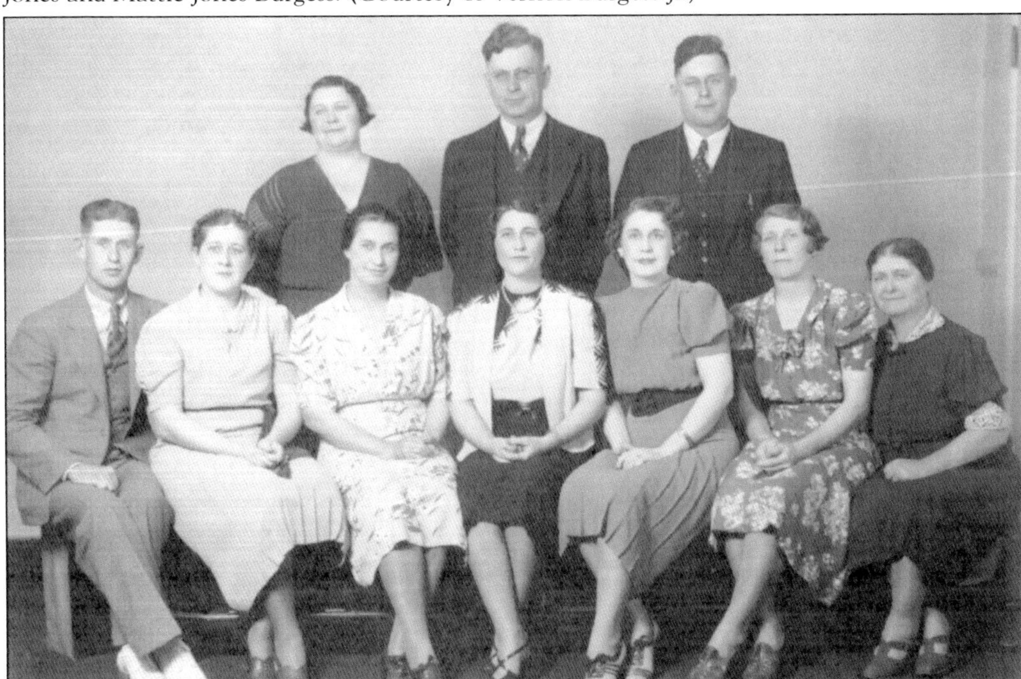

Members of the Bartlett family are, from left to right, (first row) Charlie Bartlett, Pollie Bartlett Stevens Mathews, Susie Estelle "Stella" Bartlett Cox, Vivian Bartlett Stevens Whitfield, Louise Bartlett Alexander, Manie Bartlett Cartwright Duncan, and Bettie Bartlett Seymour; (second row) Essie Bartlett Dough, William Bartlett, and Dennis Bartlett Jr. (Courtesy of Doris Dough Forehand.)

William Whitehurst "Billie" Forehand had a significant impact on preserving the history of Camden County as the Camden County historian. Through his efforts, there are old court records, board of education minutes, a record of the Camden County poorhouses, and many other artifacts and records. Forehand's specialty was genealogy and helping people find their ancestors. He had a building behind his house that served as a Camden County Museum. (Courtesy of Brian Forehand.)

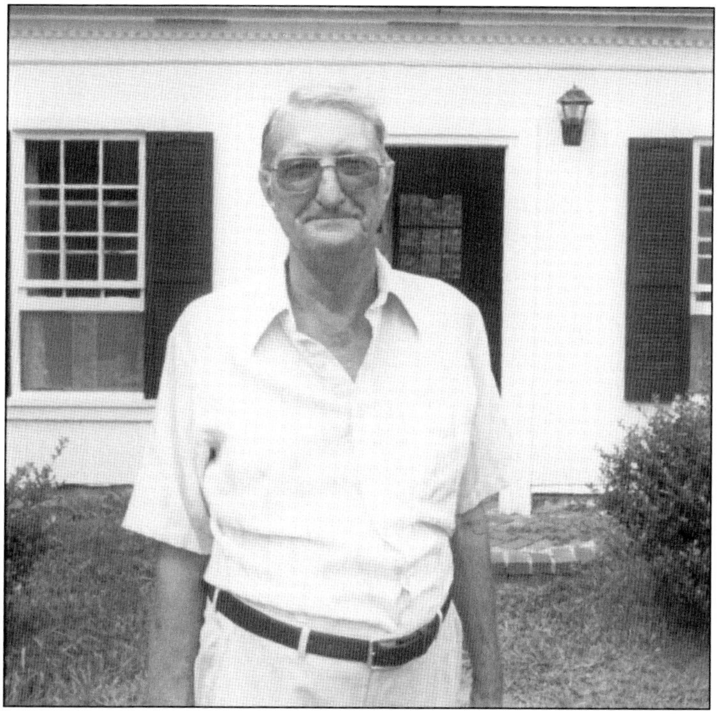

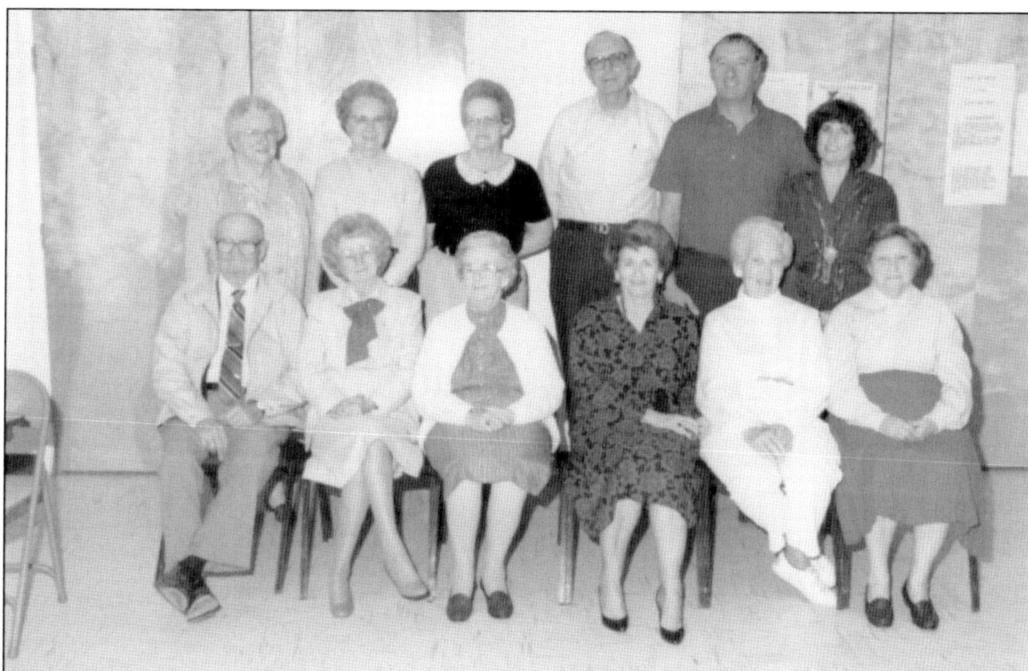

In 1959, Jesse Pugh successfully rallied the citizens of Camden County to reactivate the Camden County Historical Society. Members seen here in 1990 are, from left to right, (first row) James Whitehurst, Mary Evelyn Whitehurst, Bernice Johnson, Thelma Naomi Sawyer Forbes, Doris Leary, and Margaret Jackson; (second row) Mamie Sawyer, Thalia Jones, Beth Forbes, Charlie Forbes, Alex Leary, and Sandra Leary. (Courtesy of Thalia Jones.)

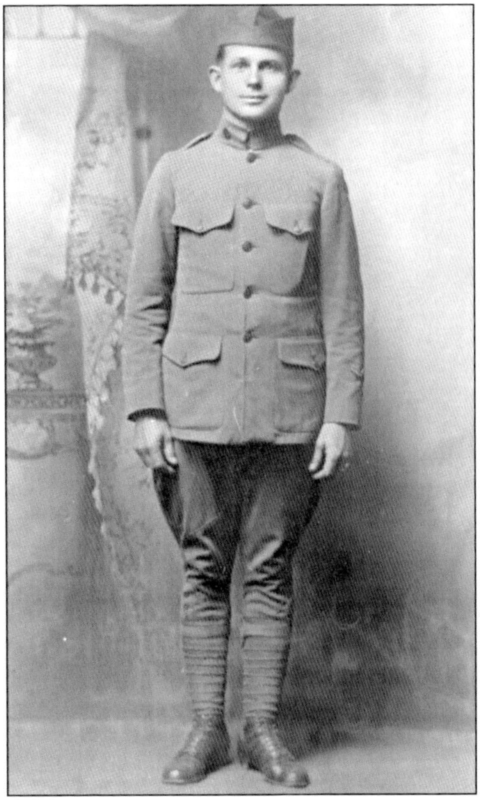

Harvey Forbes Gregory Sr., born February 3, 1890, served in the US Army and spent time in the trenches in France during World War I. After the war, he made his living as an expert carpenter, building boats, homes, and even a courthouse as far away as Georgia. He helped to finish the Edward Collings Knight Jr. hunting lodge, now known as the Whalehead Club (although a recent marketing study has recommended a name change to simply Whalehead), in Currituck County. (Courtesy of Alex Leary.)

Here is Samuel Bartlett with the children of Addie Forbes Bartlett and John Thomas "Dick" Bartlett. The children are, from left to right, Henning Bartlett, Earl Bartlett, Worth Bartlett, and Henrietta Bartlett. Henning Forbes Bartlett, born on September 1, 1920, posted a letter on the last day of mailing from the Bartlett, North Carolina, post office on July 30, 1932. (Courtesy of Linda Ann Mansfield.)

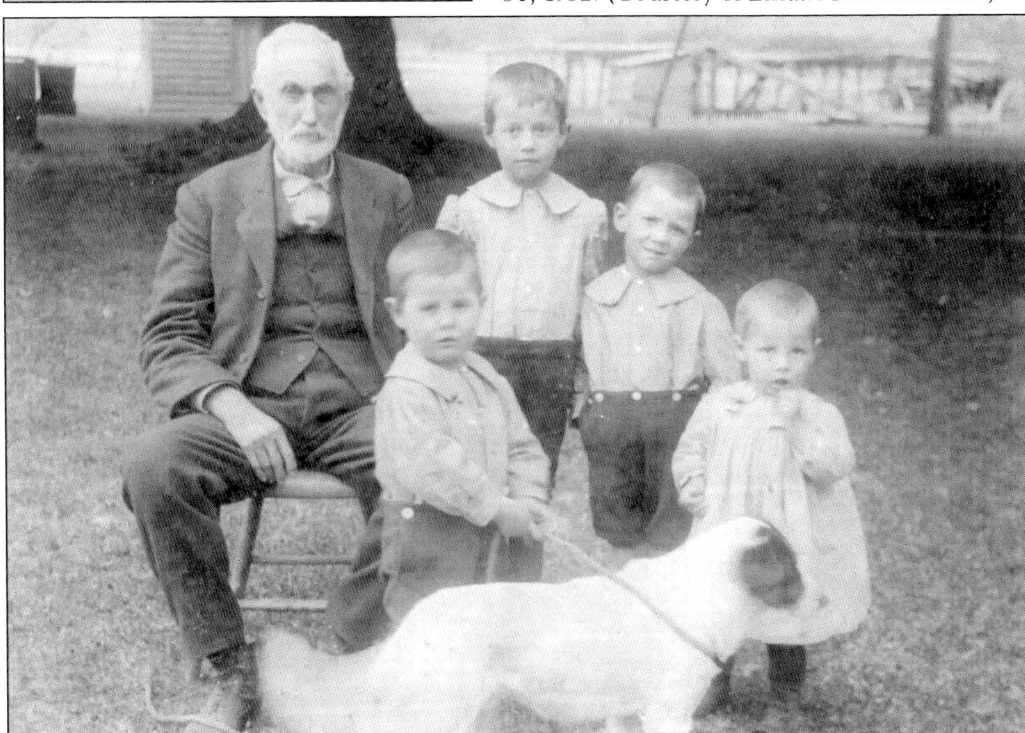

Bettie Bartlett Seymour and Silas Berry Seymour were both born around 1880 and reared eight children in Camden County. The oldest six are pictured here around 1920 and are, from left to right, (first row) Alma Lee Seymour and Mabel Inez Seymour; (second row) Fannie Louise Seymour, Silas Berry Seymour Jr., Marguerite Seymour, and Marvin Bartlett Seymour. Youngest brothers Dennis Joseph Seymour and Erving Bartlett Seymour had not yet been born. (Courtesy of Betty Brock.)

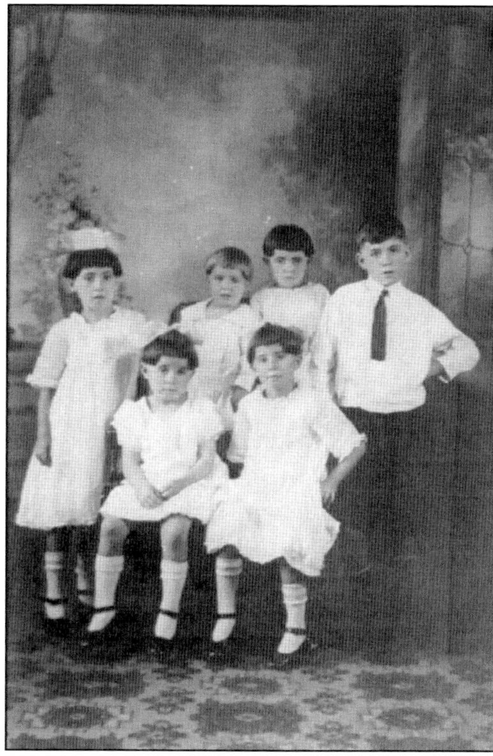

All eight children of Bettie Bartlett Seymour and Silas Berry Seymour shown here in the 1930s are, from left to right, (first row) Marvin Bartlett Seymour, Fannie Louise Seymour, Mabel Inez Seymour, Marguerite Seymour, and Alma Lee Seymour; (second row) Silas Berry Seymour Jr., Dennis Joseph Seymour, and Erving Bartlett Seymour. These eight siblings were born between 1910 and 1923. (Courtesy of Doris Dough Forehand.)

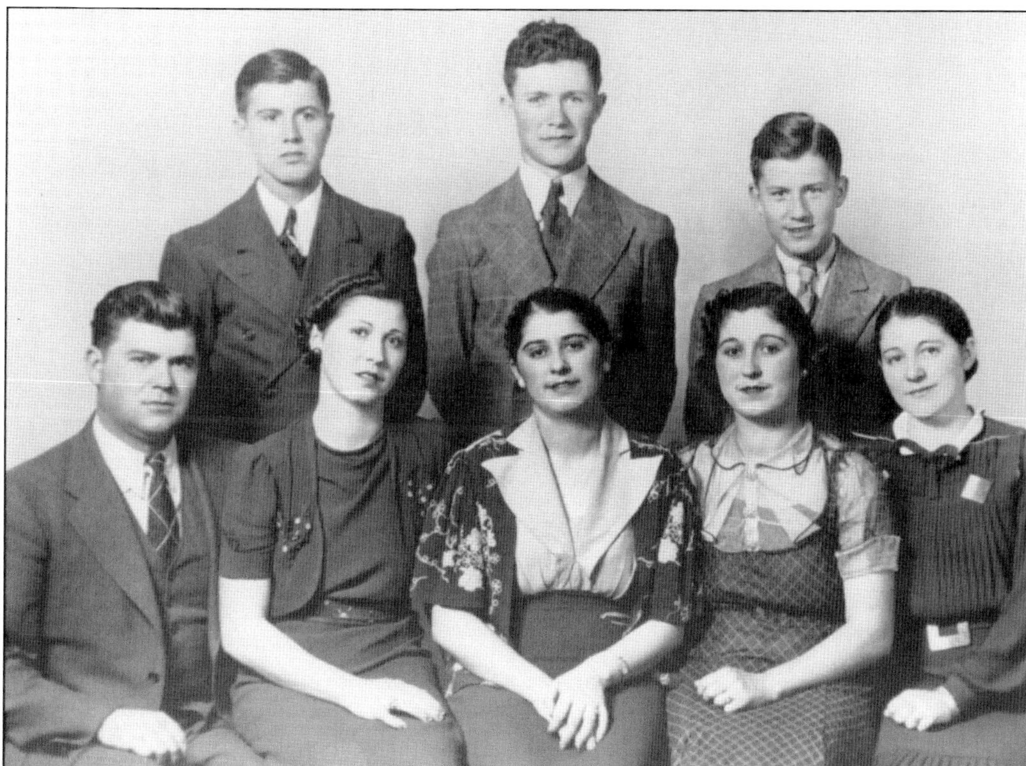

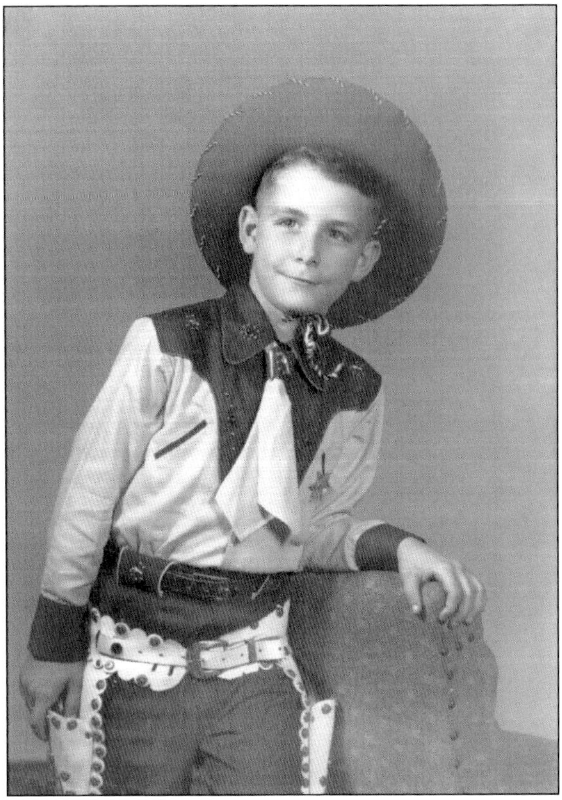

The young boy in this picture taken in February 1953 is Charles Glenn Forbes. He is the son of Elizabeth Walston Forbes and Charlie Forbes. Charles graduated from Camden County High School in 1964. A month after his graduation, he died tragically in a diving accident at a popular swimming spot in Riddle. (Courtesy of Anita Whitehurst.)

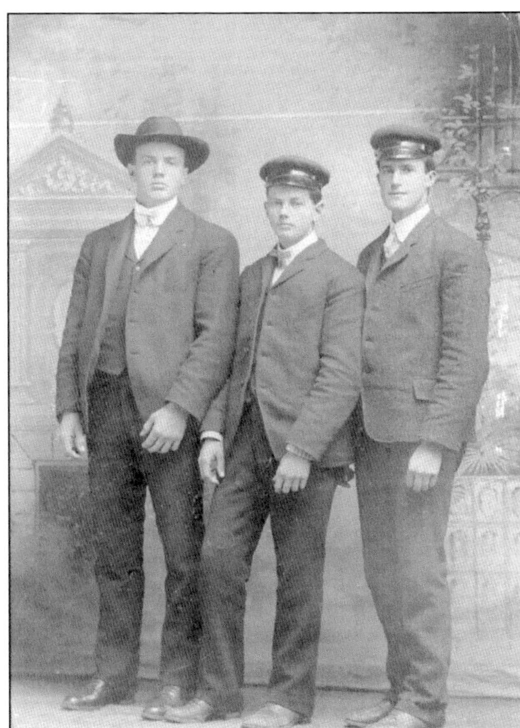

Joseph Forbes Mercer (right) began work with the US Lighthouse Service in 1898 and retired in 1932. He was keeper at both North River Lighthouse and Wade Point Lighthouse. Mercer sent out the message that the North River Lighthouse had been seriously damaged by the big freeze of 1917–1918. North River Lighthouse was purchased by Dare County and moved to Rodanthe in 1920 for use as a schoolhouse. (Courtesy of Thelma Naomi Sawyer Forbes.)

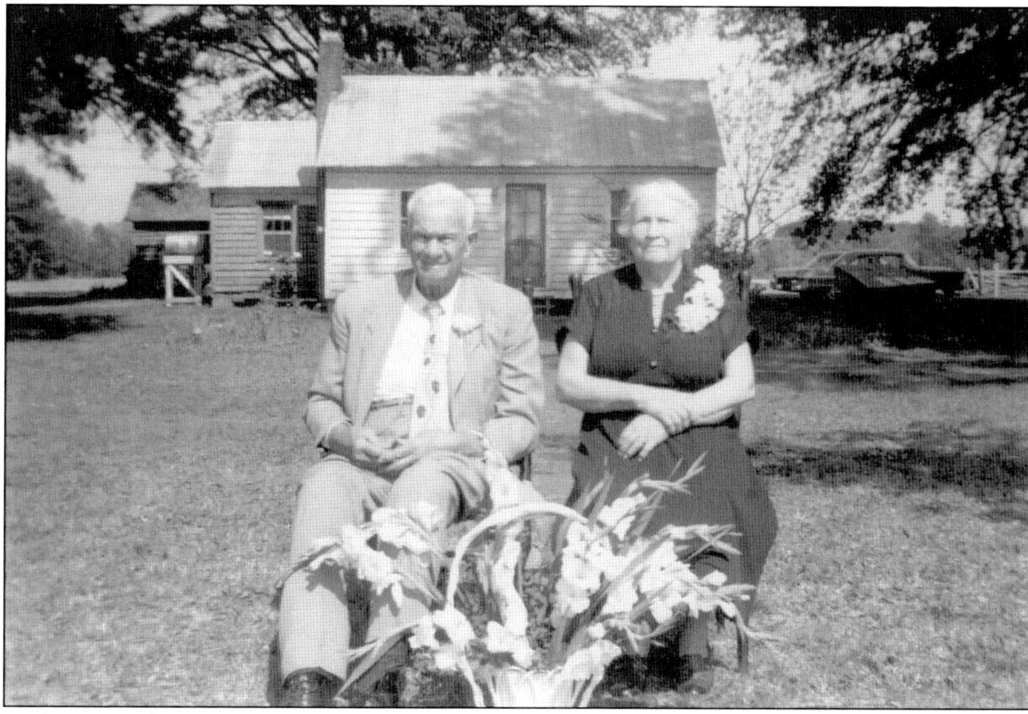

In this 1959 photograph, Chessie and George Pearce celebrate their 58th wedding anniversary at their home on Muddy Road in Pearceville. The flowers were given to them by McBride Methodist Church, of which they were longtime members. It is interesting to note the outbuildings of the small farm, especially the intact milk house at the right side of the photograph. (Courtesy of Martha Ann.)

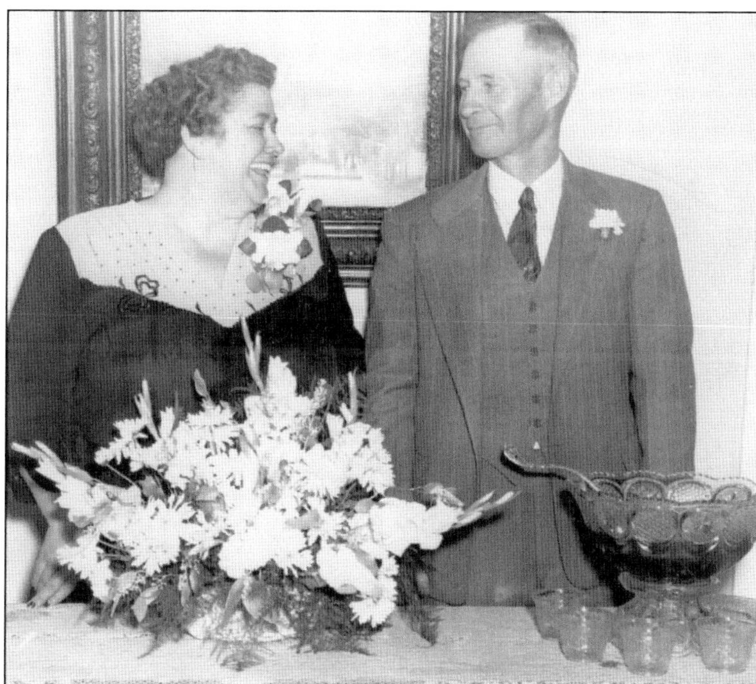

Essie Sears Bartlett married William Williams "Will" Dough on December 18, 1922. Their three children were Doris Elizabeth Dough (Forehand), William Ishmael Dough, and Alton Bartlett Dough. Essie and Will celebrated their 25th wedding anniversary at their home on North Trotman Road in Indiantown in 1947, surrounded by family and friends. (Courtesy of Doris Dough Forehand.)

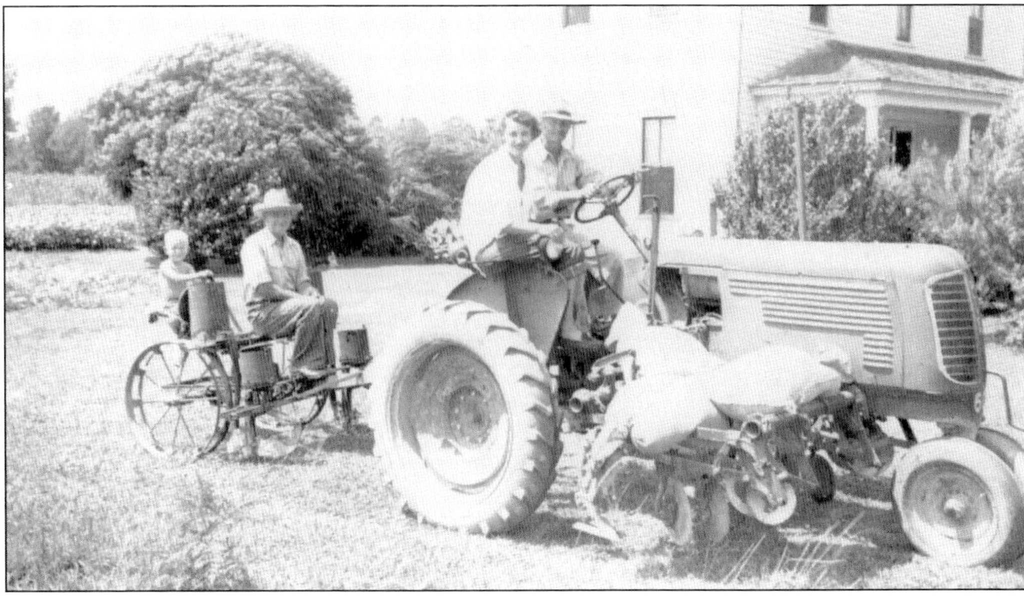

From left to right are Terry Forehand, Grady Dough, Donna McDonnell Dough, and Will Dough riding on a 1945 Model 60 Oliver row crop tractor pulling a two-row seed planter. Bags of seed or fertilizer are lying across the discs and plows mounted to the underside of the tractor. The ground was broken open with the plows, and the planter dropped seed and/or fertilizer. (Courtesy of Doris Dough Forehand.)

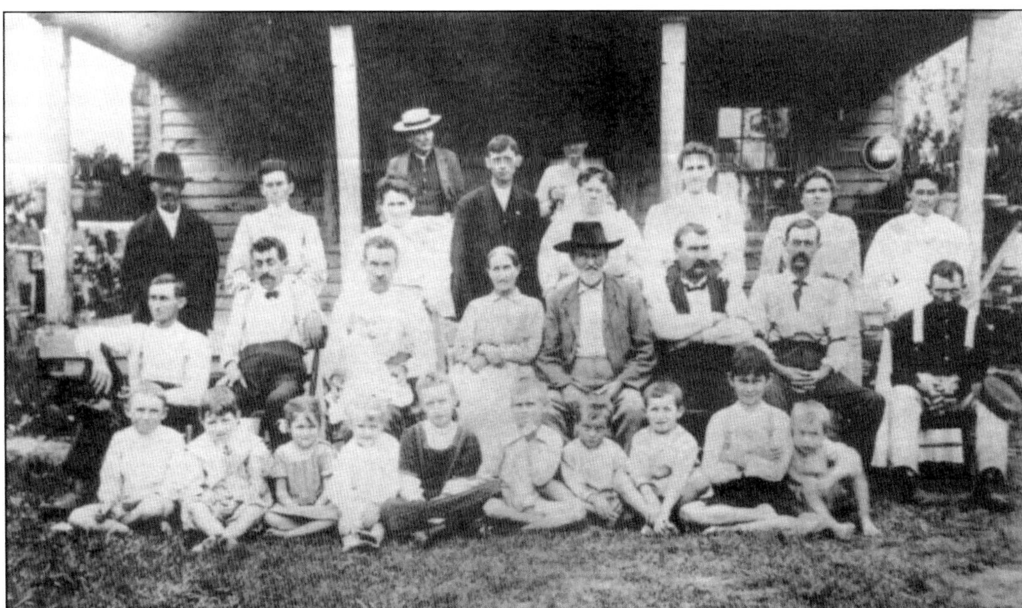

This is the family of Mary Jane Perkins, born in 1841, and William Sawyer Jones, born in 1838, who are seated between their six sons in front of their house in Pearceville around 1907. Those in the second row are, from left to right, Malichi Crowder Jones, William Dozier Jones, George Nelson Jones, Mary Jane Perkins Jones, William Sawyer Jones, Charles Willey Jones, James Franklin Jones, and Wilson Raynor Jones. (Courtesy of Bob Jones.)

Montelle Bulloch Williams, born on October 21, 1903, is the only law enforcement officer of Camden County ever to have been lost in the line of duty. Deputy Williams died on November 9, 1966, at the age of 63 after 20 years of service with the Camden County Sheriff's Office. He was survived by his wife and two children. (Courtesy of the Camden County Sheriff's Office.)

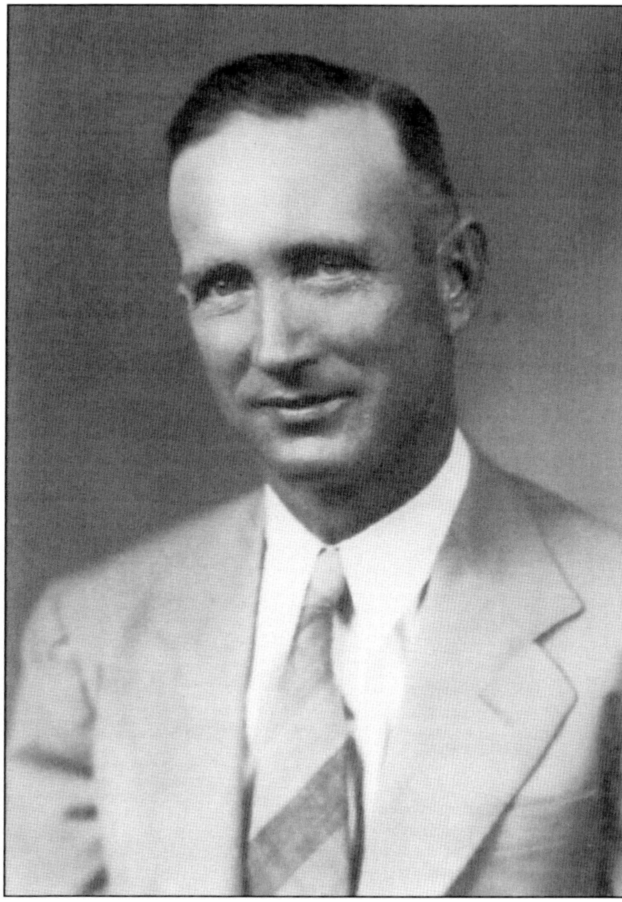

These children are, from left to right, Catherine Pugh, Edward Pugh, and Gladys Pugh. Their parents were Nettie and John Pugh. Theirs was a simple rural childhood when children used their imaginations playing together. The girls were lucky to have dolls. It was customary at the time to keep boys in dresses until they no longer wore diapers. (Courtesy of Joyce Mitchell Cuthrell.)

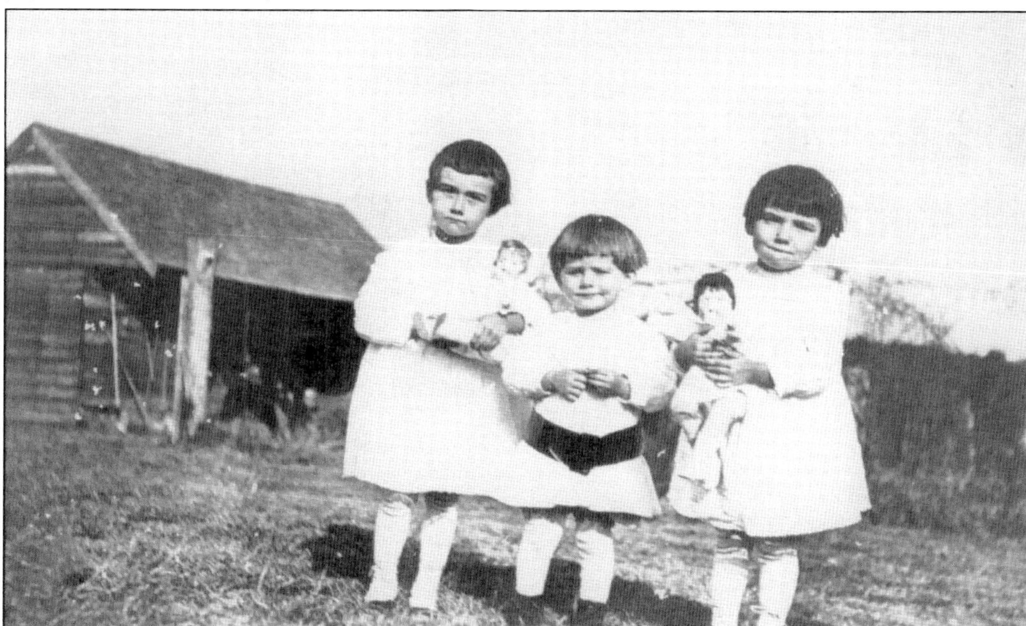

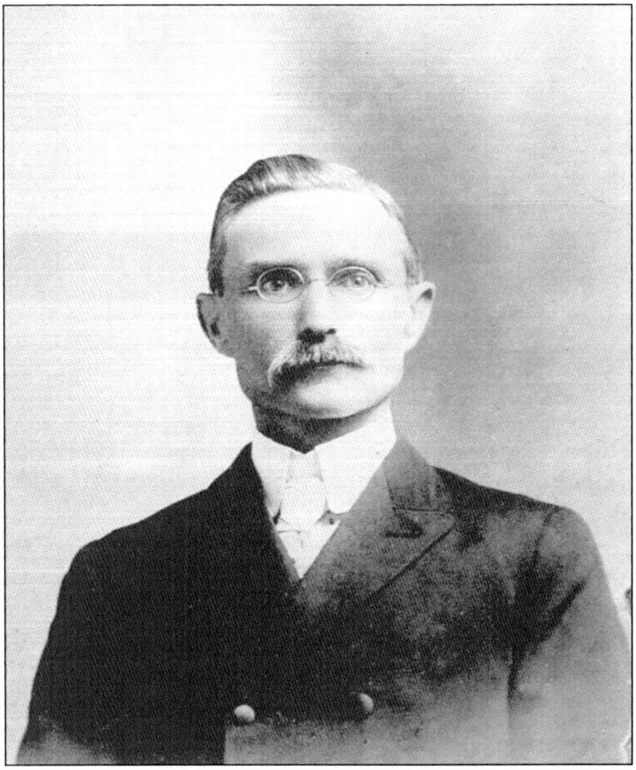

Dennis Forbes Bartlett Sr. was born in Shiloh in 1868 and married Pollie Jarvis Sears in 1889, parenting 10 children. Bartlett, a carpenter, served as justice of the peace and as Camden County's representative in the North Carolina State Legislature in 1911 and 1913 where he served on agriculture, fish, and fisheries; game; and "deaf and dumb" committees. He was a respected arbitrator and humanitarian. (Courtesy of Anita Whitehurst.)

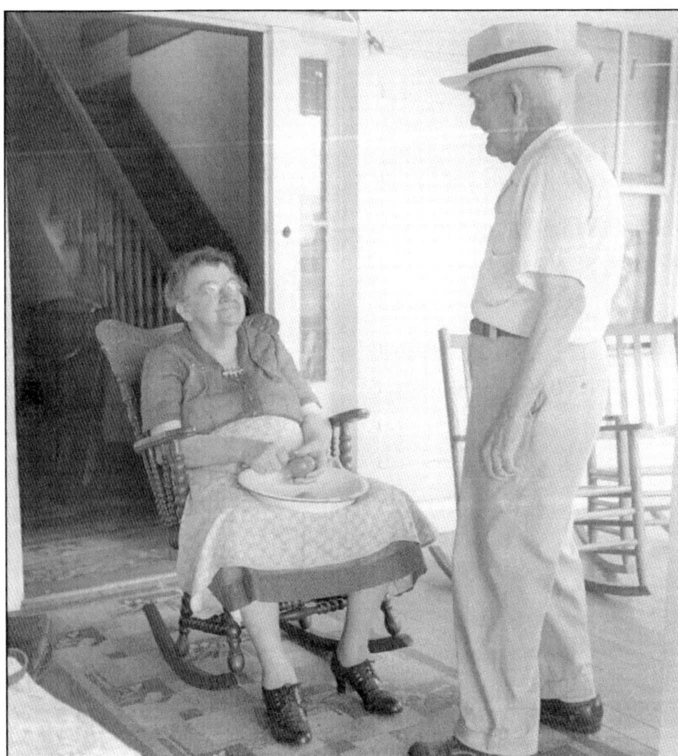

Polly Burgess, born in 1880, was the daughter of Sarah Burgess and Wilson Bartlett Burgess and married Willie Jasper Burgess. She sits on her front porch visiting with her brother. Hezekiah Burgess was born in May 1875 to Elizabeth Burgess and Wilson Bartlett Burgess and married Sophia Forbes. Hezekiah died in 1961, and Polly followed in 1967. (Courtesy of Portia Lee and Wilse Burgess.)

Addie Dorothy Pearce and William Robert Pritchard had a kennel in South Mills where they bred champion Norwegian elkhounds. The Pritchards had an only child, Robert, who was blind and mentally handicapped but had outstanding musical ability and played piano. Here are Addie and Robert standing in front of McBride United Methodist Church, where he would play the piano. (Courtesy of Martha Ann.)

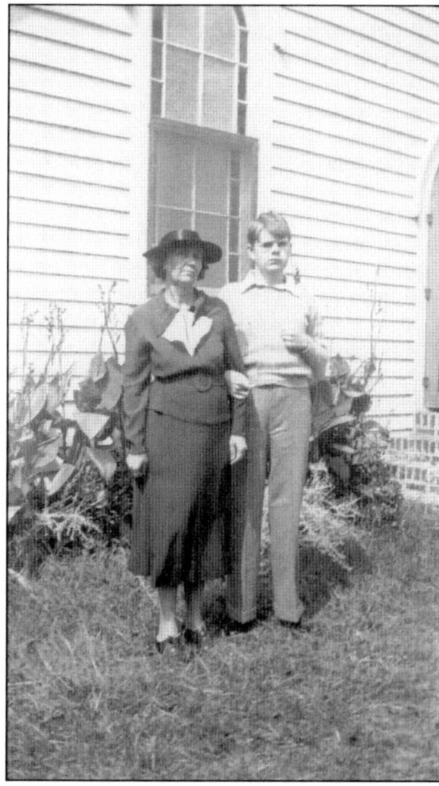

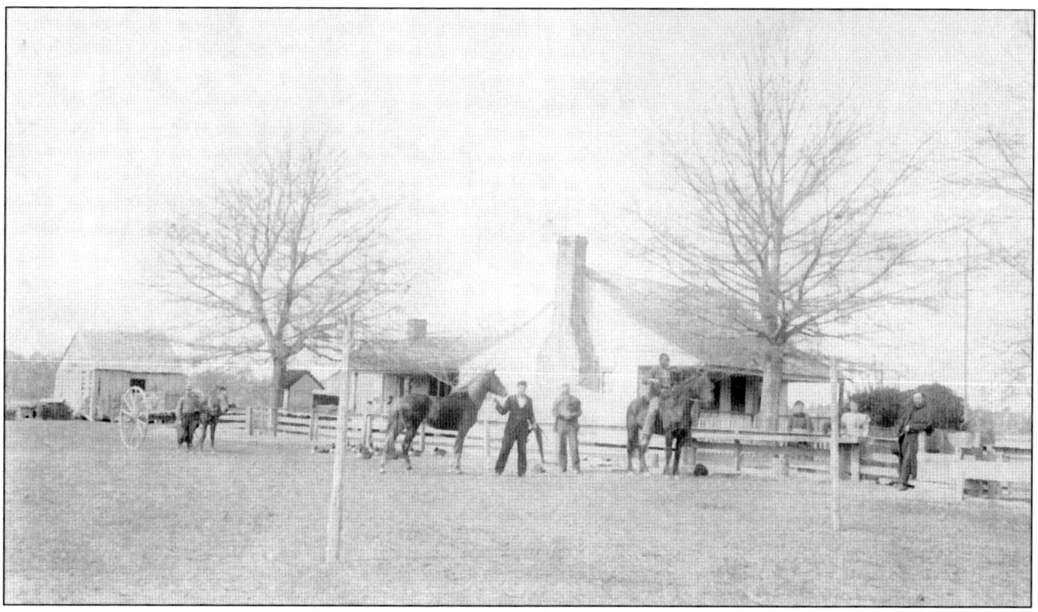

The Mercer family from Old Trap around 1900 are, from left to right, Burvil F. Mercer, Joe F. Mercer, Benjamin Franklin Mercer, Buck Gallop, Meddie Forbes Mercer, Mary Mercer Baker, and John Baker, a schoolteacher. Photographers Zoeller and Morgan from Elizabeth City traveled through the countryside, producing this sort of image that documented the family, farm, and horses for tax purposes. Teachers boarded with families. (Courtesy of Thelma Naomi Sawyer Forbes.)

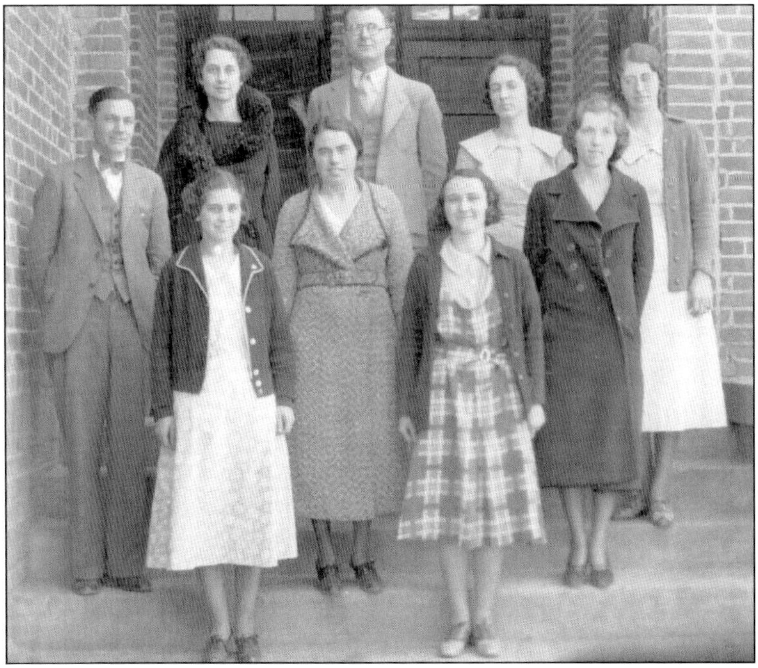

The faculty of Shiloh High School during the 1930s are not limited to but include, from left to right, (first row) Eloise Forbes, Nannie Pugh, Gertie Basnight, and Pauline Jordan; (second row) Mr. ? Barefoot, Ruby Adams, Joe Brothers (principal), Geneva Forehand, and Elizabeth Forbes. Camden County teachers moved to fewer and more centralized schools as consolidation occurred. (Courtesy of Linda Ann Mansfield.)

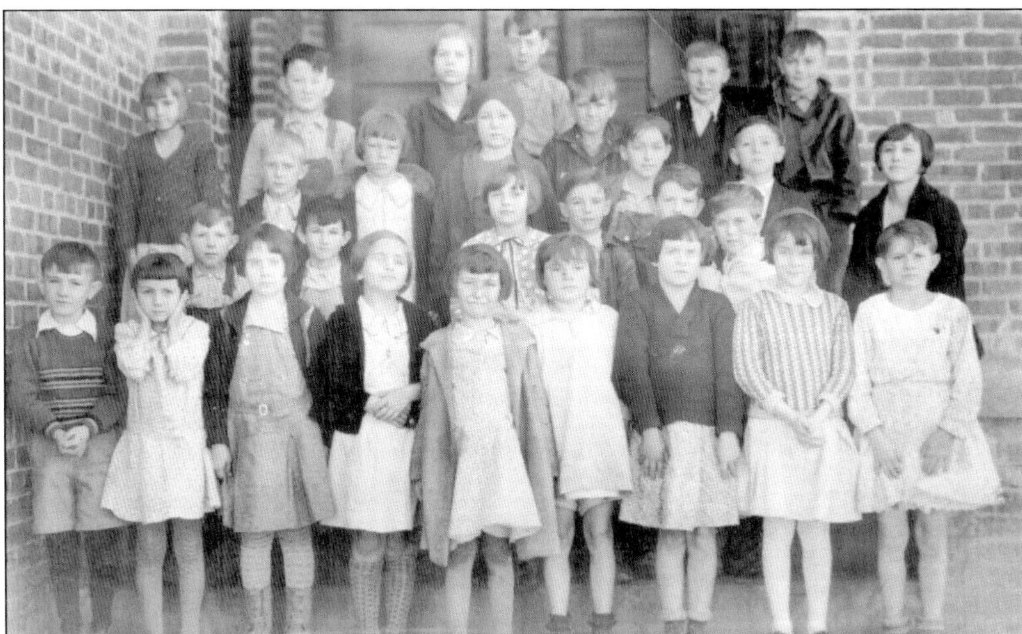

Shiloh School's 1932 third grade is made up of, from left to right, (first row) Calvin Sawyer, Reba Harrison, Wilma Bray, Ellen Barnard, Alma Forbes, Alma Seymour, Mary Riggs, Ellen Forehand, and Virginia Harrison; (second row) John Harrison, James Harrison, Bertha Wilson, Clifton Burgess, Jesse Bell, Levy Kight, and teacher Mary Burgess; (third row) Marvin Jordan, Lucille Burgess, Florence Dowdy, Norman Pierce, Marshall Riggs, and Winfred Owens; (fourth row) Isabelle Forbes, Julian Squires, Henrietta Forbes, Norman Lee, Obie Reynolds, and Dennis Burgess. (Courtesy of Dewey Burgess.)

Two

South Mills and the Dismal Swamp Canal

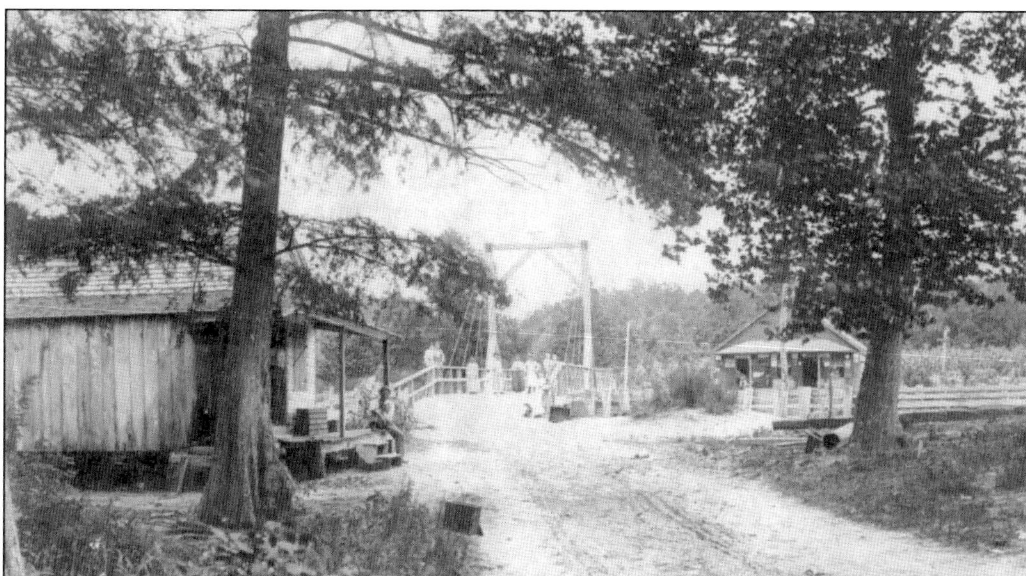

The D.S. Williams store was located at River Bridge, about a mile below South Mills lock. Built over the Pasquotank River early in the 1800s, the bridge was destroyed during the Civil War and then rebuilt by Union brigadier general Edward A. Wild's troops during his infamous raid. It was rebuilt once more during the Reconstruction period. (Courtesy of Joyce and Durward Medlin.)

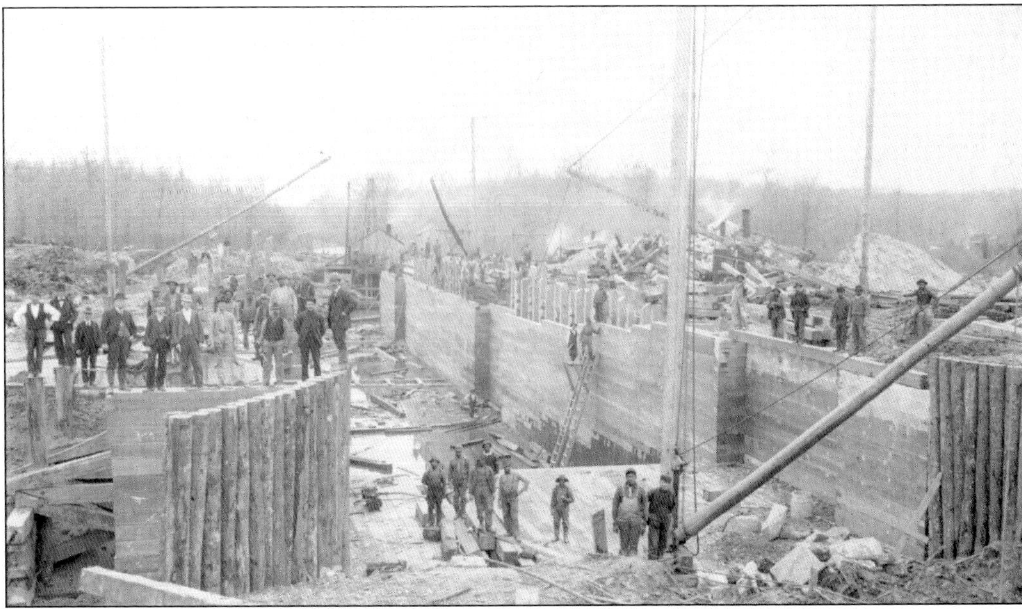

Between 1896 and 1899, the Lake Drummond Canal and Water Company widened the Dismal Swamp Canal to 60 feet wide and deepened it to 10 feet. Northwest and Culpepper locks were removed and South Mills and Deep Creek locks were rebuilt of timber with chambers of 250 feet by 40 feet. This photograph was made in 1896 by Zoeller, Morgan Company. (Courtesy of Alex Leary.)

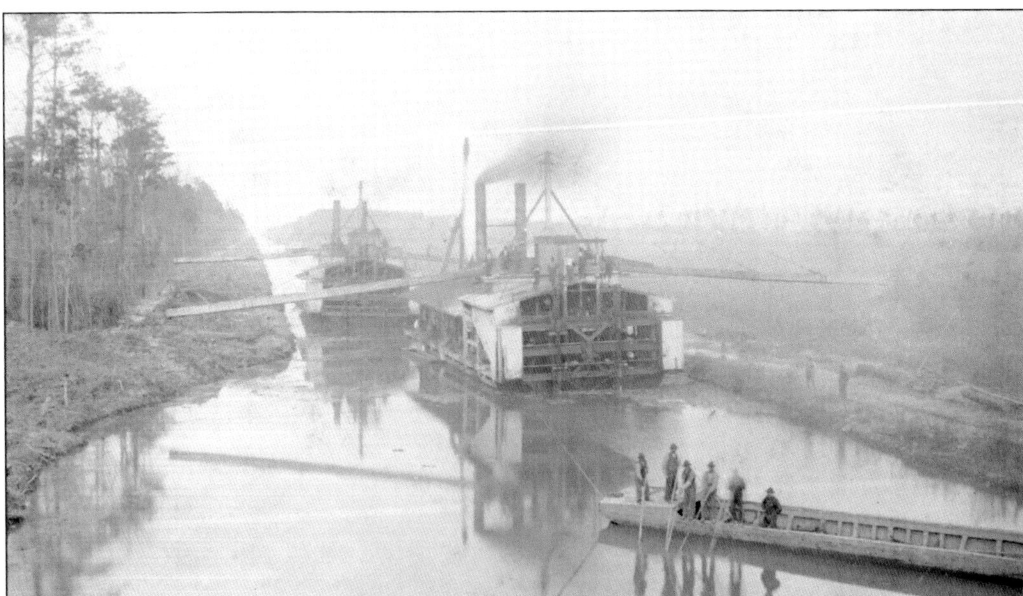

Original construction of the Dismal Swamp Canal began in 1793. This photograph was made around 1896 by Zoeller, Morgan Company from Elizabeth City. The Lake Drummond Canal and Water Company used steam-powered dipper dredges and hydraulic dredges to dig out the canal. Large barges were used as moving platforms, which floated the dredges and steam engines used to power them. (Courtesy of Alex Leary.)

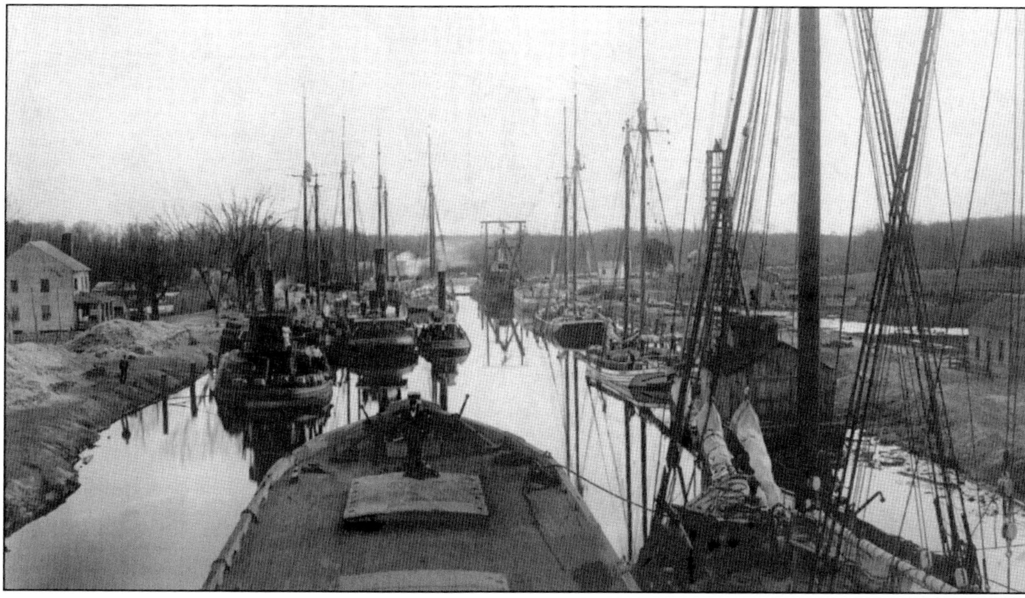

This photograph was taken by Zoeller around 1900, soon after the major widening of the Dismal Swamp Canal and rebuilding of the of the lock at South Mills, and shows a number of southward-bound ships waiting to lock through down to Elizabeth City. Piles of dirt from the recent widening can still be seen along the left bank. (Courtesy of the author.)

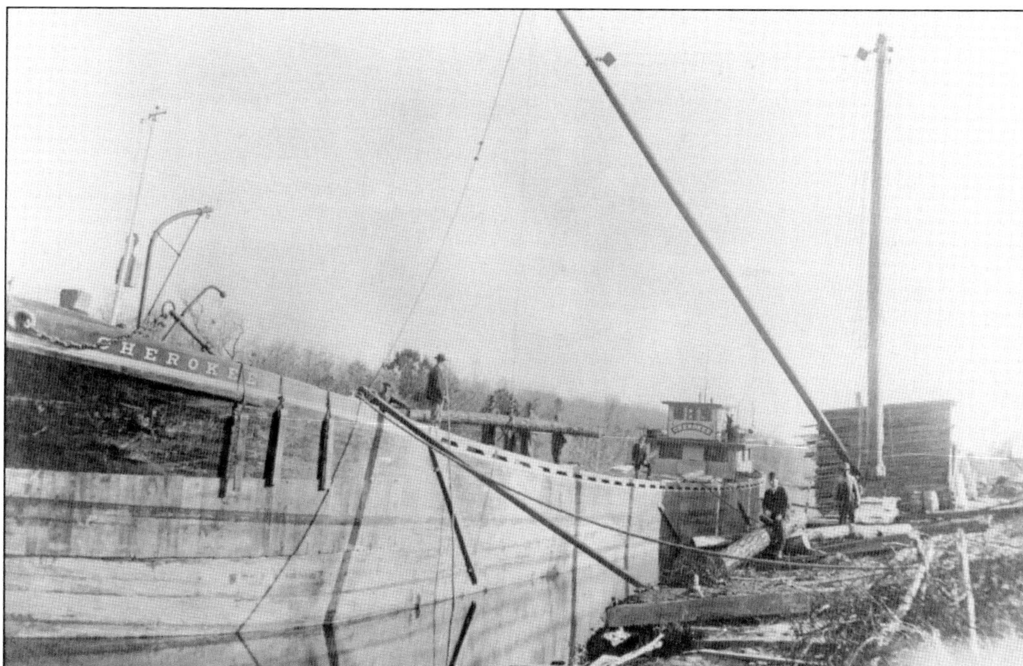

Ships carried tons of logs and milled lumber through the Dismal Swamp Canal. The enormous *Cherokee* is shown here docked alongside the canal bank with a crane being used for loading and unloading. Countless boats and barges loaded with logs and lumber locked through South Mills to travel the canal between the Pasquotank and Elizabeth Rivers. (Courtesy of the Outer Banks History Center, Dismal Swamp Canal and South Mills Collection.)

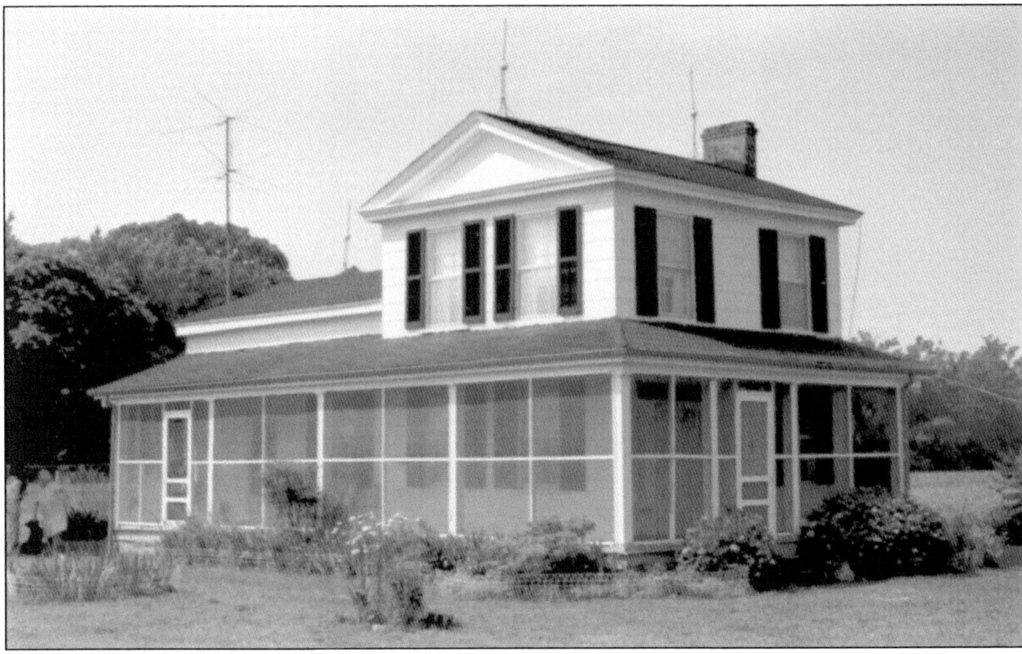

This house is located off the road on the west side of Highway 343 between the village of Camden and South Mills and was built by carpenter James H. Sawyer about 1858. Sawyer also did much of the work of building Geneva Baptist Church, organized at Burnt Mills in 1860 and named for Geneva Bell. Sawyer also ran the ferry landing near here. (Courtesy of the State Archives of North Carolina.)

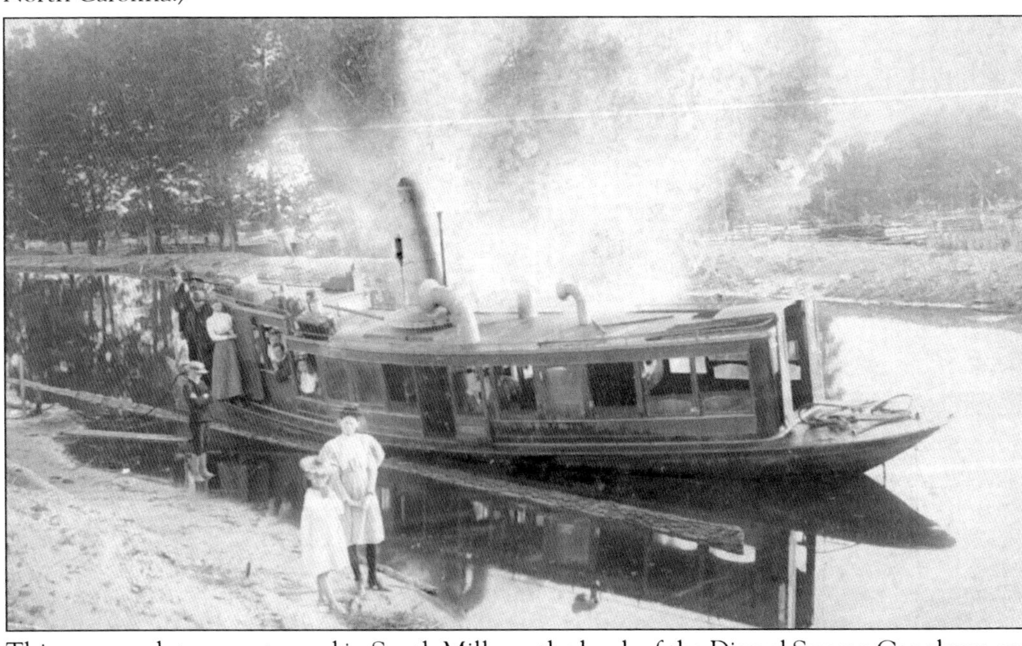

This unnamed steamer stopped in South Mills on the bank of the Dismal Swamp Canal was one of many that provided regular passenger and mail services to many destinations. The steamers and railroad lines were affiliated with one another and made regularly scheduled connections at various ports and railway depots. (Courtesy of the Dismal Swamp Canal Welcome Center.)

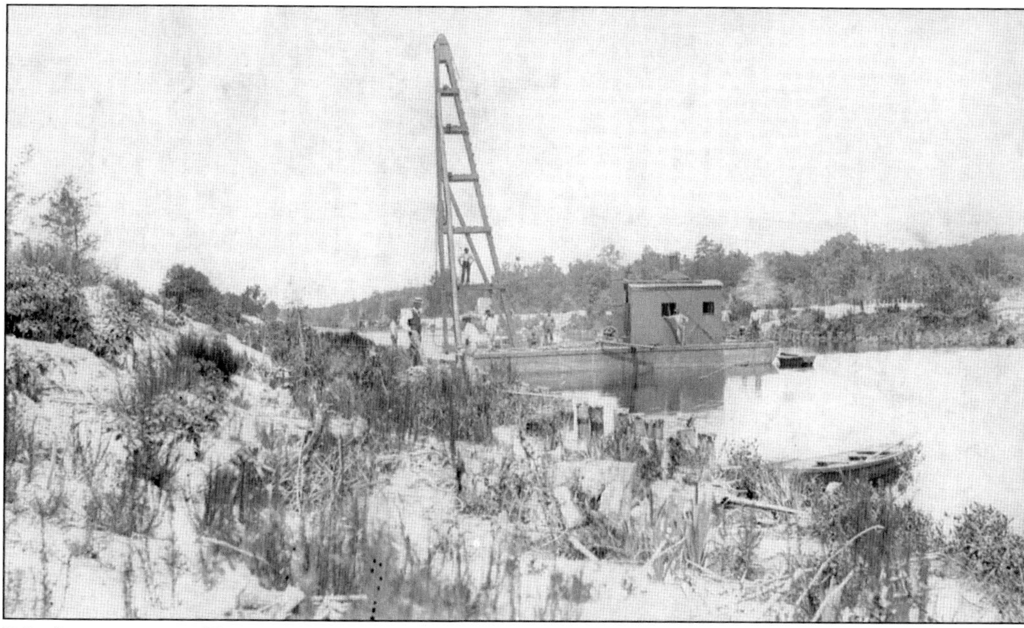

Pile drivers powered by steam engines were used for driving the pilings necessary to prevent collapse and erosion of the banks of the newly widened Dismal Swamp Canal. Multiple pile driving barges were used, and one other can be seen in the distant background. In the foreground, the newly driven bulkhead can be seen. (Courtesy of the Dismal Swamp Canal Welcome Center.)

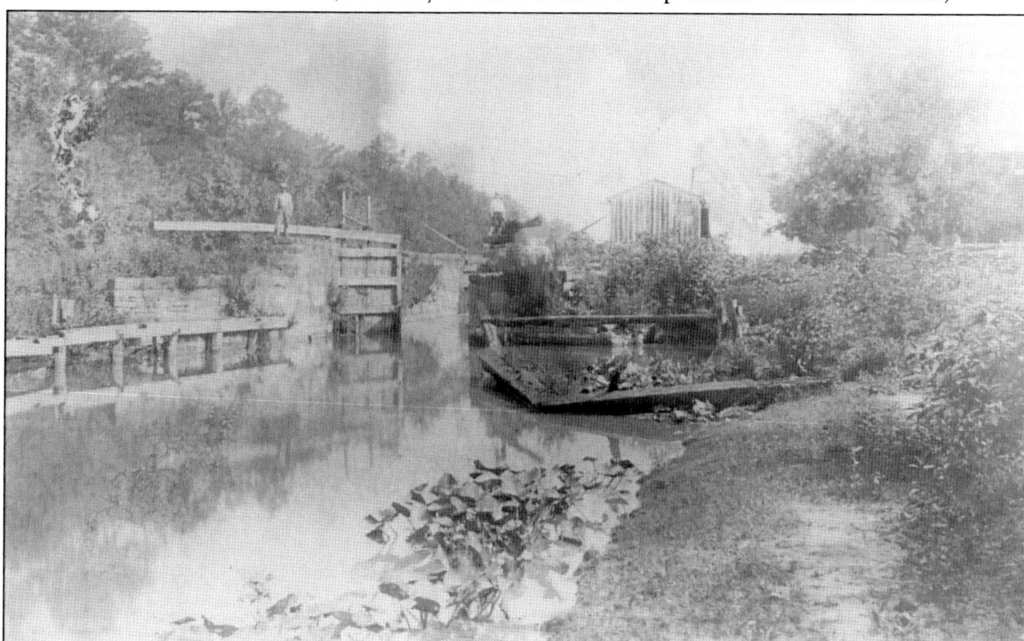

The Dismal Swamp Canal was enlarged and rebuilt entirely by 1899, dropping the level of the canal by eight feet. Culpepper lock, pictured here, was no longer necessary after the rebuilding. The lock at South Mills narrowly escaped total destruction by explosives during the Civil War, but Confederate forces were able to defend it from the Union attack at the Battle of South Mills. (Courtesy of the Dismal Swamp Canal Welcome Center.)

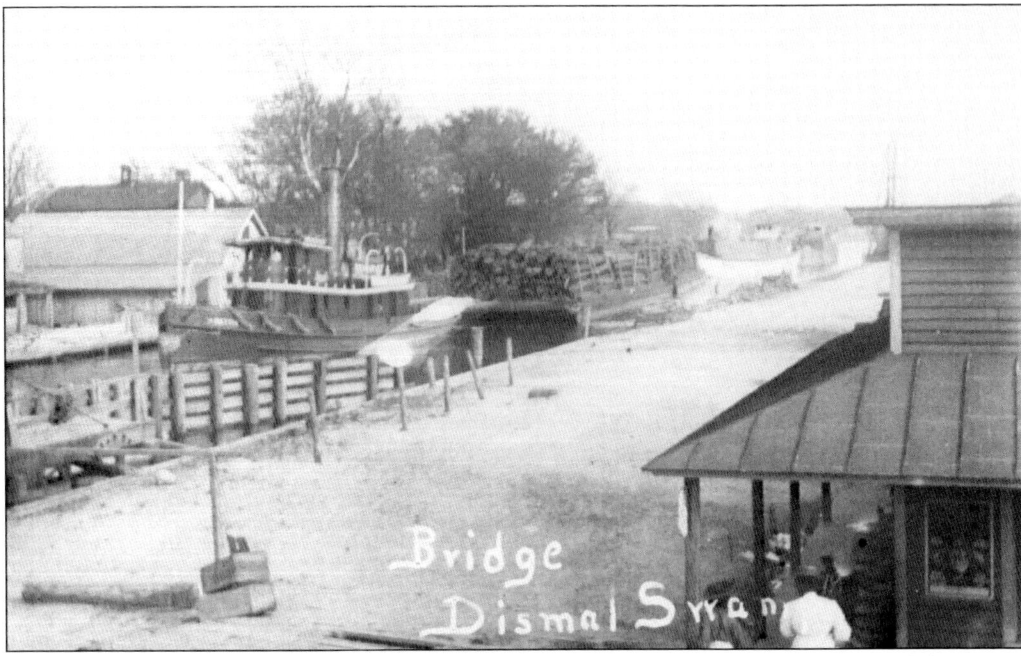

Just north of the lock in South Mills, a bridge, shown here in the open position, crossed the Dismal Swamp Canal. Around 1900, a wooden swing bridge was still in use. When a boat needed to pass through, a bridge tender pulled a lever that activated gears, causing the bridge to open in the middle, and each side would swing open towards the bank. (Courtesy of Vernon Burgess Jr.)

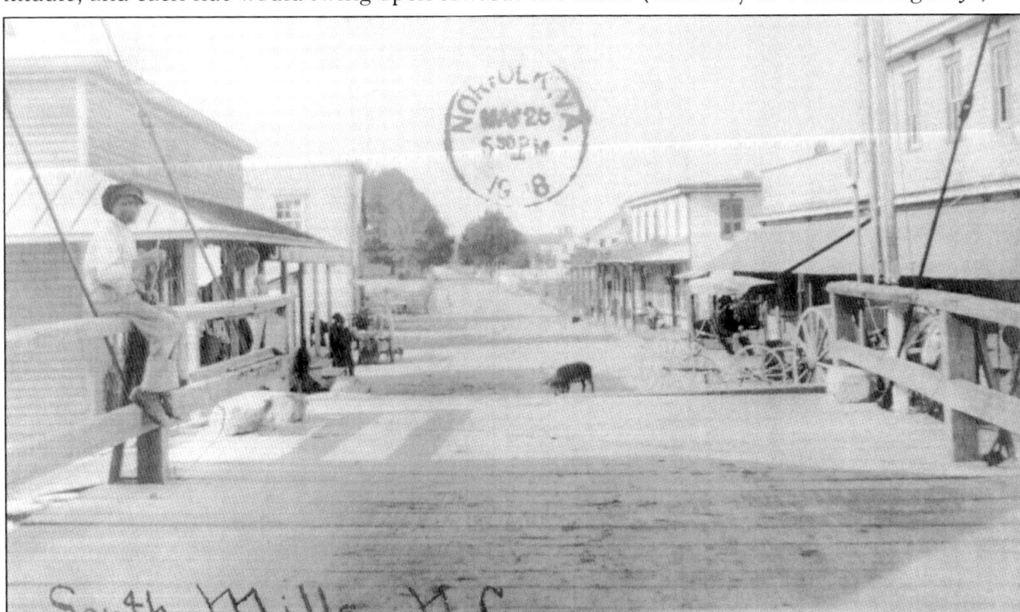

This real-photo postcard was made from the bridge that crosses the Dismal Swamp Canal at South Mills and looks down Main Street. The card was posted in Norfolk, Virginia, in 1928, just prior to the beginning of construction on the new steel drawbridge. South Mills was known as a "marriage mill" because couples would come down from Virginia so that they could marry with no waiting period. (Courtesy of Thalia Jones.)

In the 1920s, pedestrians were still using the top of the spillway at the South Mills lock as a walkway. The spillway was used to control the level of the water in the canal above the lock with the number of open and closed wickets regulating the flow of the wasteway. More wickets were open during wet weather, flowing continually when necessary. (Courtesy of the author.)

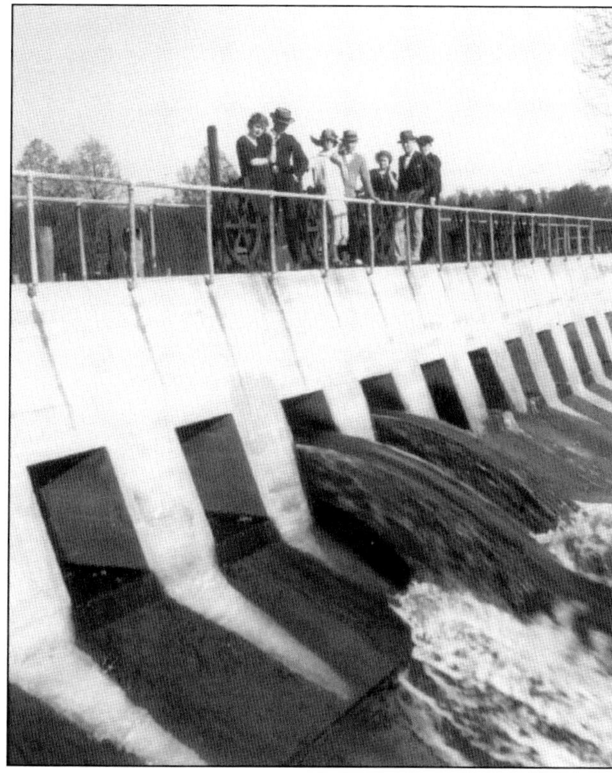

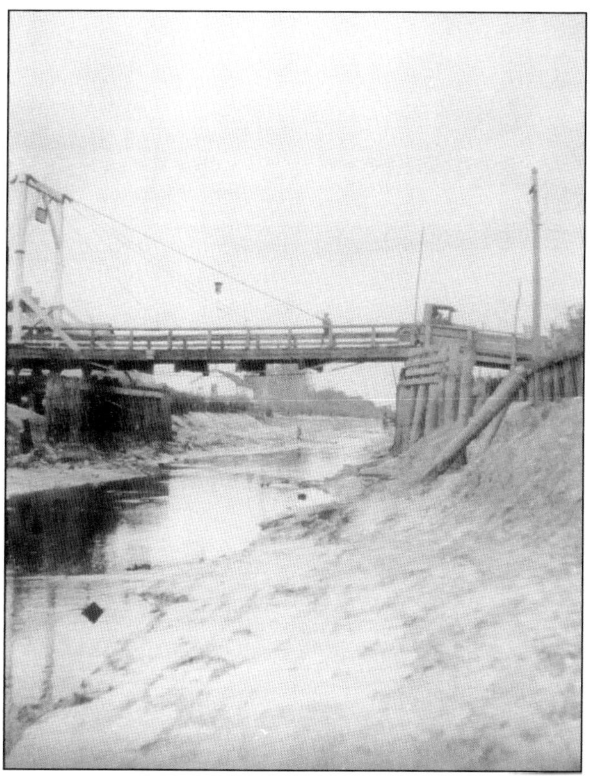

At some time during the 1920s, the spillway at the South Mills lock failed, causing most of the water above the lock to drain out of the canal. This photograph was taken from down inside of the almost empty canal and the view looks up at a car crossing the same bridge where the James Adams Floating Theatre would tie up and perform for one week during the summer. (Courtesy of the Dismal Swamp Canal Welcome Center.)

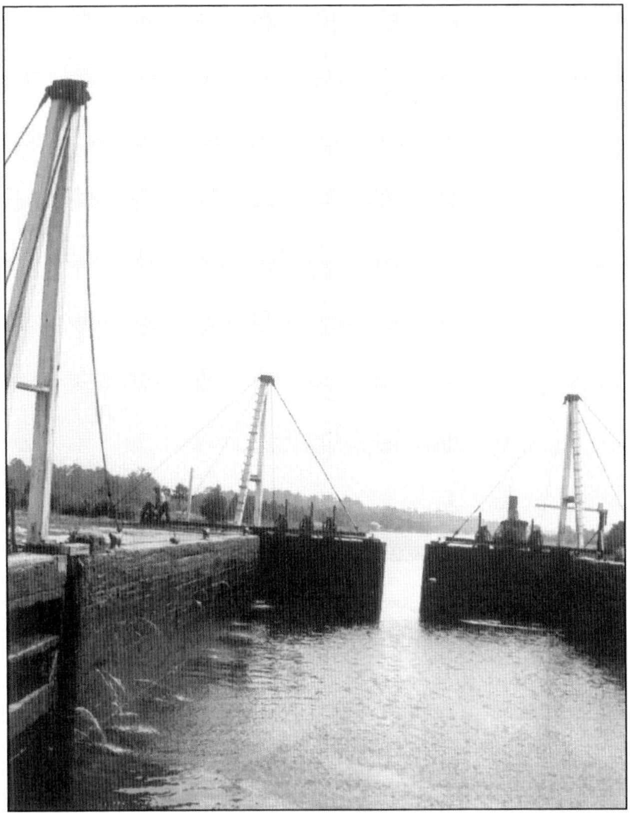

The lock gates at the South Mills lock are shown in the 1920s. The Dismal Swamp Canal is the oldest surviving man-made waterway in the United States, linking South Mills with Deep Creek, Virginia. The golden age of the canal was from 1839 until 1860. Ansel Adams once traveled and photographed the canal, which is still used today as part of the Intracoastal Waterway. (Courtesy of the author.)

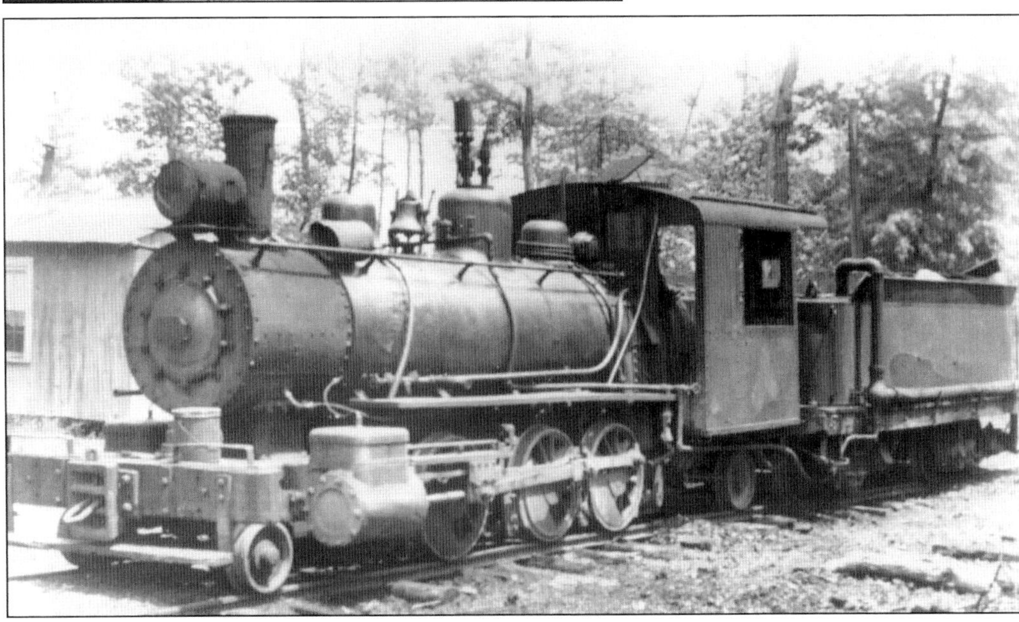

Along with industrial development came small-gauge railroads and locomotives, or "lokis," which replaced draft animals for hauling logs out of the swamp. Lumber companies owned large tracts of timberland in the swamp and employed many men to cut and haul lumber. This locomotive was in use in 1948. (Courtesy of the Dismal Swamp Canal Welcome Center.)

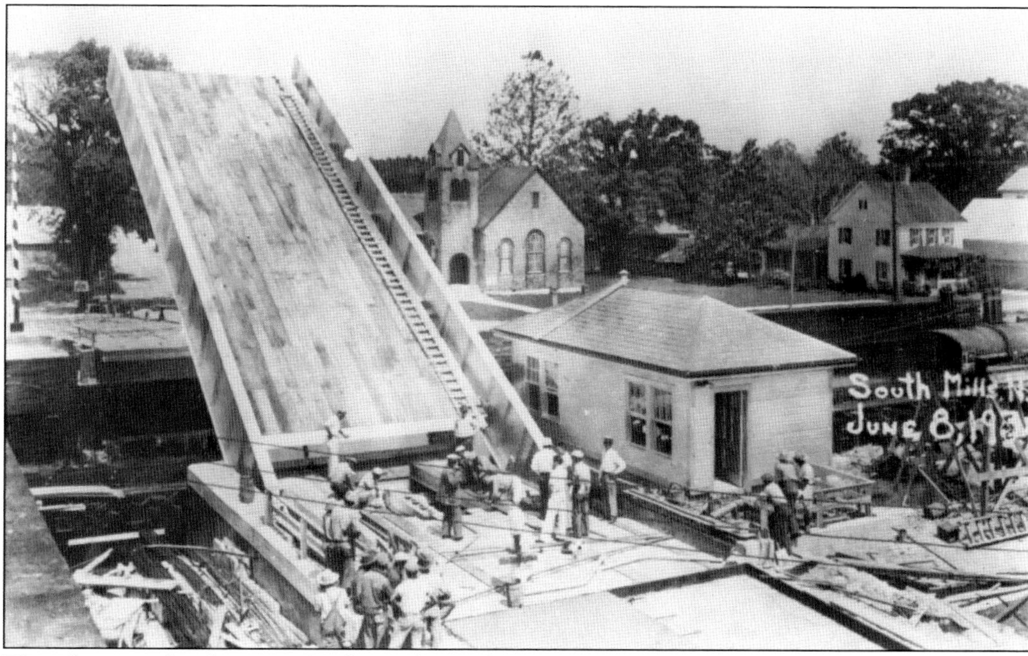

This photograph taken in 1934 shows the workers nearing completion of the new steel drawbridge over the Dismal Swamp Canal in South Mills. Only a month later, the new bridge would officially open for the first time. This canal crossing has had much strategic value since its first use. (Courtesy of the Outer Banks History Center, Dismal Swamp Canal and South Mills Collection.)

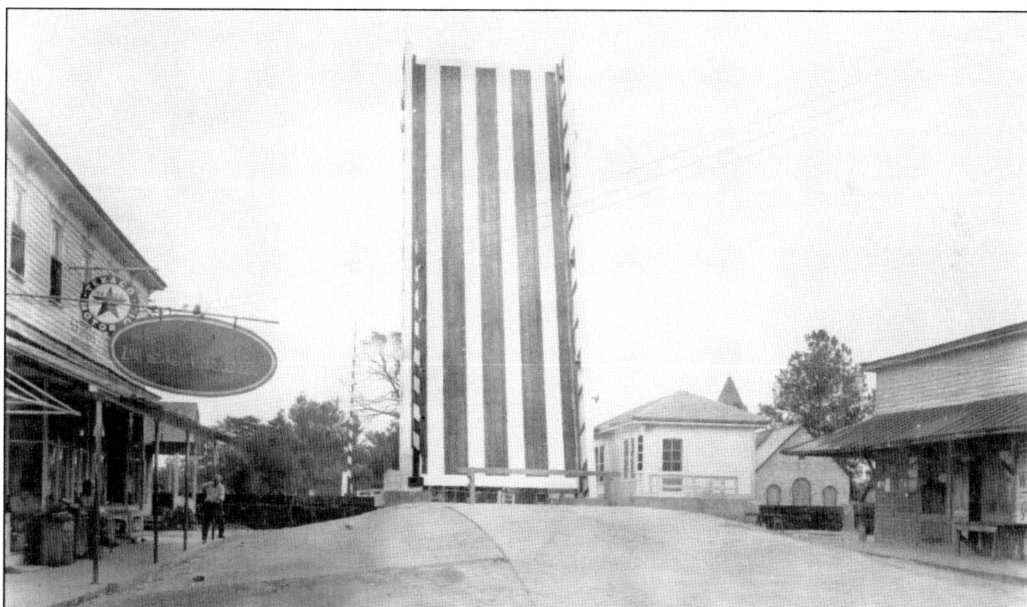

The steel lift drawbridge over the canal in South Mills was officially opened on July 6, 1934, as pictured here. From the west side of the canal, the businesses along the street can be seen, and in the background, to the right of the span, the peak of the steeple and part of the Ebenezer Baptist Church are visible. (Courtesy of Vernon Burgess Jr.)

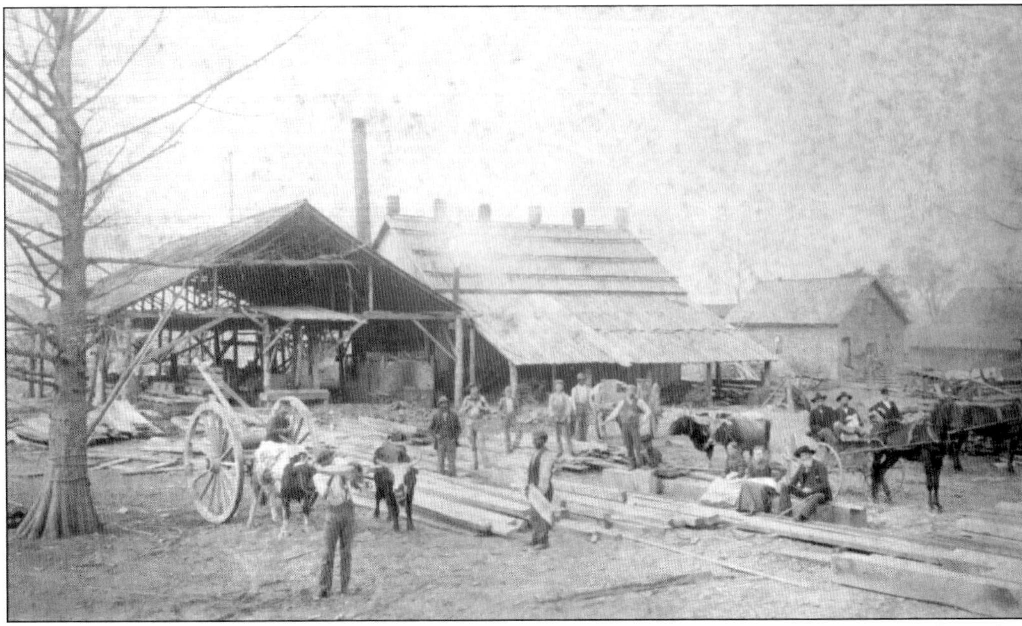

Because of its convenient proximity to the Great Dismal Swamp, the lumber industry has flourished in Camden County. Depicted here is a typical sawmill, many of which were operating in the county around 1900. Lumber cut here was dragged out of the swamps with oxcarts. Two yokes of oxen and a cart can be seen in this photograph. (Courtesy of the author.)

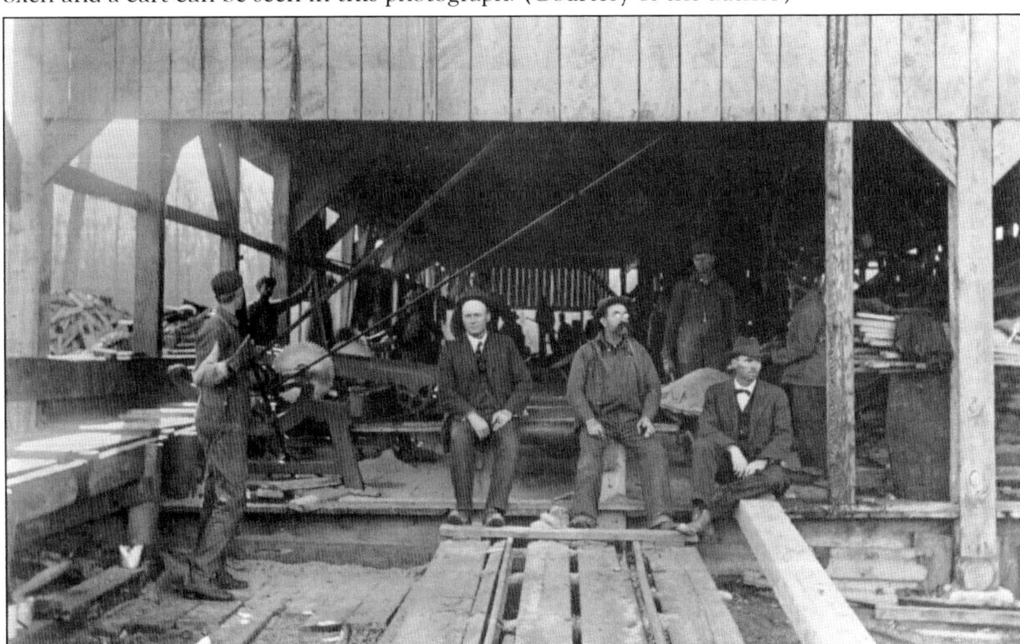

The D.E. Williams sawmill, located near River Bridge in an area that has also been known as Joppa, was in operation between 1910 and 1925. The men seated are, from left to right, Daniel Edward Williams, William Thomas Sawyer, and Frank Williams. Daniel, "Danel" or "Mr. Dan'Led," as he was called, owned and operated this mill. (Courtesy of the Outer Banks History Center, Dismal Swamp Canal and South Mills Collection.)

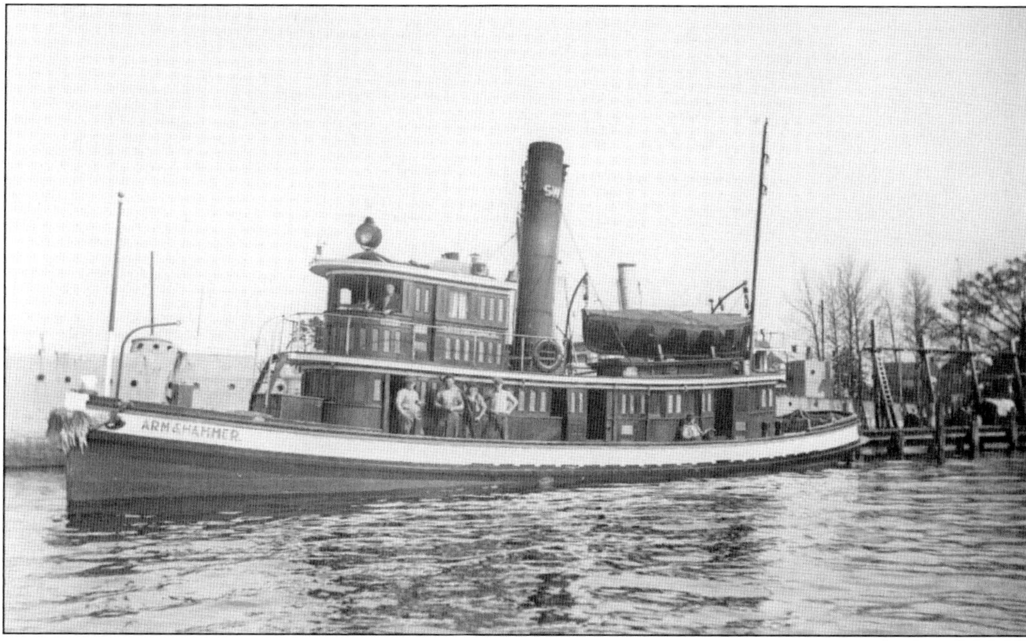

This beautiful tugboat, the *Arm & Hammer*, was owned by Daniel E. Williams from South Mills. Because he owned and operated a sawmill, Williams became involved in the transportation of his products and bought the tugboat to move barges filled with lumber. This photograph appears to have been taken on the Elizabeth City waterfront around 1920. (Courtesy of Joyce and Durward Medlin.)

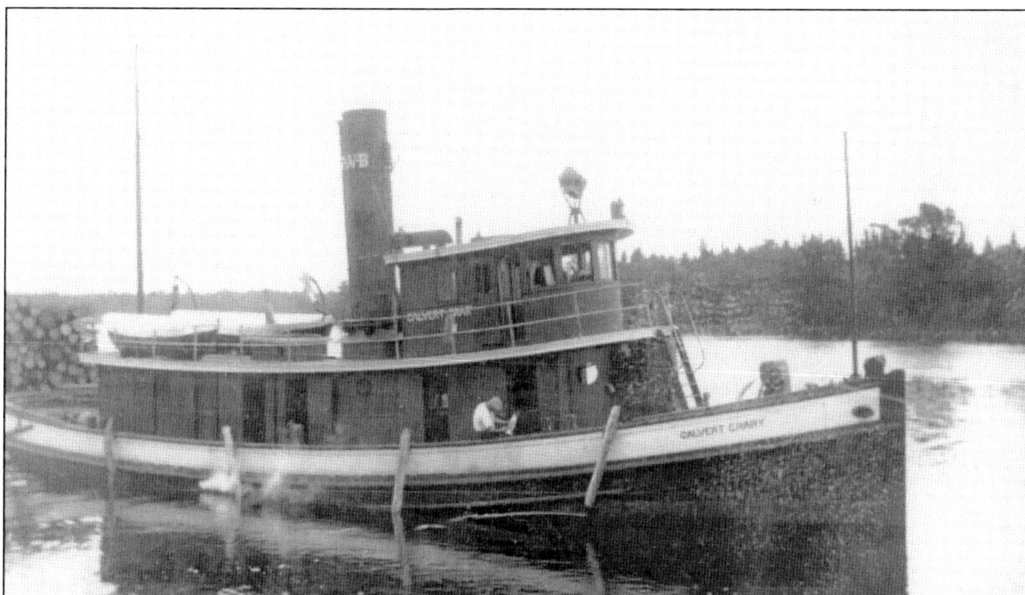

The tugboat *Calvert Crary*, owned at one time by Daniel E. Williams, was seen around 1915 towing three barges—*Dare Devil*, *Dare Belle*, and *Dare Maiden*—loaded with logs. The loads were headed from North Carolina to Norfolk, Virginia, by way of the Elizabeth River. Tugboats and barges were essential for moving timber and lumber to buyers of Camden County forestry products. (Courtesy of Joyce and Durward Medlin.)

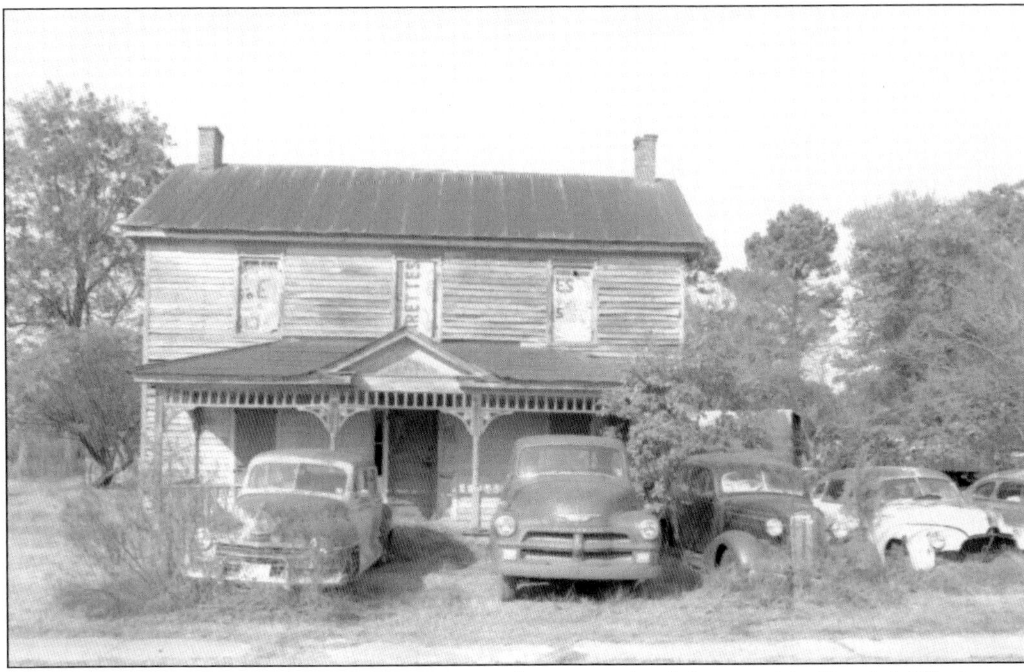

This old house was located on Main Street on the west side of the canal in South Mills. It once belonged to Capt. James "Jim" Johnson and his wife, Sue. Folks would go visit and enjoy Sue's player piano. Durward Medlin restored old cars and had these old models—from the 1930s up to about 1960—for sale out front until around the early 1980s. (Courtesy of the State Archives of North Carolina.)

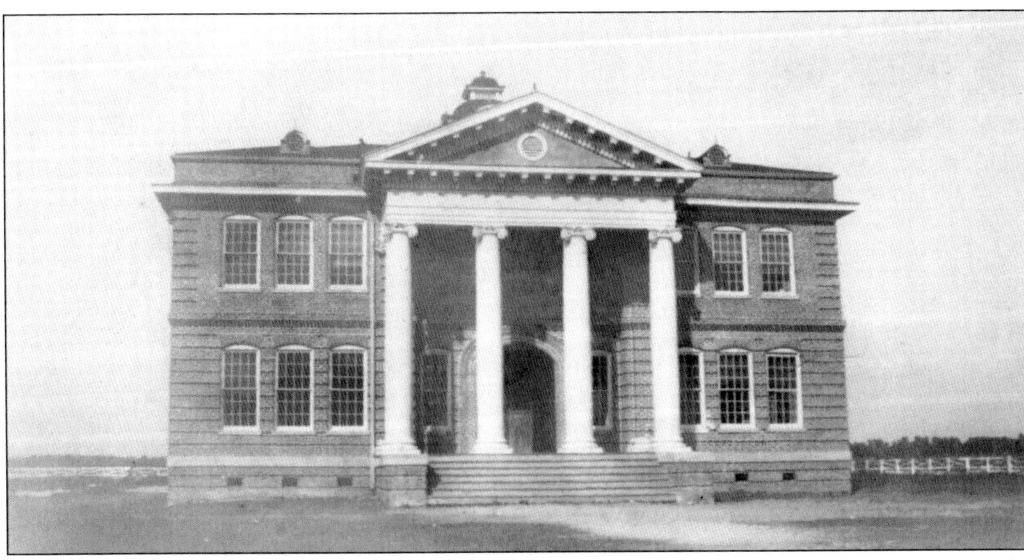

This is the original building of the South Mills High School, which was completed in 1914. The structure burned in October 1933. It was rebuilt without the Colonial columns, and two wings were added around 1934. High school classes were held at the school until 1952. Elementary grades continued until about 1961. (Courtesy of Vernon Burgess Jr.)

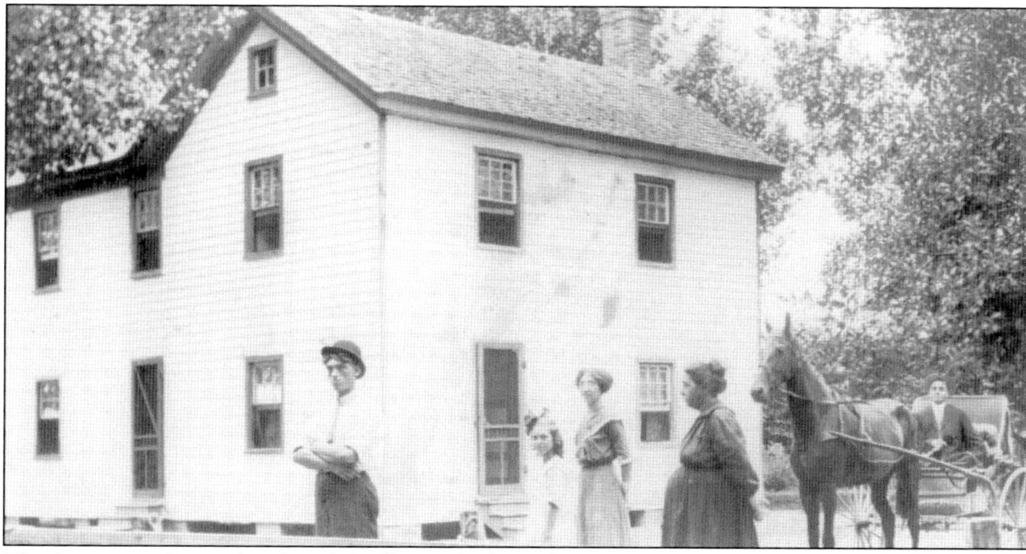

This home was located in South Mills not far from the Bartlett Boarding House. Because so many travelers passed through South Mills, both by boat and highway, there were several guesthouses or hotels in the little town. Many marriages were recorded in Camden County because couples would come down to South Mills from Virginia to be wed without the waiting period required by the Commonwealth of Virginia. (Courtesy of Linda Ann Mansfield.)

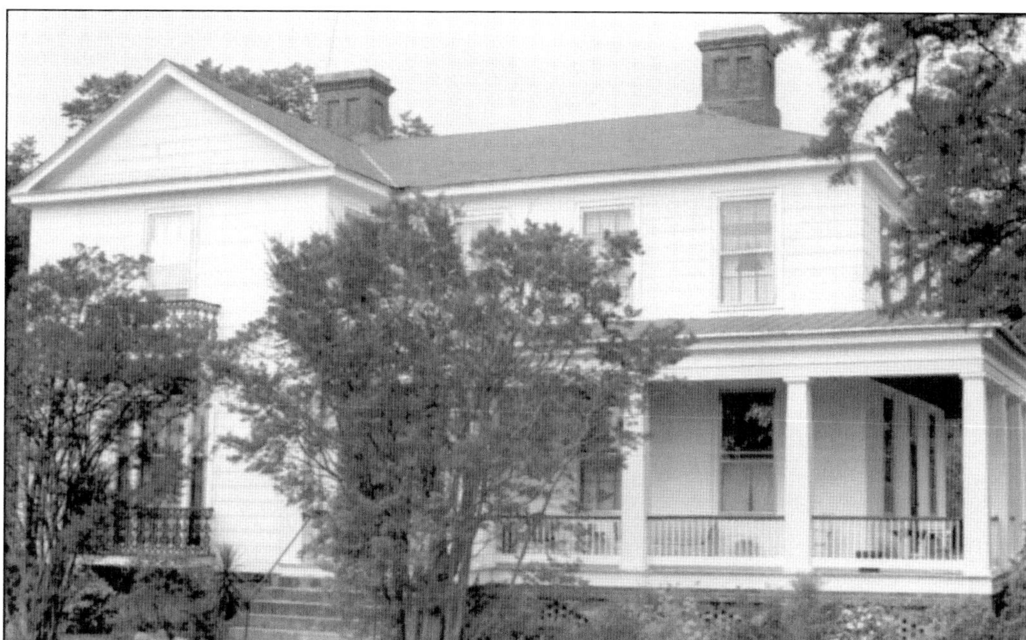

This home, still standing today, once belonged to Confederate colonel Dennis Dozier Ferebee, who graduated with a degree in law from the University of North Carolina in 1839. He opposed secession as unconstitutional but later took charge of the 1st North Carolina Brigade, part of which successfully defended the Dismal Swamp Canal locks from destruction by Union troops under Gen. J.L. Reno on April 19, 1862. (Courtesy of the State Archives of North Carolina.)

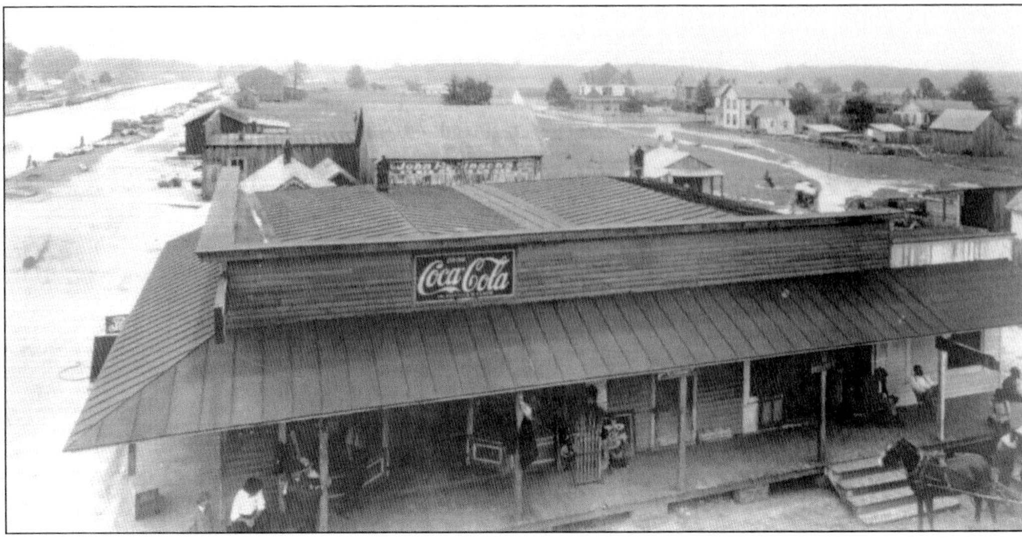

The original Coca-Cola formula was invented in 1886, and the script trademark seen here was registered with the patent office in 1893. By 1895, the company claimed that the drink was being consumed in every state in the Union. This view of South Mills looks toward the lock, which is barely visible in the background. (Courtesy of Joyce and Durward Medlin.)

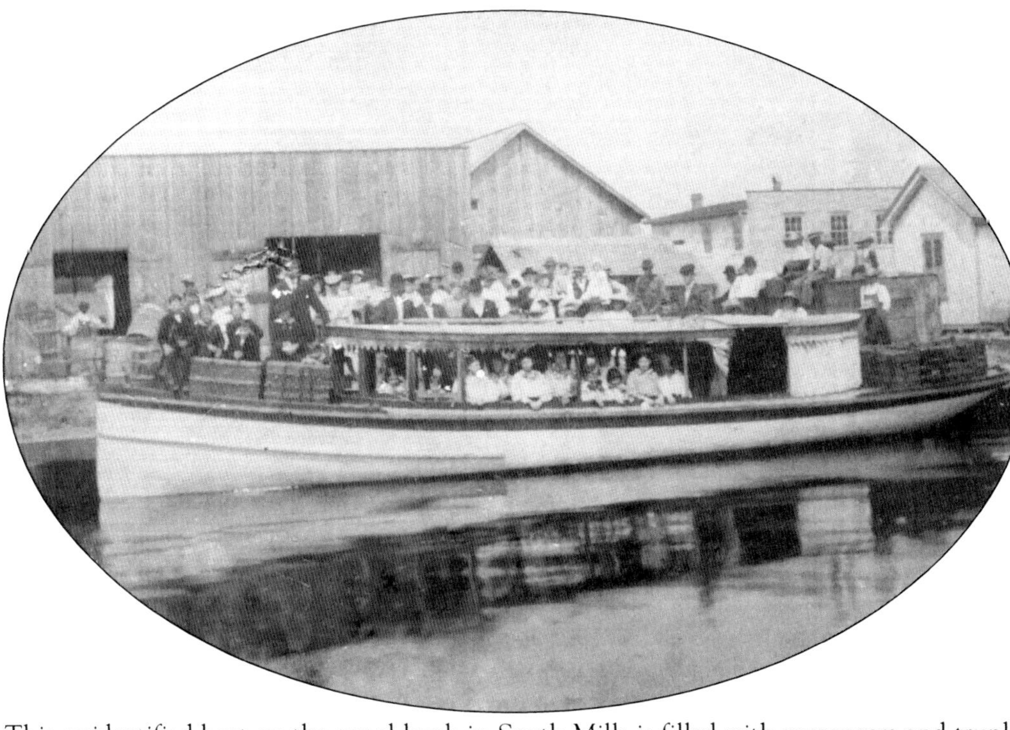

This unidentified boat on the canal bank in South Mills is filled with passengers and trunks. A crowd has gathered along the street between the canal and the warehouse. Barrels used for shipping a variety of goods can be seen outside of the warehouse door on the left. Barrels were needed for shipping everything from potatoes to china dishes, cushioned by excelsior or wood shavings. (Courtesy of Linda Ann Mansfield.)

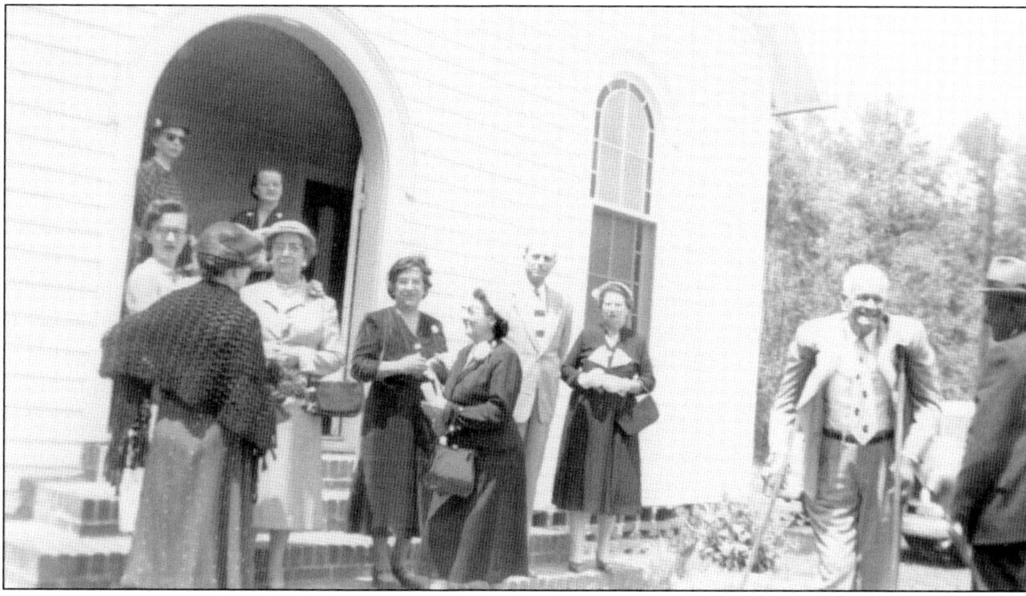

In June 1956, some of the members of the congregation of the oldest Methodist church in Camden County, McBride United Methodist Church, established in 1784, socialize. A marble plaque on the church reads, "McBrides M. E. Church. Erected 1792 A.D. Rebuilt 1837. Remodeled and Rebuilt 1882." "Forke Chapel" was permitted a house of worship for joint use of the Methodist Society and the Episcopal Church of America beginning in December 1792. (Courtesy of Bob Jones.)

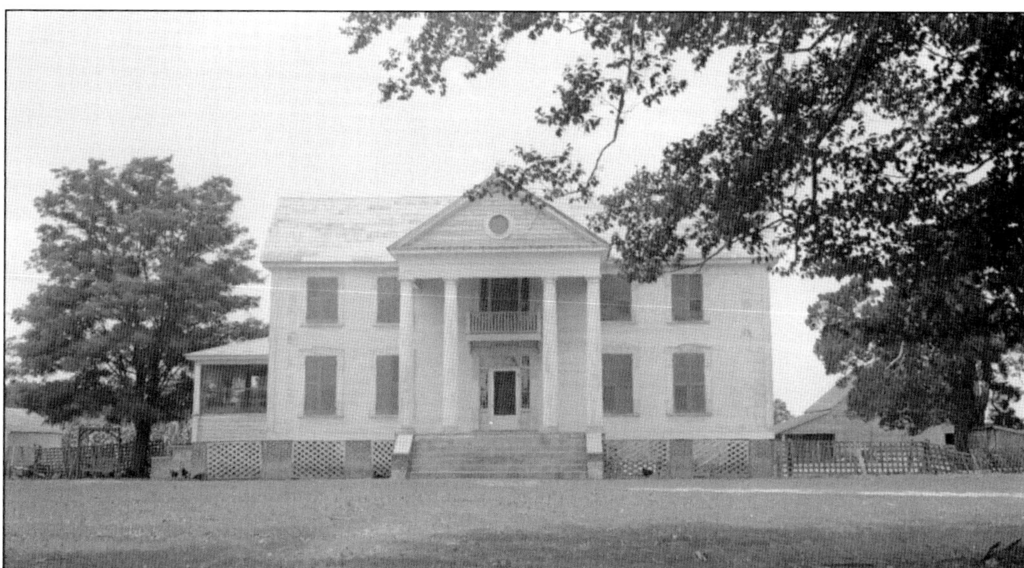

The Nosay House was built by William Riley Abbot in 1840 and was eventually sold to Henry Nosay. It is a familiar landmark on Nosay Road in South Mills and is visible from Highway 343 North. Because it is located so near the site of the Battle of South Mills, fought on April 15, 1862, it is reported to have been used as a battlefield hospital. (Courtesy of the Library of Congress.)

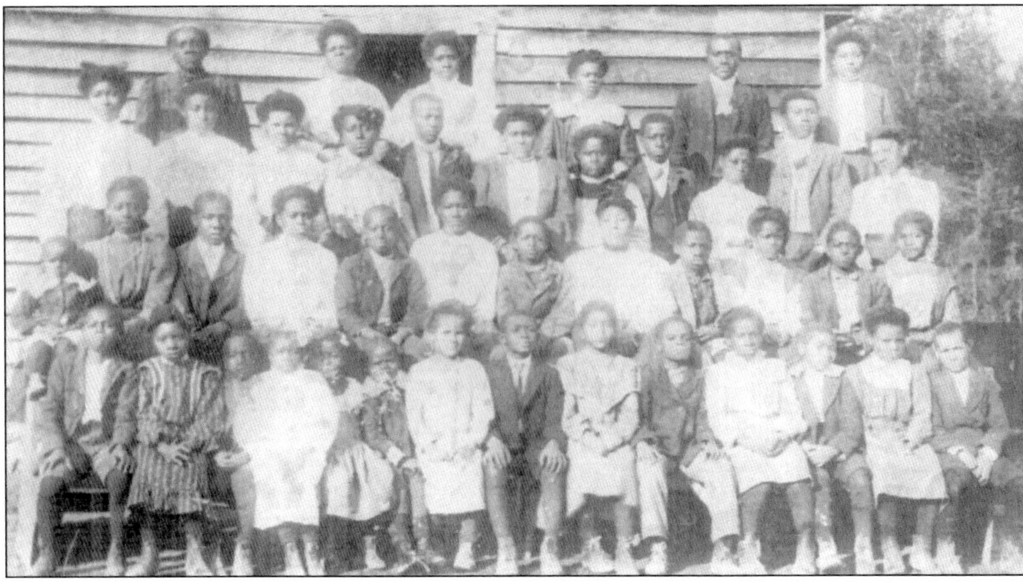

Seven Bridges School in South Mills was one of many small neighborhood schools located throughout the county. Until the 1920s, when school buses came into use, schools had to be located within walking distance of students. Children were sometimes sent to live with relatives who lived near schools. When children became old enough to work on the farms, it often ended their education. (Courtesy of Alex Leary.)

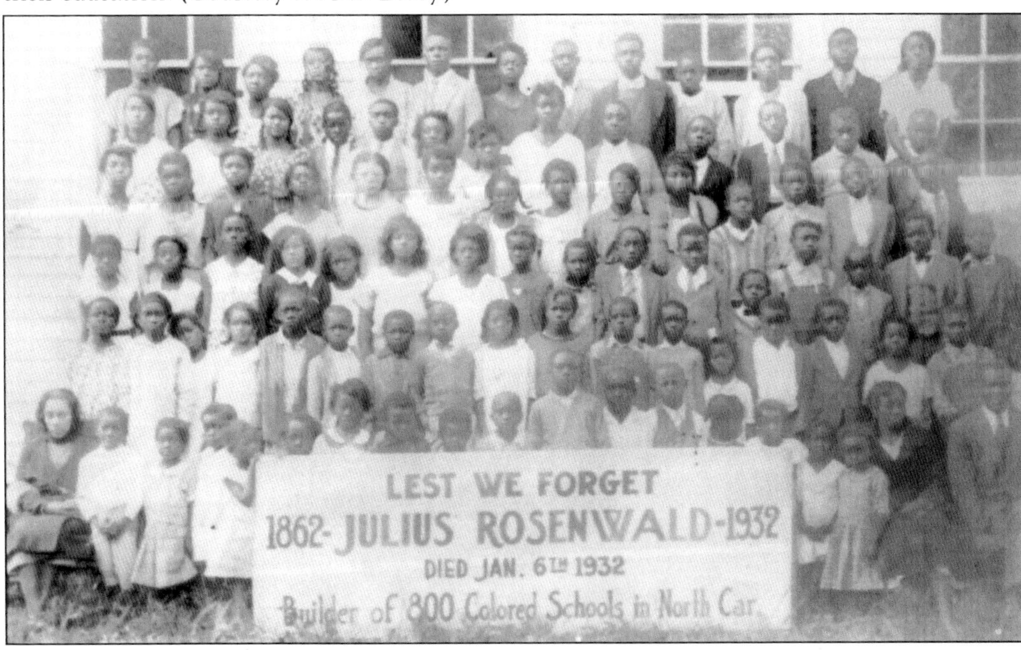

The Rosenwald school in South Mills was one of 800 schools built in North Carolina with funding provided by Julius Rosenwald, who lived from 1862 until 1932. The Rosenwald school in South Mills continued to operate until the opening of Sawyer's Creek High School, which was soon renamed as Marian Anderson High School—after Marian Anderson, a classical contralto who was the first African American female to perform in the Metropolitan Opera, in 1955. (Courtesy of Alex Leary.)

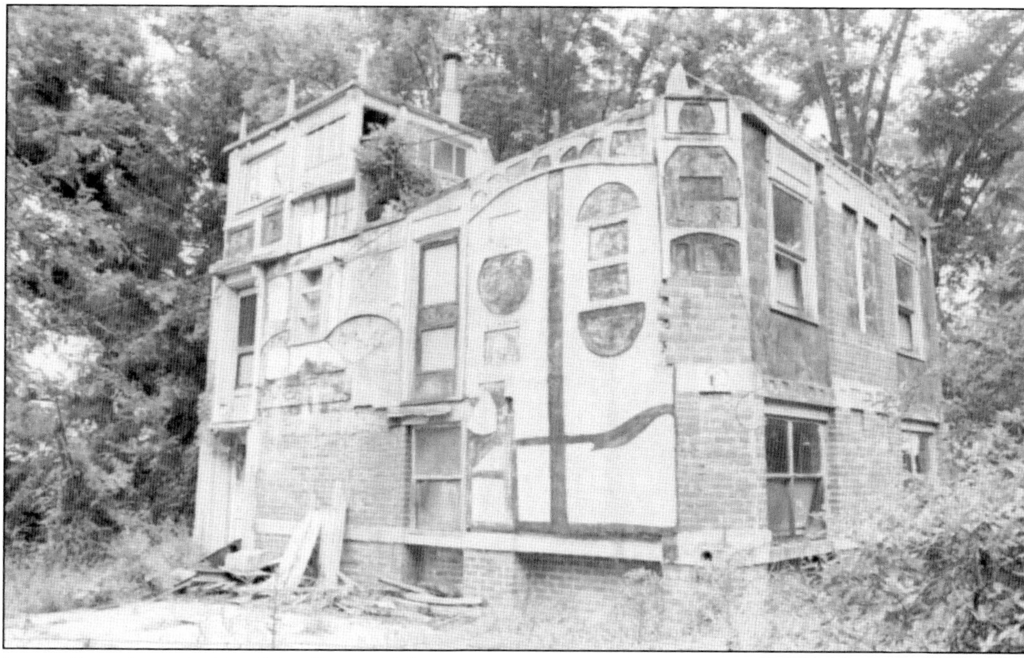

James Butt, born in South Mills in 1894, was given a lot on the corner of Bass Lake and Old Swamp Roads on which to build his dream house, which became known as the "bottle house" or "glass house." He was a creative soul with a love for history who would have a dream and then build a new room by recycling discarded materials. (Courtesy of the State Archives of North Carolina.)

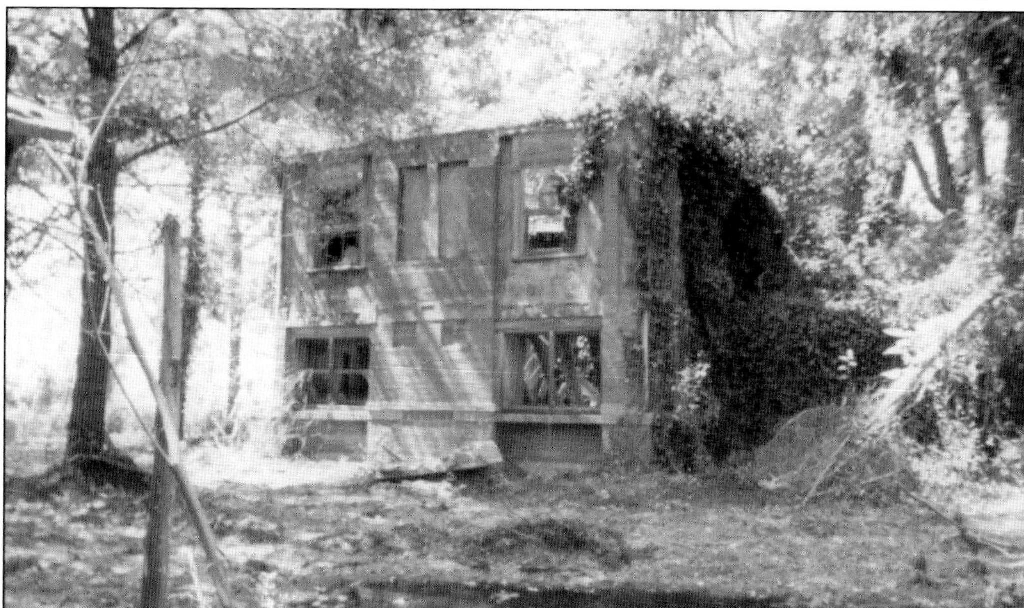

James Butt lived with his wife and son in a modest home next door to his dream house, which was an awesome array of historical tributes surrounded by lovely gardens. After Butt passed away in 1973, his beautiful dream house had been a work in progress for two decades. The unattended house and garden had deteriorated by the time this photograph was taken in 1998. (Courtesy of Joyce and Durward Medlin.)

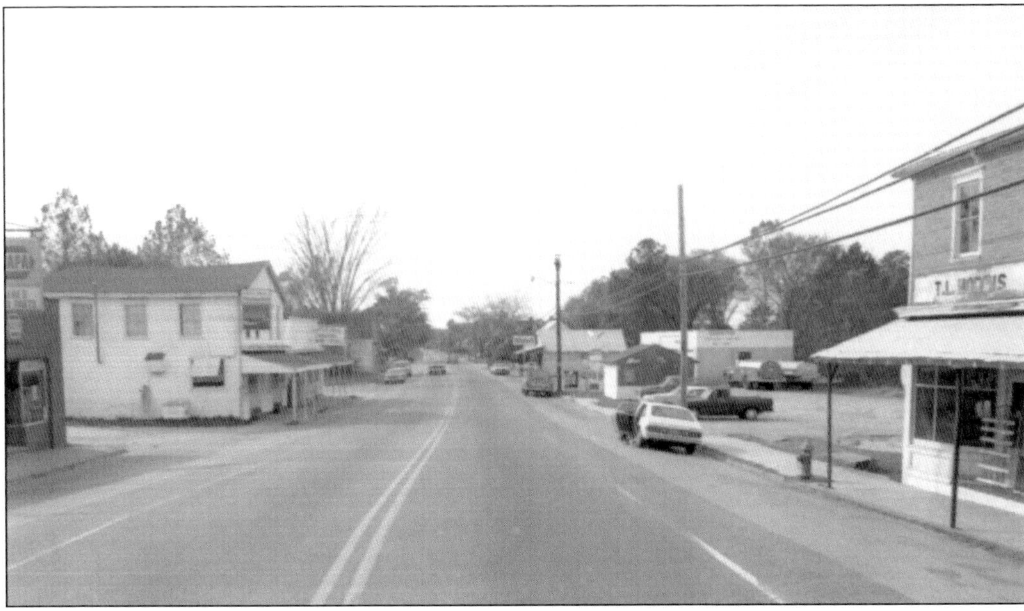

Looking west from the drawbridge in South Mills, one can see the T.L. Norris Grocery on the right, which initially began operating off and on in 1840 and began full-time operation at the close of the Civil War. By 1979, it was the oldest known general merchandising store in the state, and its contents read like the pages of a history book. (Courtesy of the State Archives of North Carolina.)

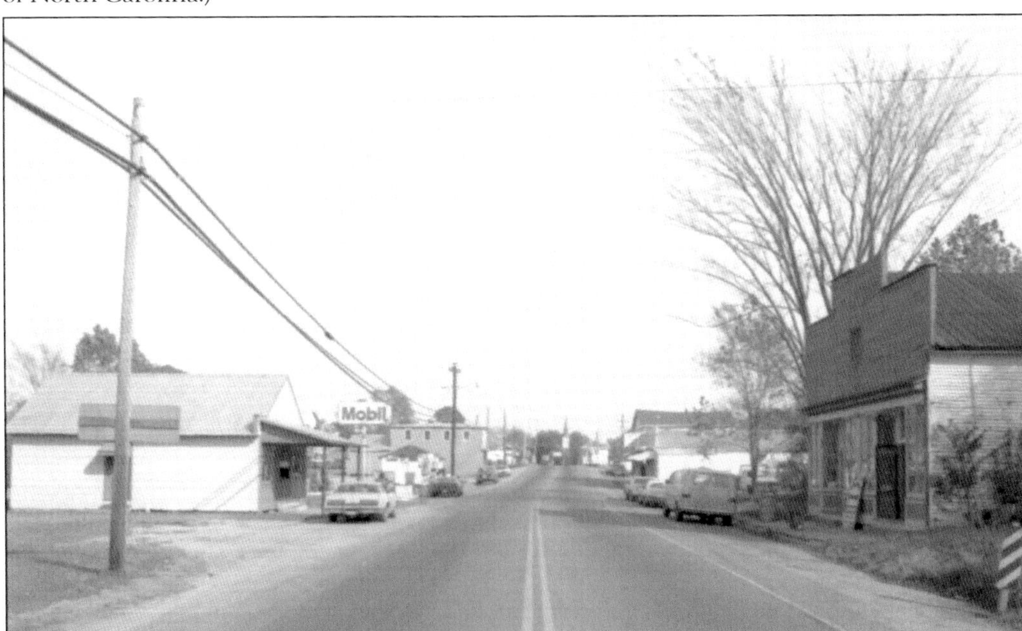

In this view looking east through the business district of South Mills, the steeple of Trinity United Methodist Church is rising above the highway behind where it crosses the Dismal Swamp Canal. Some local businesses remembered through the years included a guesthouse, post office, shoe shop, T.L. Norris Store, South Mills Restaurant, Minton's Mobile Station, an auto parts store, appliance store, barbershop, feed store, and others. (Courtesy of the State Archives of North Carolina.)

Three

Camden County Courthouse District

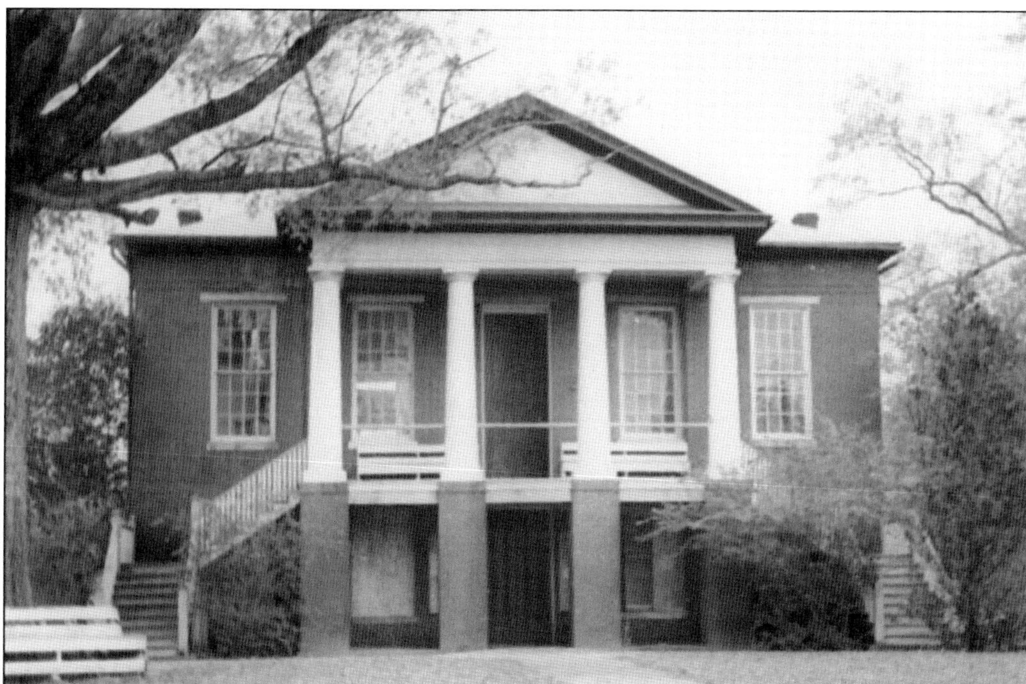

On March 15, 1782, Thomas Sawyer and his mother, Margaret Sawyer, sold a one and one-quarter acre plot of ground to commissioners Lemuel Sawyer, Isaac Gregory, Dempsey Burgess, Caleb Grandy, and Joseph Jones for the purpose of building a courthouse, prison, and stocks for Camden County. The courthouse, which was constructed in 1782, was replaced in 1847 by the present Camden County Historic Courthouse. (Courtesy of the Outer Banks History Center, David Stick Collection.)

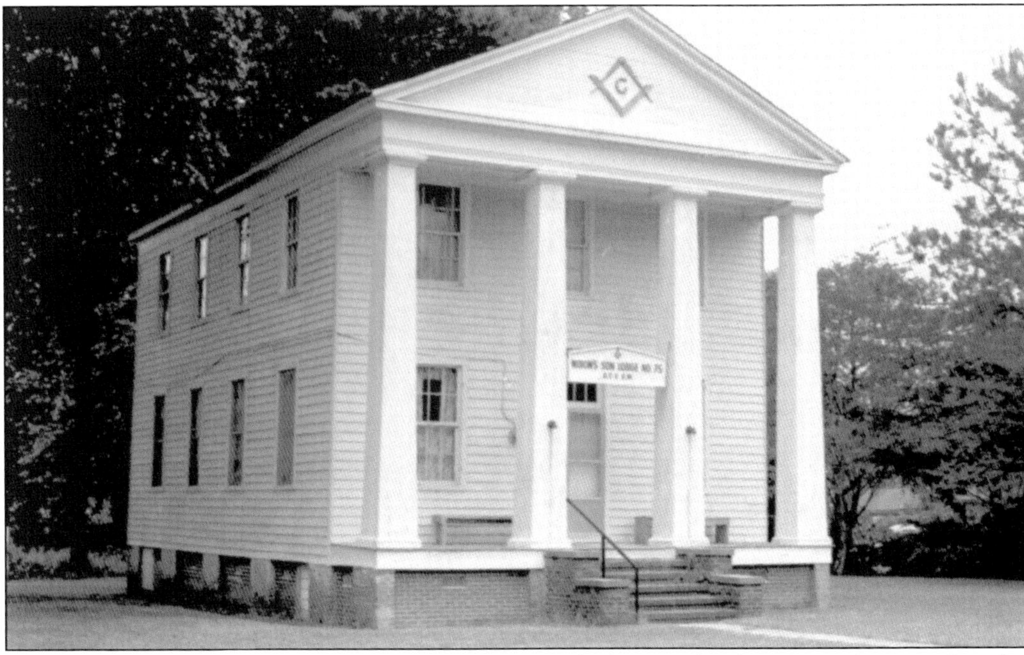

On January 6, 1820, eighteen Master Masons met in the home of Wilson B. Webster in Camden County to form Widow's Son Lodge No. 75. After meeting in homes and other locations, the lodge members erected a new building near the Camden County Courthouse, and it was dedicated on November 7, 1856. In the early 1900s, the structure was used as a school. (Courtesy of the State Archives of North Carolina.)

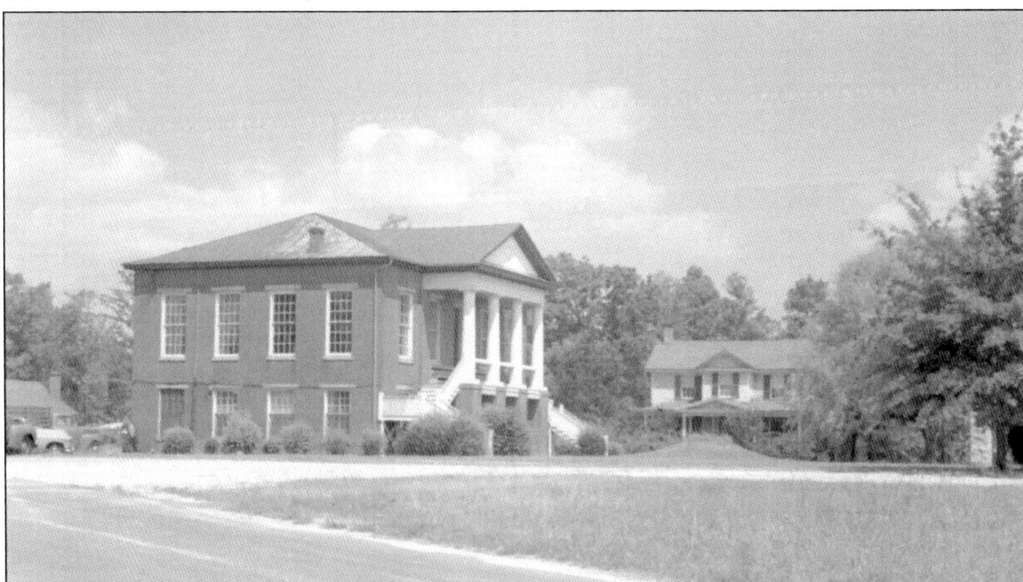

This view of Camden County Courthouse in 1955 shows the house that was located at the north end of the courthouse. For a time, it served as an inn and meals were provided for those at the courthouse. After the Cuthrell family sold the house, it was used as the Camden County Department of Social Services for a while and then was moved to Sleepy Hollow Road. (Courtesy of the State Archives of North Carolina.)

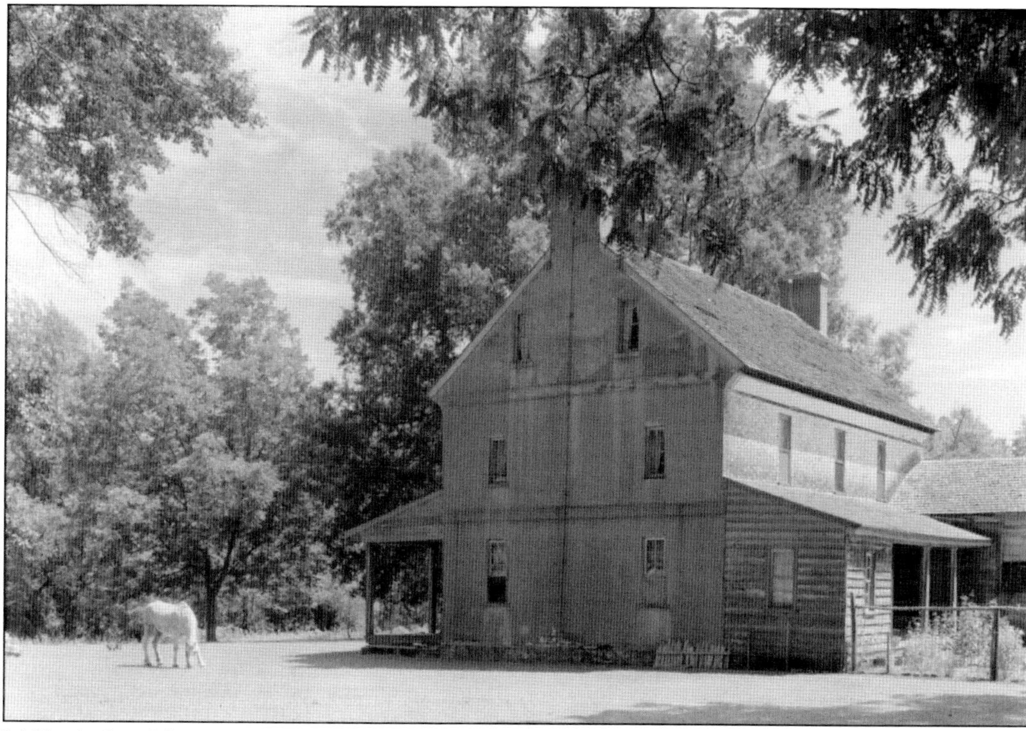

Milford, the oldest two-story brick home in North Carolina, was built by Thomas or William Palin in 1746 on land deeded to them by their grandfather Thomas Relfe. The house, still standing on Shipyard Road, is listed in the National Register of Historic Places, and a brick found in the north chimney of the third floor is dated 1746. (Courtesy of the Library of Congress.)

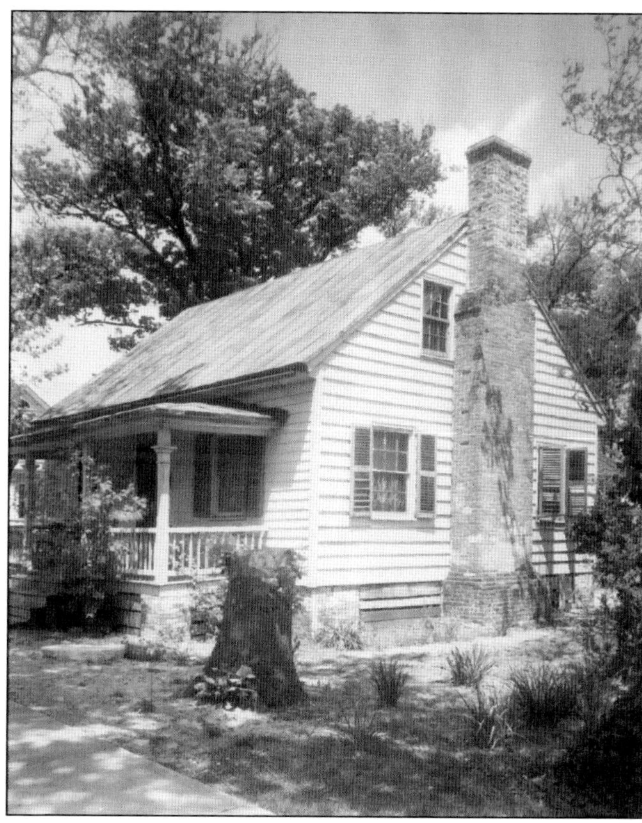

This loom house once stood behind Milford, which was built before Camden County had separated from Pasquotank County in 1777. During the Colonial period, one source of income for the colonists was the export of linen, wool, and cotton cloth. Linen and wool was blended into yarn and woven on looms. (Courtesy of the Library of Congress.)

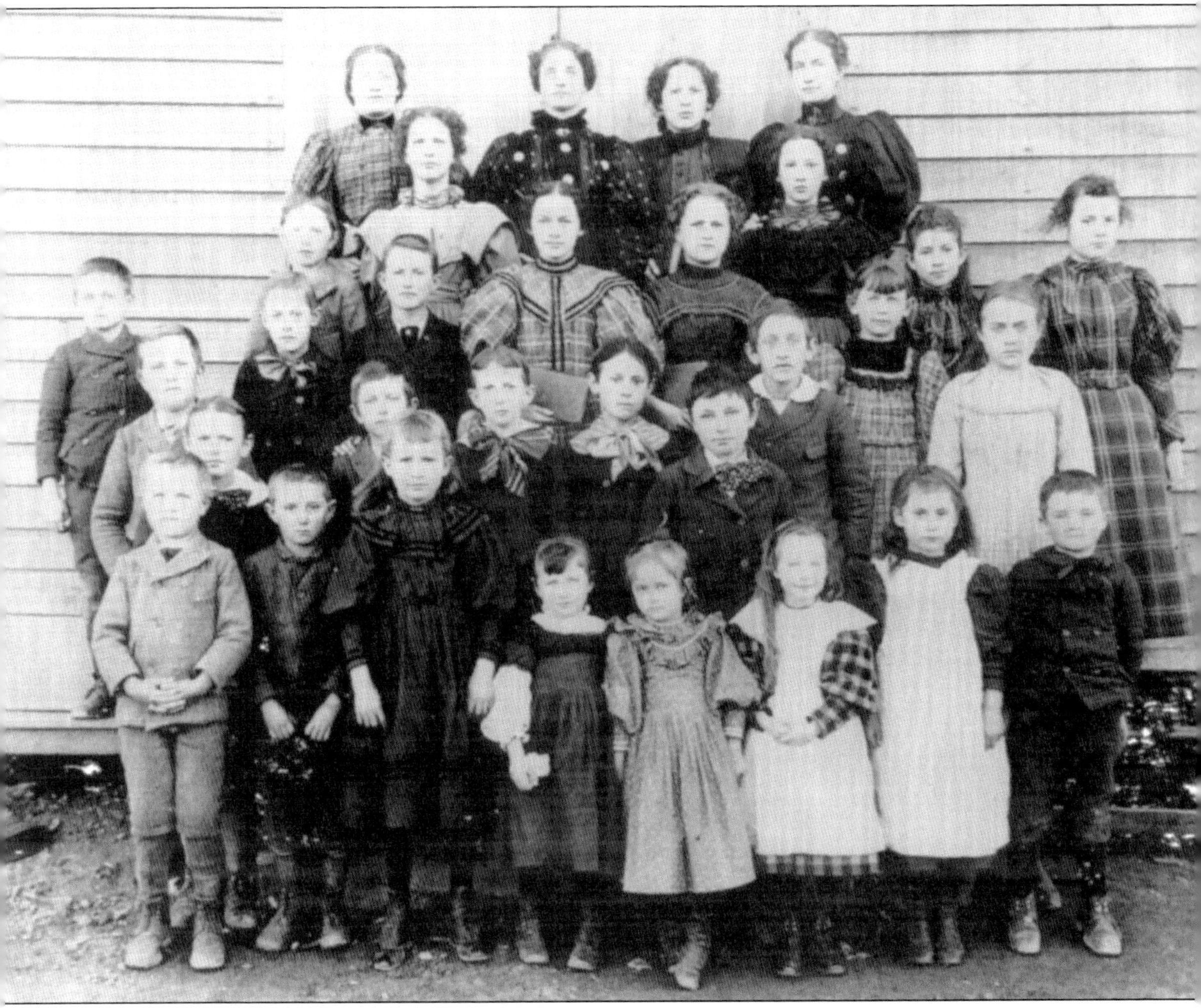

The Belcross Academy was located beside Sawyer's Creek Baptist Church, which was founded around 1790. The students of Belcross Academy pictured in 1897 are, from left to right, (first row) Walter Tarkington, Henry Evans, Willie Evans, Melissa Williams, Florence Sawyer, Mary Gilbert, Mary Brown, and Tommie Sawyer; (second row) Sam Tarkington, Sam Sawyer, Charlie Tarkington, Frank Sawyer, Claude Berry, and Talmon Berry; (third row) Grover Gilbert, Milton Sanderlin, Jakie Garrett, Lula Sanderlin, and Lula Sawyer, (fourth row) Edwin Sawyer, Curtis Tarkington, Hortense Sanderlin, Beulah Trafton, Annie Gilbert, Bettie Sanderlin, Lizzie Brown, and Carrie Brown; (fifth row) Emma Gilbert, Iredel Kight, and Melissa Sanderlin, along with teacher Ella Gilbert. (Courtesy of Alex Leary.)

St. Joseph Episcopal Church, which once stood across from the Camden County Courthouse was built shortly after 1715 on land donated by Thomas Sawyer. From left to right are C.C. Tarkington, Minnie Morrisette, Bill Morrisette, unidentified, Lizzie O. Bell, Sallie O. Tarkington, and Jennie Morrisette. In 1829, Tamozine Eustace was married to Tully Dozier by this church. Tamozine later moved to Illinois, married George Donner, and died in the Donner Pass. (Courtesy of Thalia Jones.)

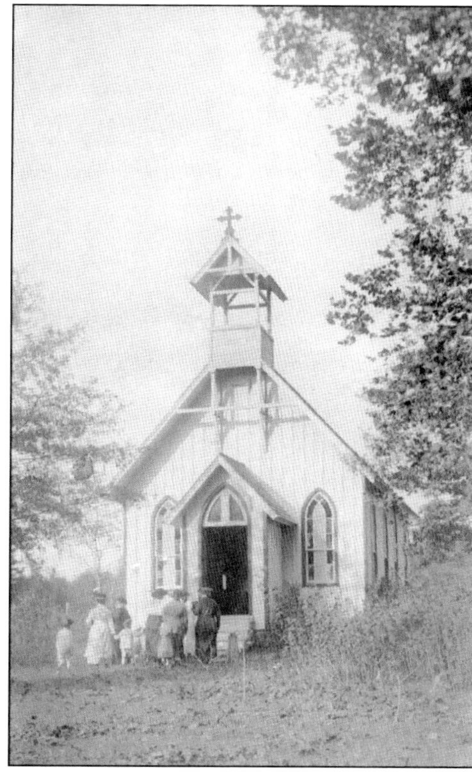

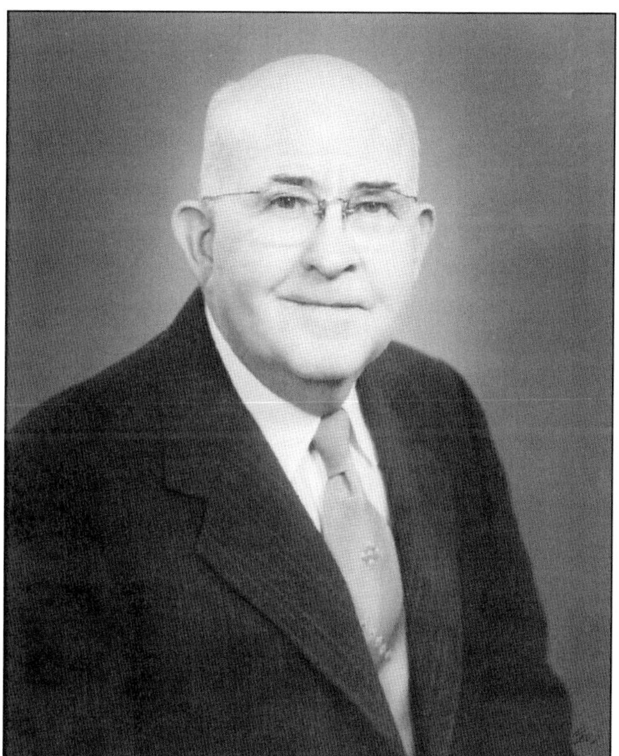

George Frank Hill was the rector of Christ Episcopal Church in Elizabeth City for 35 years. On Sunday afternoons, he would take a boat from Elizabeth City and come up Sawyer's Creek and dock where the creek crosses the highway. He walked the short distance up the road to St. Joseph Episcopal Church. (Courtesy of the Family Research Society of Northeastern North Carolina, Inc.)

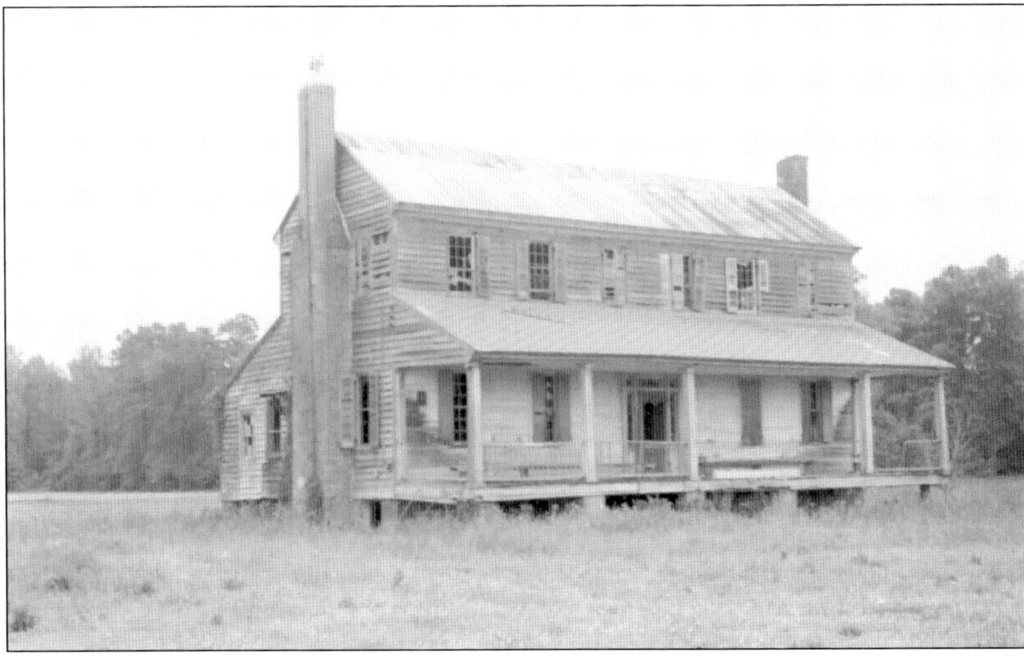

The William Sanderlin House was one of two very similar homes built near each other on the east side of Belcross Road by brothers William and Joseph Sanderlin. Both houses eventually fell into disrepair. Since the William Sanderlin House was considered to be in the worse condition of the two, it was left to ruin and disappear. (Courtesy of the State Archives of North Carolina.)

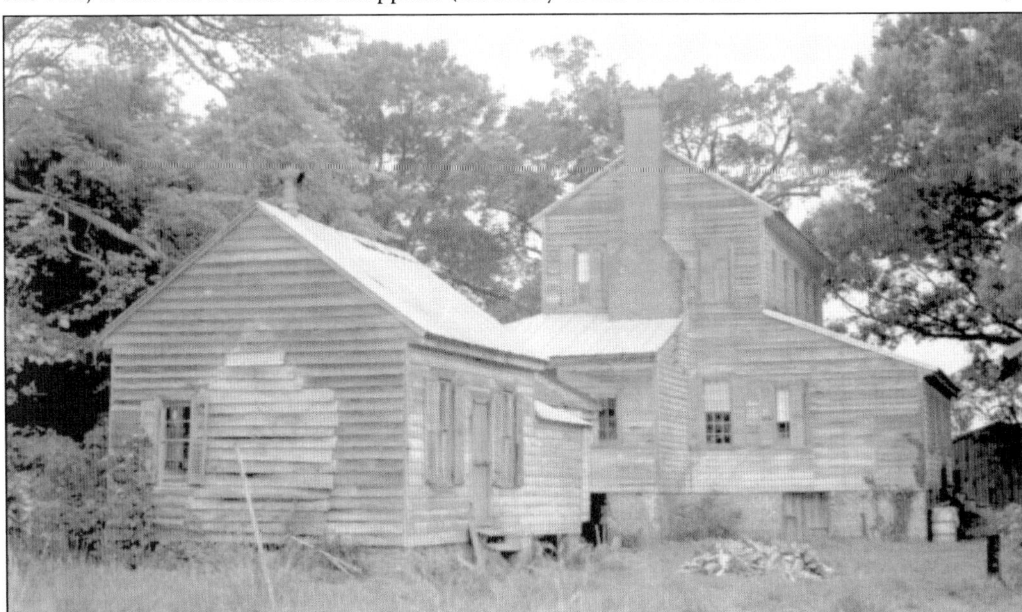

In 1851, Joseph Sawyer Sanderlin built this house for his 19-year-old bride, Margaret Homer. After Irene Pritchard, the last family member to occupy the house, died in 1984, three separate attempts were made to restore the home. After the restoration was finally complete, Hurricane Isabel dropped a huge tree into the house in 2003, and the old Sanderlin-Pritchard House had to undergo major repair. (Courtesy of the State Archives of North Carolina.)

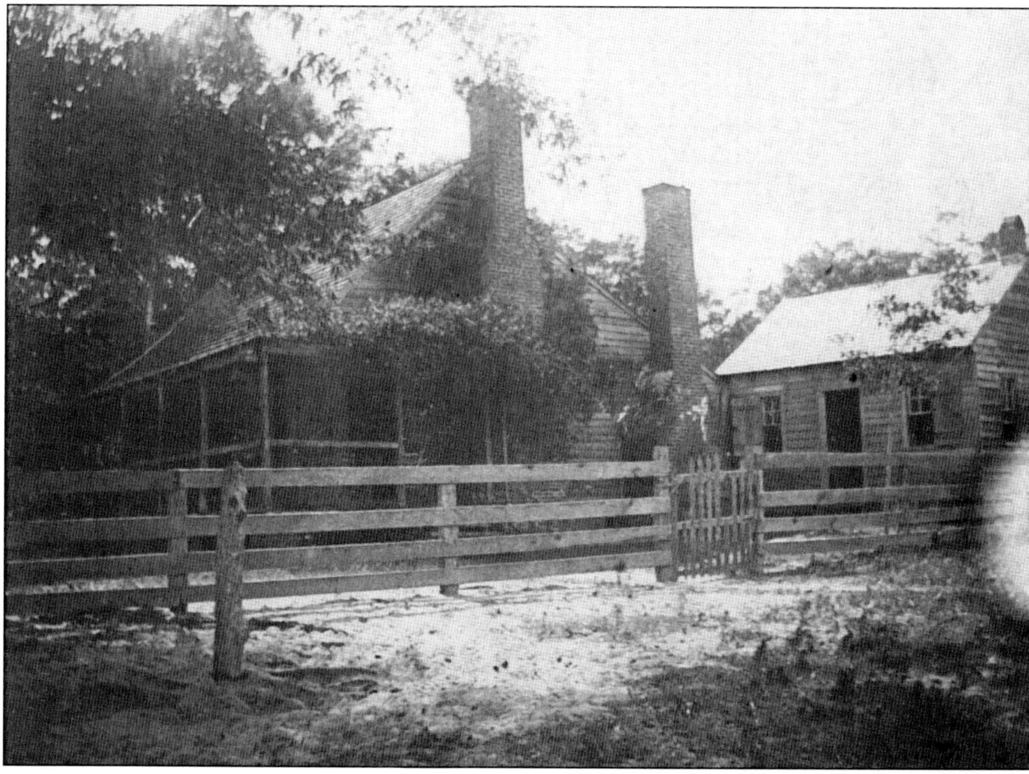

This is the home of Walter Raleigh Gilbert, a farmer and soldier in the Civil War born in 1830, and his wife, Rebecca Jones Gilbert, born in 1850, as it looked in 1899. Rebecca married Walter Gilbert in 1871, and their children Annie, Grover, and Mary were attending Belcross Academy in 1897. (Courtesy of Sarah Forbes Hamilton.)

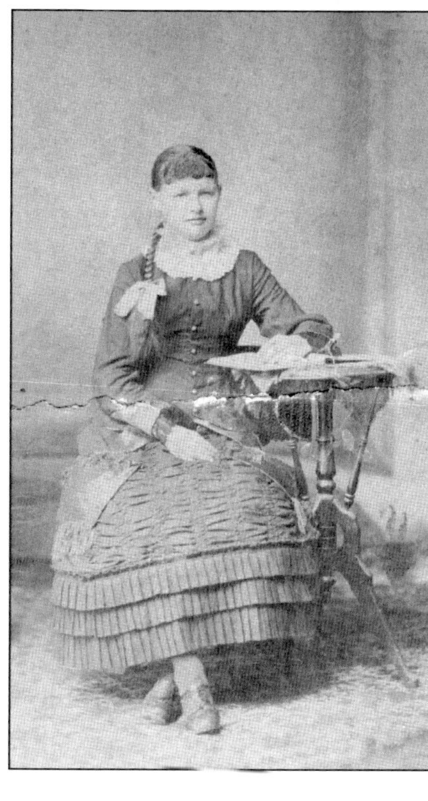

Lela Sanderlin was the daughter of Betty Trafton Sanderlin and Joseph Sanderlin and was born on June 11, 1867. At the time this portrait was made in Norfolk, Virginia, in 1880, Lela would have been 14 years old. She married Robert Lee Forbes, and together, they reared two children—Robert Jr. and Lillie—in the Homer-Aydlett House. (Courtesy of Sarah Forbes Hamilton.)

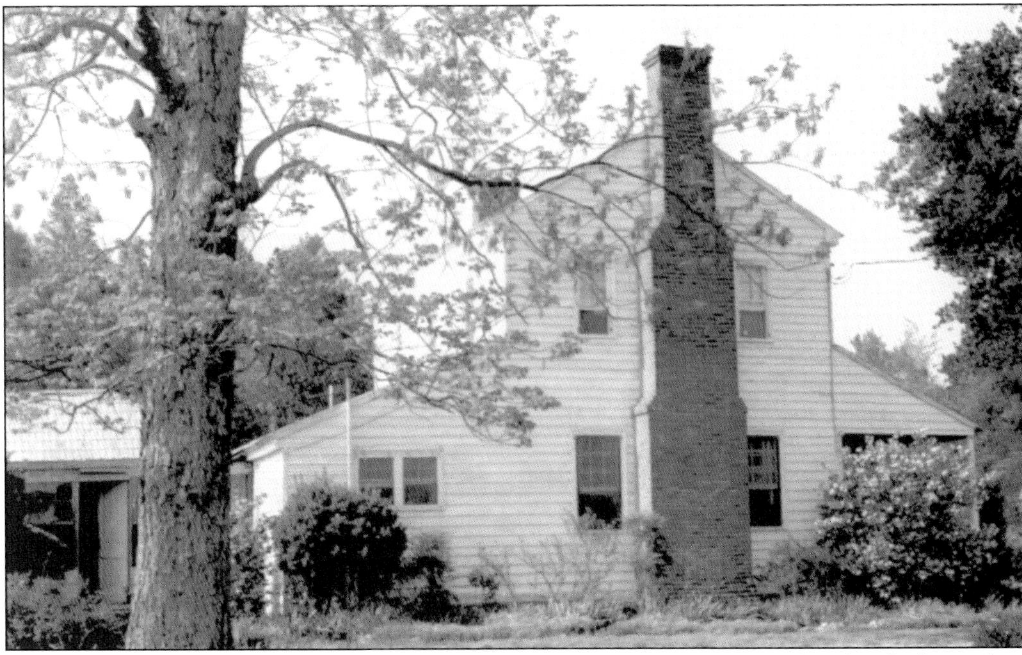

The J.W. Homer House was built prior to 1790 near Sawyer's Creek Baptist Church. The house later passed into the Aydlett family and became known as the Sleepy Hollow Farm. Three generations of the Forbes family lived in the home before the pegged construction became too unstable to salvage. (Courtesy of the State Archives of North Carolina.)

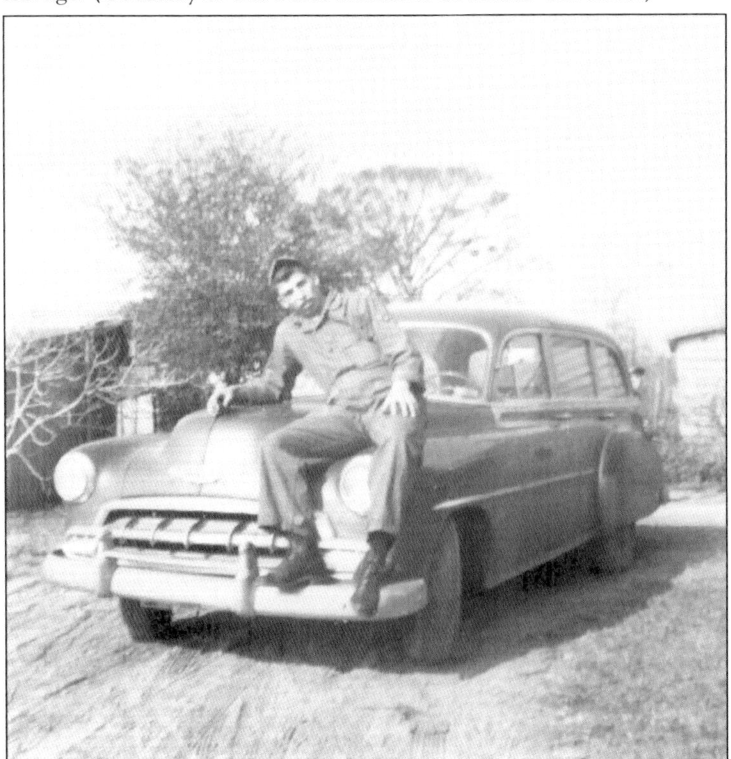

Robert Layden Forbes, the son of Cecile Marie Layden and Robert Lee Forbes Jr., grew up with his three sisters and one brother in the Homer-Aydlett House near Sawyer's Creek Baptist Church. He was known for his excellent driving and mechanical skills. Forbes sits on the hood of a 1954 Chevrolet 210 Handyman station wagon. (Courtesy of Sarah Forbes Hamilton.)

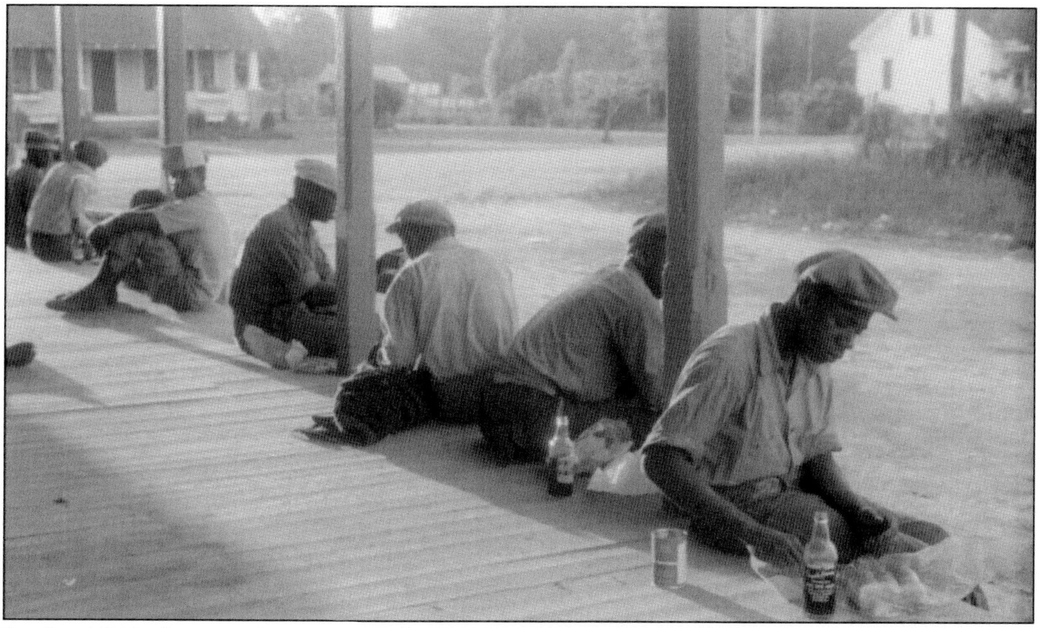

In this 1940 photograph, a group of migratory laborers enjoys lunch on the porch of Edwin Sawyer's store, one of several stores in Belcross where a potato grader and a cotton gin were located. Rich peat in the area is ideal for growing potatoes. Since this photograph was made, thousands of acres have been cleared in the nearby area known as Hales Lake. (Courtesy of the Library of Congress.)

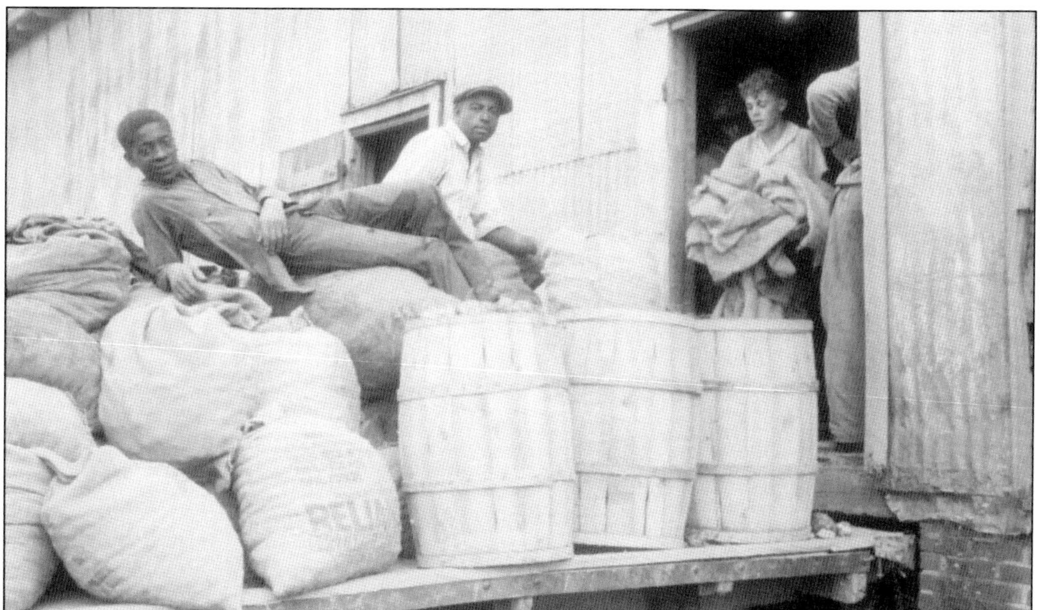

Local farm boys worked beside the migratory laborers at the hot, dirty, and backbreaking labor of harvesting, grading, packing, and loading potatoes onto the waiting boxcars. In 1830, Josiah Hales bought 100 acres in the Great Dismal Swamp, and what began as a small, isolated, communal farm is now thousands of acres of cleared farmland. Hales Lake has become one of the most productive potato producing regions in North Carolina. (Courtesy of the Library of Congress.)

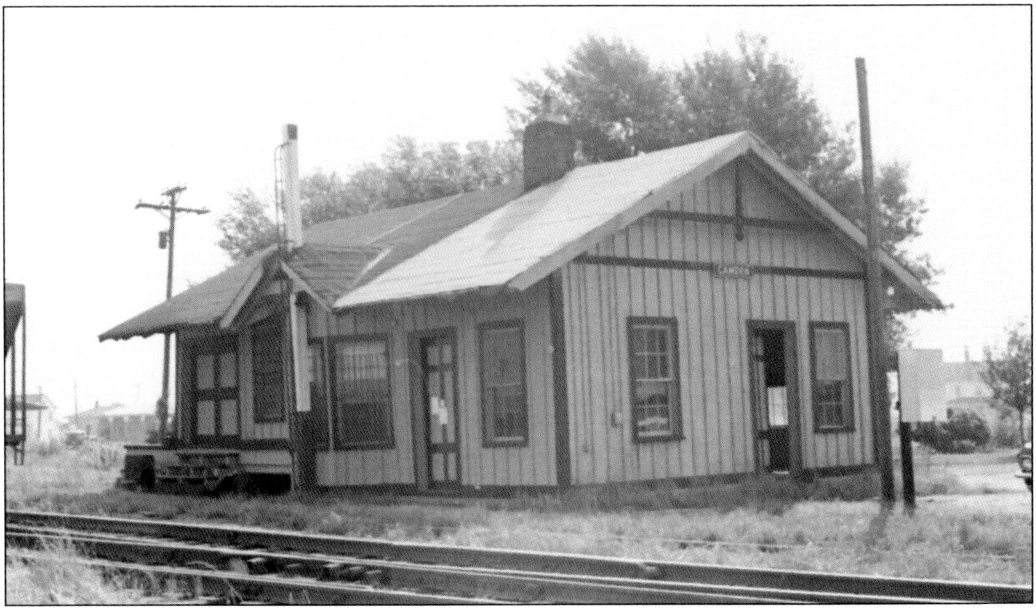

The Camden Railroad Depot was located on Gumberry Road near the loading dock of the potato grader and the grain elevator. Mail came and went by train, and many barrels of potatoes and tons of grain were loaded onto boxcars parked on sidetracks near the depot. Passenger service was at its height between 1900 and 1950. (Courtesy of the State Archives of North Carolina.)

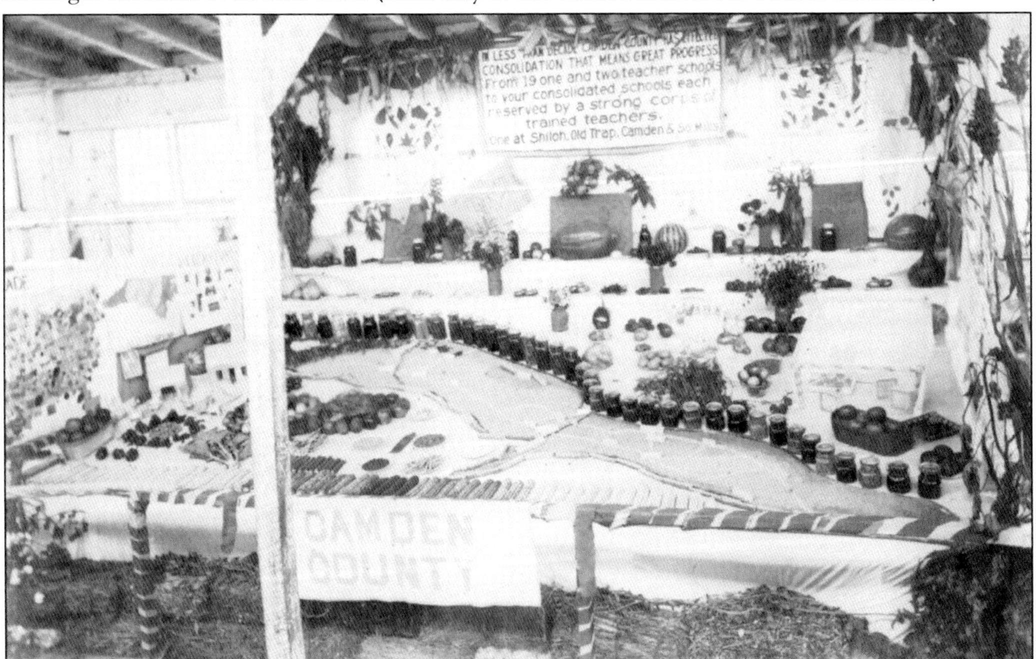

Sometime around 1930, a Camden County Fair was held at Elwyn Leary's potato-grading shed on Gumberry Road. The sign on this educational display proudly proclaims, "In less than a decade Camden County has effected consolidation that means great progress. From 19 one and two teacher schools to your consolidated schools each reserved by a strong corps of trained teachers. One at Shiloh, Old Trap, Camden, and South Mills." (Courtesy of Betty Brock)

Marvin Seymour (left), born in 1910, was the eldest of eight siblings of Bettie Bartlett Seymour and Silas Berry Seymour. Seymour and his friend Eddie A. Whaley (right) are parked at W.W. Morriesette General Merchandise at the intersection of Highways 343 and 158. (Courtesy of Vernon Burgess Jr.)

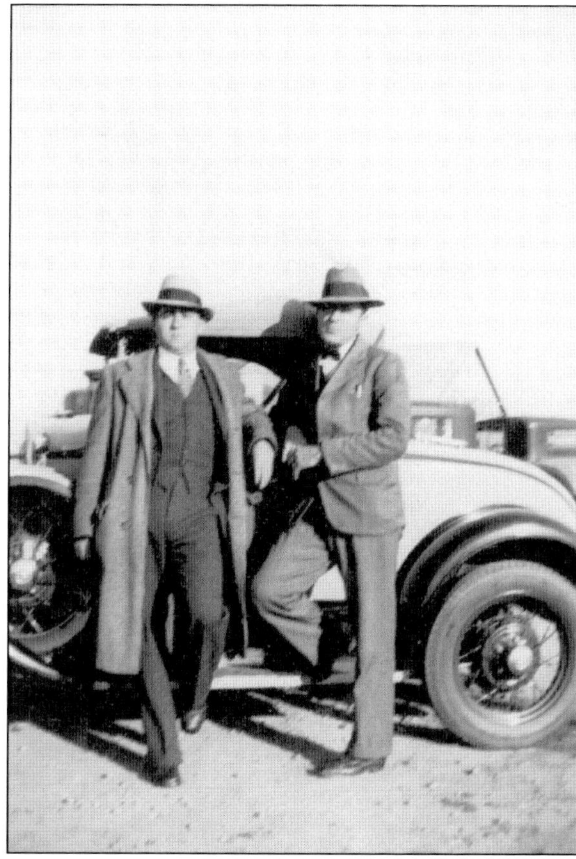

This gas station, owned by Freshwater P. Wood and located in Camden between the railroad tracks and Camden County High School, is typical of many that existed in Camden County during the early to mid-1900s. In 1950, there were at least 100 gas stations and stores in Camden County. Most sold commonly needed items along with petroleum products, and some served as post offices. (Courtesy of the Library of Congress.)

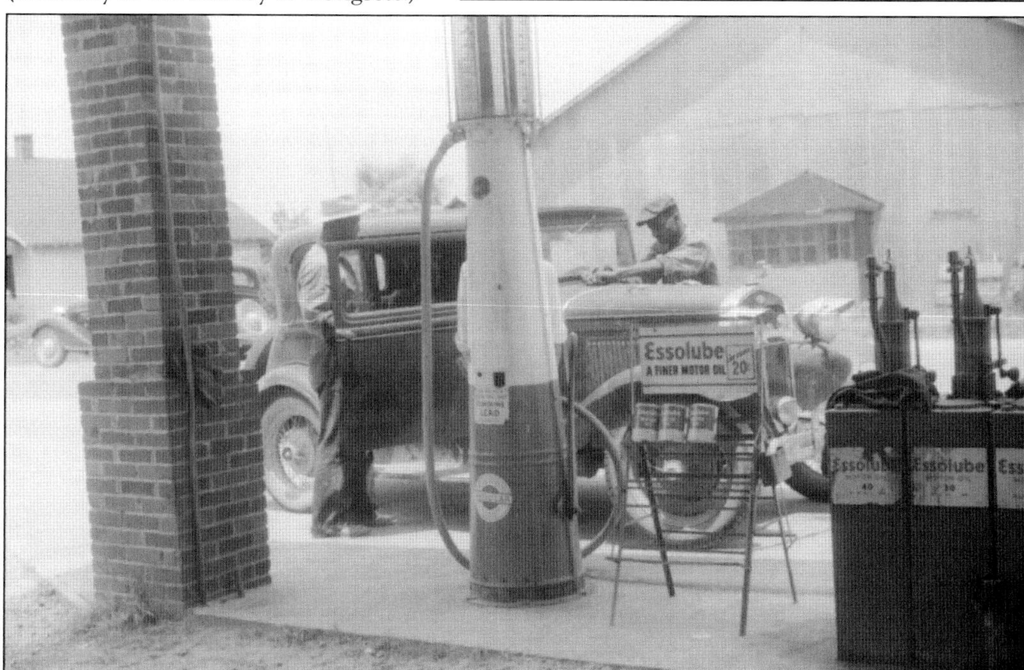

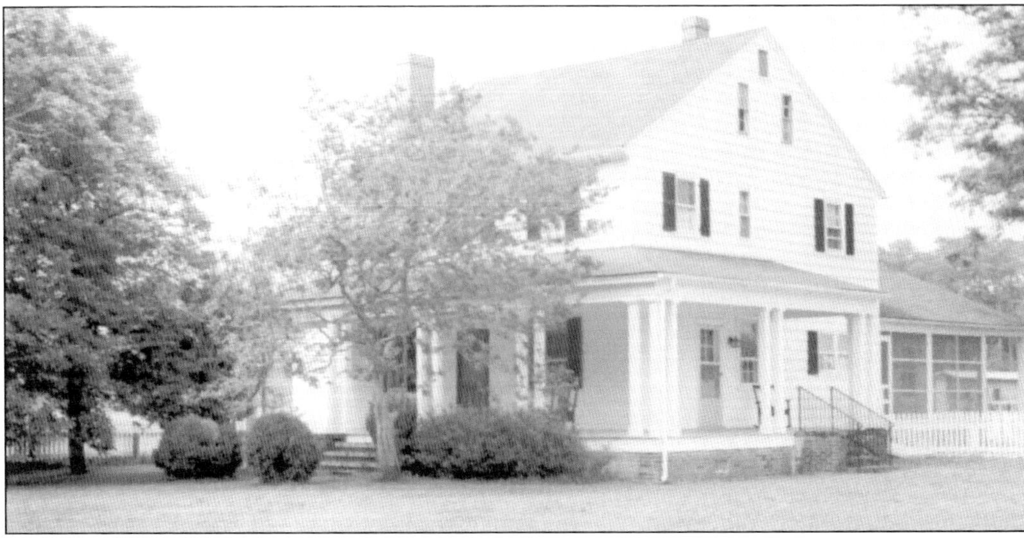

The Lamb-Ferebee House was a Federal dwelling built in the 1820s by Miles Lamb, who was born in 1798 and married Marietta Matilda Grandy Lamb, born in 1810. Miles and his wife, Marietta, and three of their children—Miriam G. Lamb Ferebee, Mary Matilda Lamb Jarvis, and Henry C. Lamb—are buried on the property. (Courtesy of the State Archives of North Carolina.)

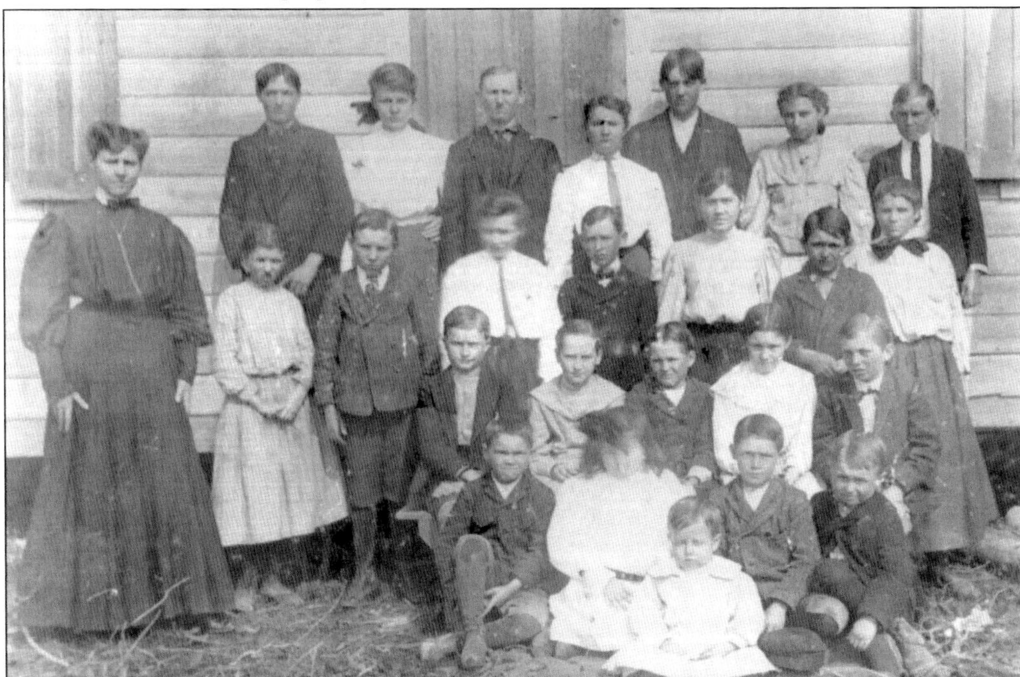

This image of students of the Herring School in 1908 includes, from left to right, (first row) Gaston Williams, unknown, Nellie Hastings, and two unidentified students; (second row) Sammy Hastings, Ruth Hastings, and three unidentified students; (third row) teacher Mary Elliott, Minnie Dunford, Harry Ferebee, Dora Brown, Joe Hastings, Etta Hastings, Charlie Williams, and Bessie Dunford; (fourth row) Wiley Williams, Ella Ferebee, Leonard Brown, Annie Morgan, Silas Robertson, Maude Spence, and John Ferebee. (Courtesy of Thalia Jones.)

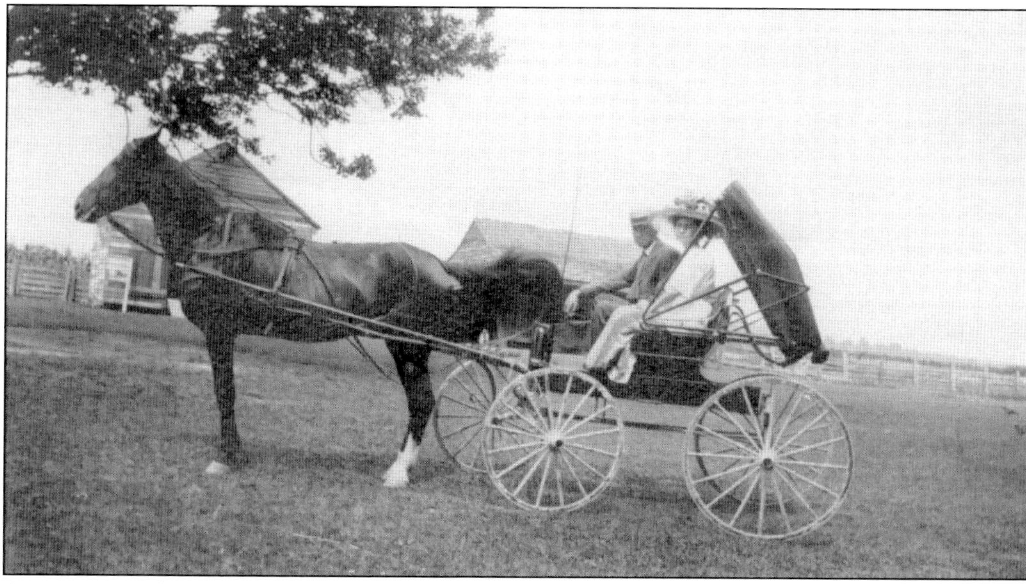

Curtis Lee Tarkington and Sally Clark Overton are seen courting prior to their marriage in 1911. Tarkington not only served two terms as a representative in North Carolina General Assembly, he also ran the Camden Post Office, F.P. Wood General Store, and tended the cotton gin across the road from the store. He was known for being a helpful and hardworking man. (Courtesy of Thalia Jones.)

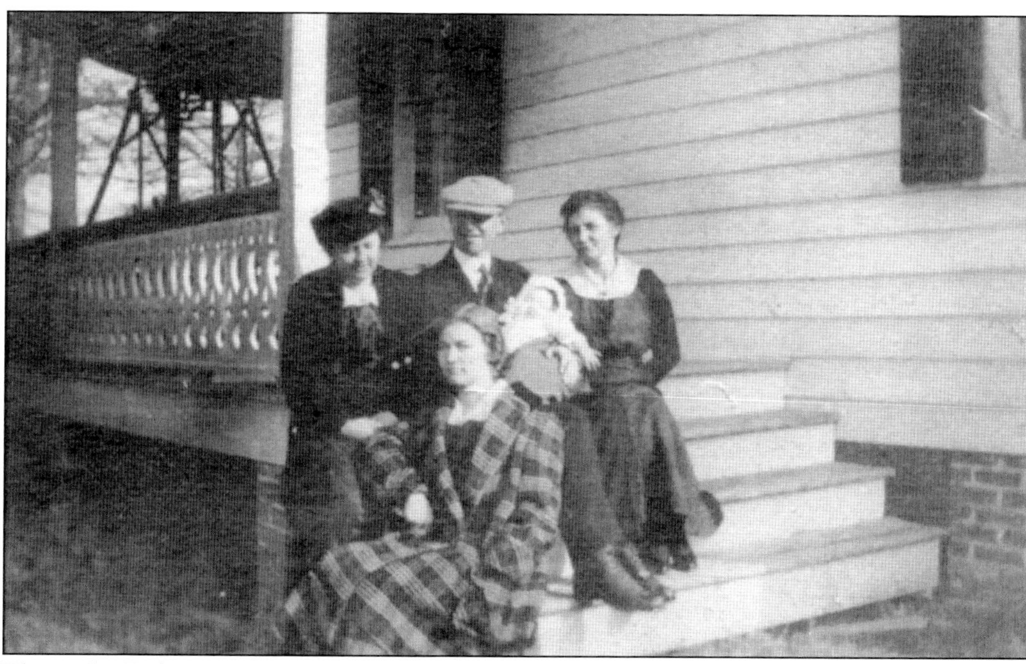

This is the Tarkington family on the porch of their Camden home. The woman sitting in front is unidentified, but from left to right are Sadie S. Robertson, Curtis Lee Tarkington holding Curtis Clark Tarkington, and Sallie Clark Overton Tarkington. Sallie married Curtis Lee in 1911 and their son, Clark, was born on November 7, 1912. (Courtesy of Thalia Jones.)

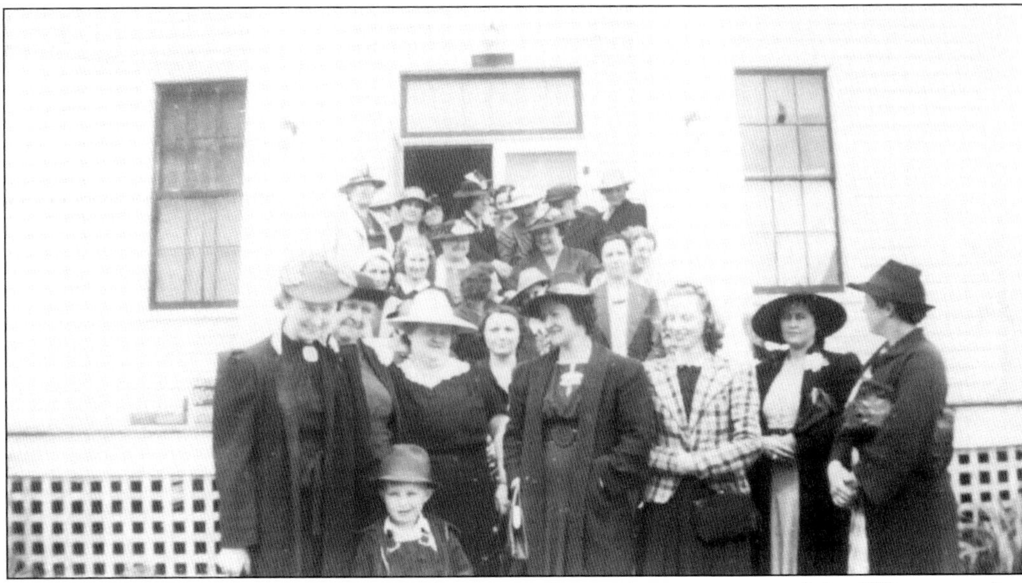

Farm women's clubs gradually became known as home demonstration clubs. What was then known as Home Demonstration became the Family and Consumer Sciences department of the North Carolina State University Cooperative Extension Service, and the farm boys' and girls' clubs became 4-H Clubs. The Camden County Home Demonstration Club is seen exiting the Widow's Son Masonic Hall, where it met in the 1940s. (Courtesy of Thalia Jones.)

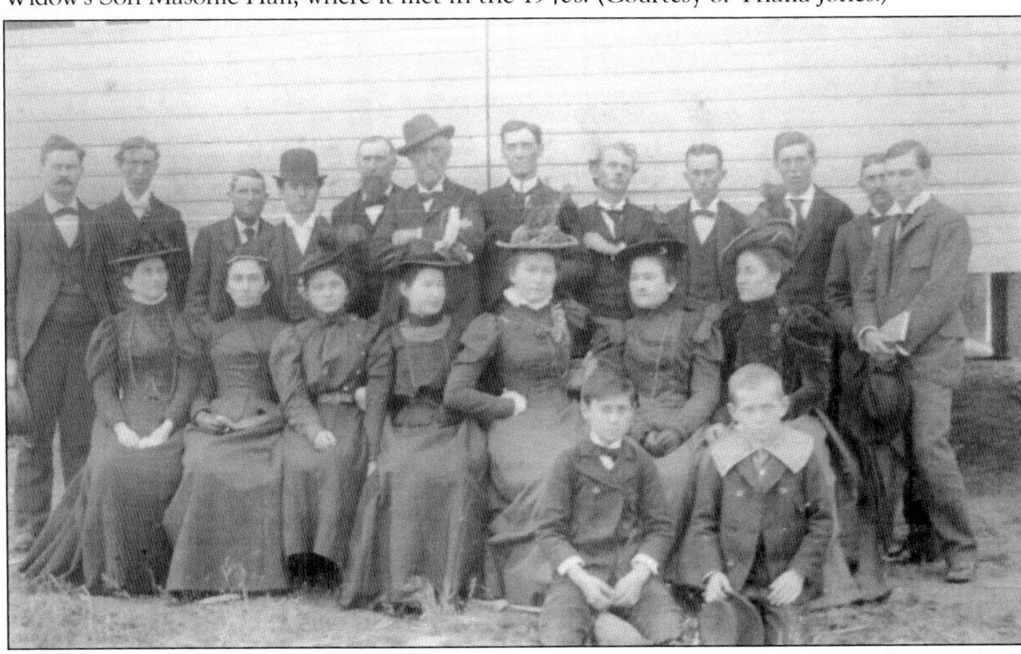

A photograph of Camden County teachers in 1895 includes, from left to right, (first row) two unidentified boys; (second row) Minnie Ferebee, Blanche Ferebee, Bertha Harris, Lina Gilbert Burgess, Katie Harris, Annie Boushall, and Mary Wood; (second row) Charles Garrett, Celeus Ferebee, John Bell, Marshall Shelby Burgess, Walter Harris, Thomas B. Boushall, Rev. Low Wood, Willie Jasper Burgess, Caleb Ferrell, Joseph Walston, and Timothy McCox. (Courtesy of Linda Ann Mansfield.)

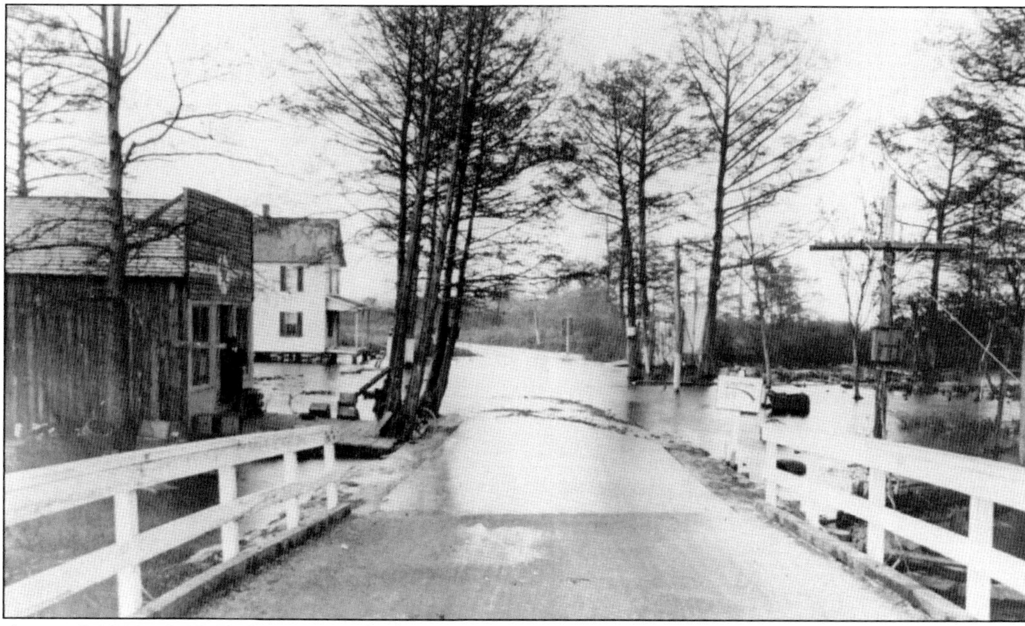

Around 1910, C.H. Robinson and Elizabeth City businessmen constructed a bridge to connect Pasquotank County with Camden County at the Narrows and built a road through the swamp using dirt, sand, sawdust, and scraps to make a roadbed. The toll bridge was completed around 1914. Because the road was frequently impassible, a new toll-free "floating road" was built around 1923. (Courtesy of the Outer Banks History Center, Fred Fearing Scrapbook Collection.)

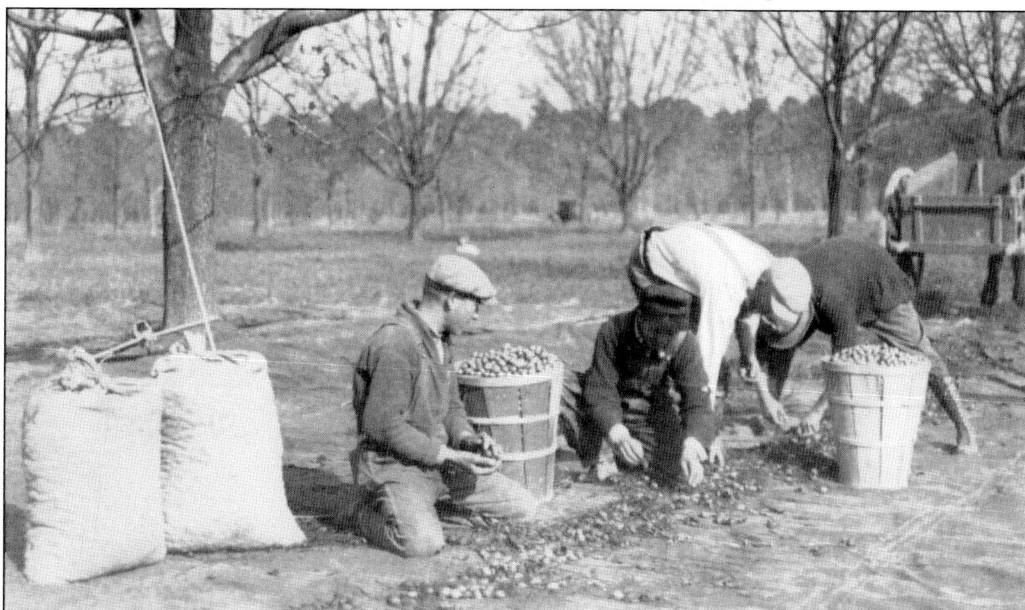

Many Camden County residents are familiar with the name Pecan Farm. This photograph depicts laborers harvesting the pecan crop at the Pecan Farm, which was located on both sides of Highway 158 at the entrance of the Camden Causeway. Today, the Pecan Farm estates are located on what was once part of this farm. (Courtesy of the Outer Banks History Center, D. Victor Meekins Collection.)

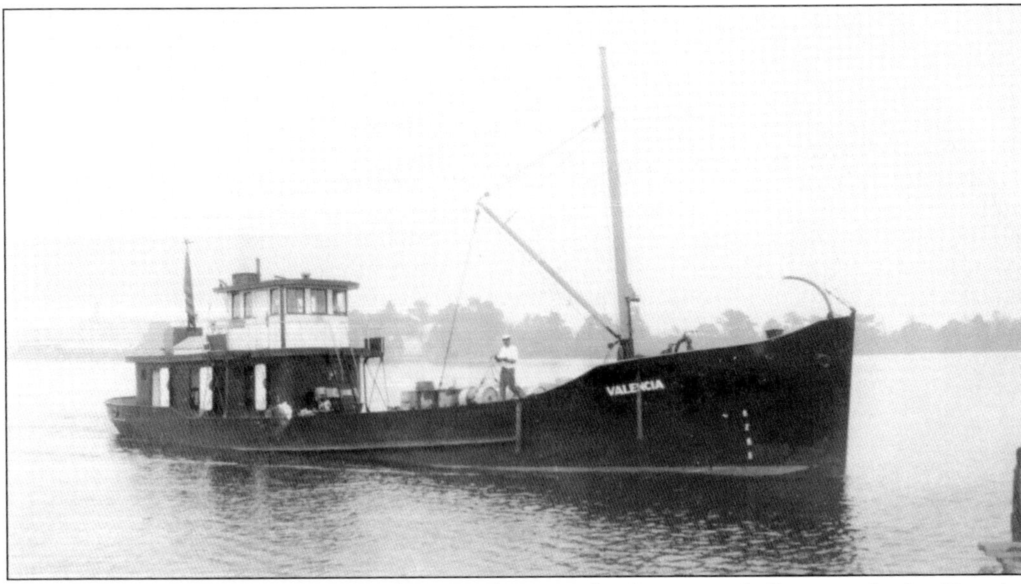

The *Valencia* was an oil tanker and is seen here in the Pasquotank River with the Camden Causeway in the background. Countless commerce and passenger vessels of all shapes and sizes have passed between the shores of Pasquotank River since Native Americans used it as a major highway for their dugout canoes made from enormous cypress trees. (Courtesy of the Outer Banks History Center, D. Victor Meekins Collection.)

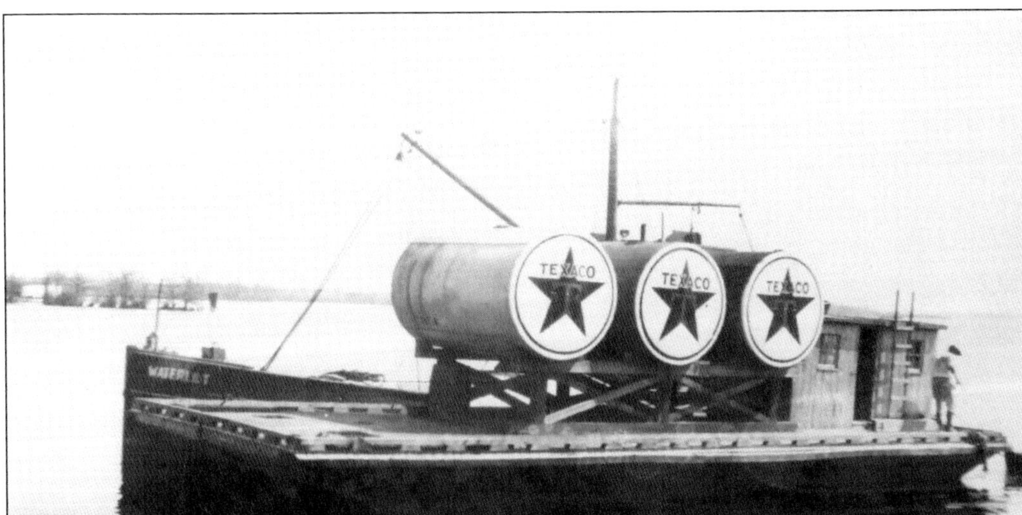

This is the Texas tanker *Waterlily* with the barge *Englehard* in the Pasquotank River at the end of the Camden Causeway. The Texaco station, which was located at the end of Milltown Road in Shiloh, was the reason that the area came to be called Texaco Beach. (Courtesy of the Outer Banks History Center, Fred Fearing Scrapbook Collection.)

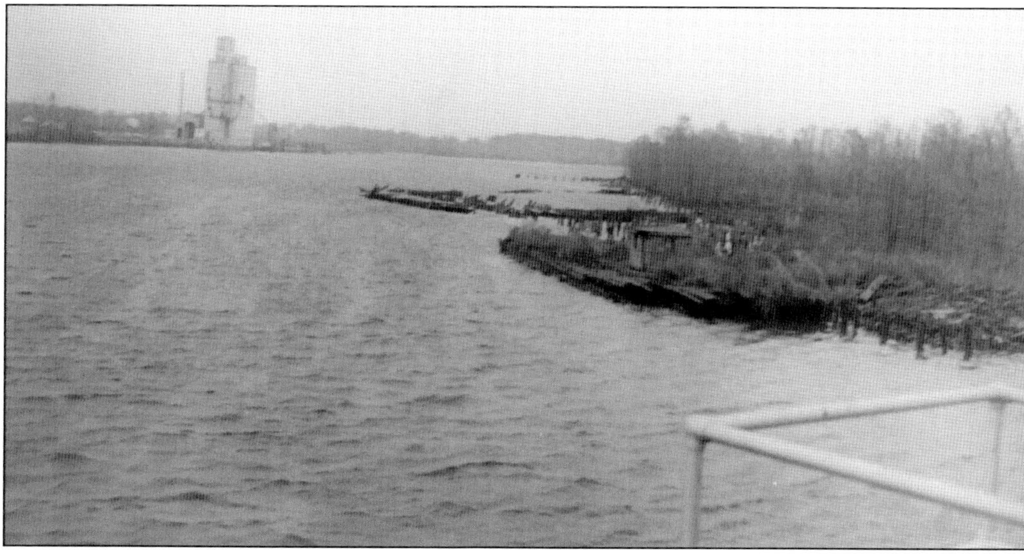

In the late 1940s, a canal was dug beside the old floating road. The canal was then filled with sand pumped in by dredge from the river and creek located at the Pecan Farm to provide a solid base for the Camden Causeway. It was built up high enough that it was not subject to frequent flooding. This photograph was taken in 1950 from the top of the Camden Bridge. (Courtesy of the Outer Banks History Center, Fred Fearing Scrapbook Collection.)

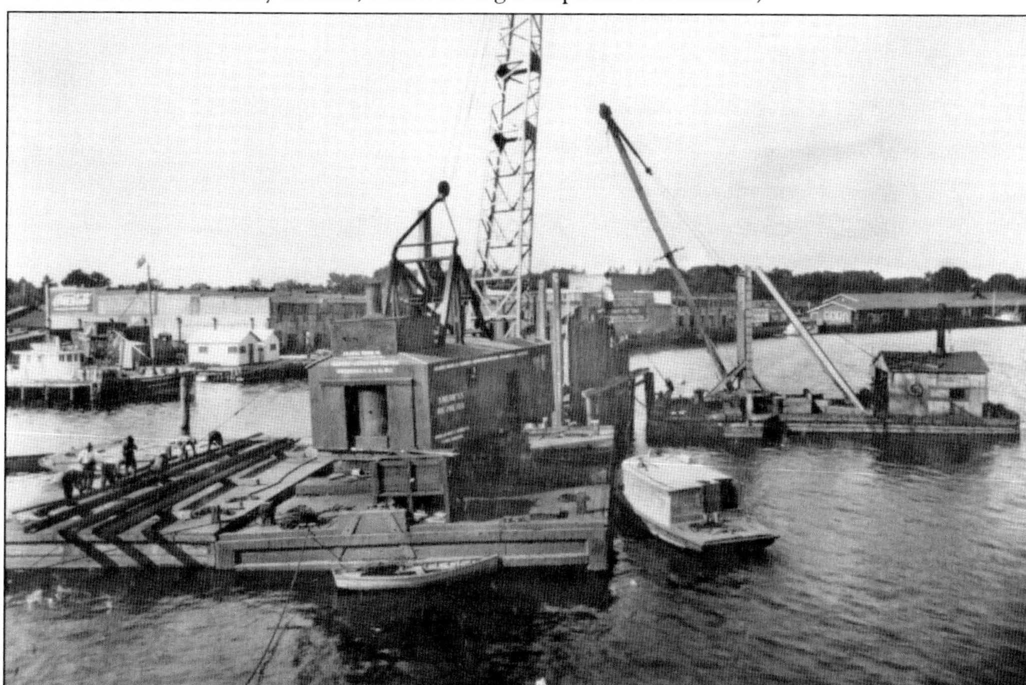

Between 1972 and 1974, a second span was added to the drawbridge over the Pasquotank River between the Camden Causeway and Elizabeth City. US Highway 158 is the main east-west route north of the Albemarle Sound and south of the North Carolina–Virginia state line. The second span marked the first time more than two lanes of traffic could flow in and out of Camden County. (Courtesy of the Outer Banks History Center, Fred Fearing Scrapbook Collection.)

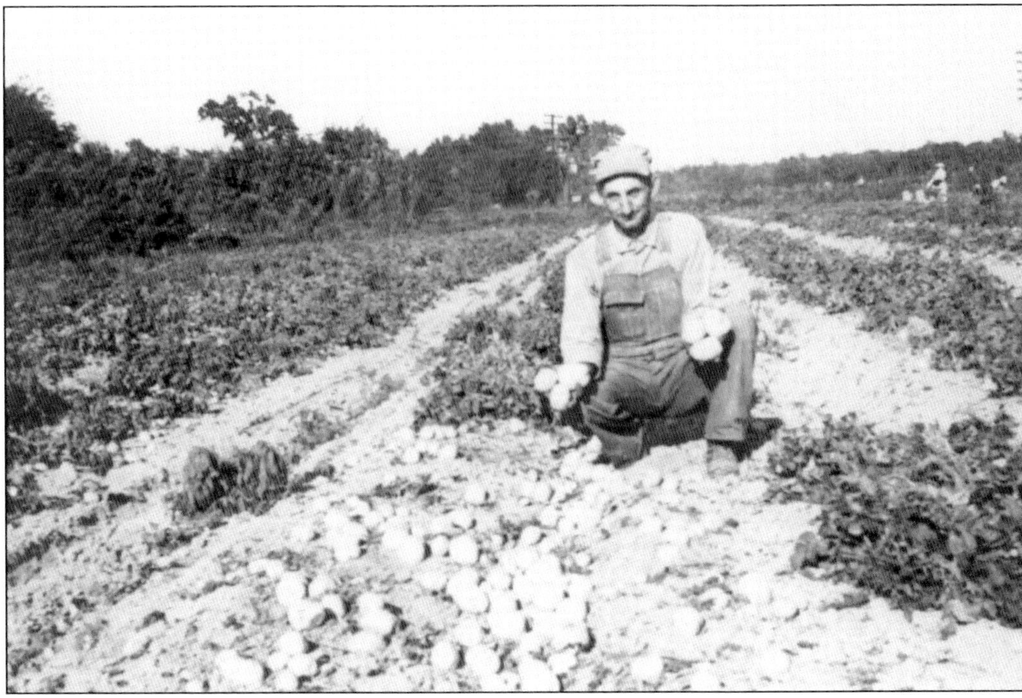

Judson Cahoon, the son of Carlista Owens Cahoon and Edward Cahoon, was born on October 10, 1901, and married Bertha Burgess. Judson is seen here in the 1940s showing off his bountiful yield of Irish potatoes in a time when the crop was still dug and collected by backbreaking human labor. (Courtesy of Anna Cahoon Boyce.)

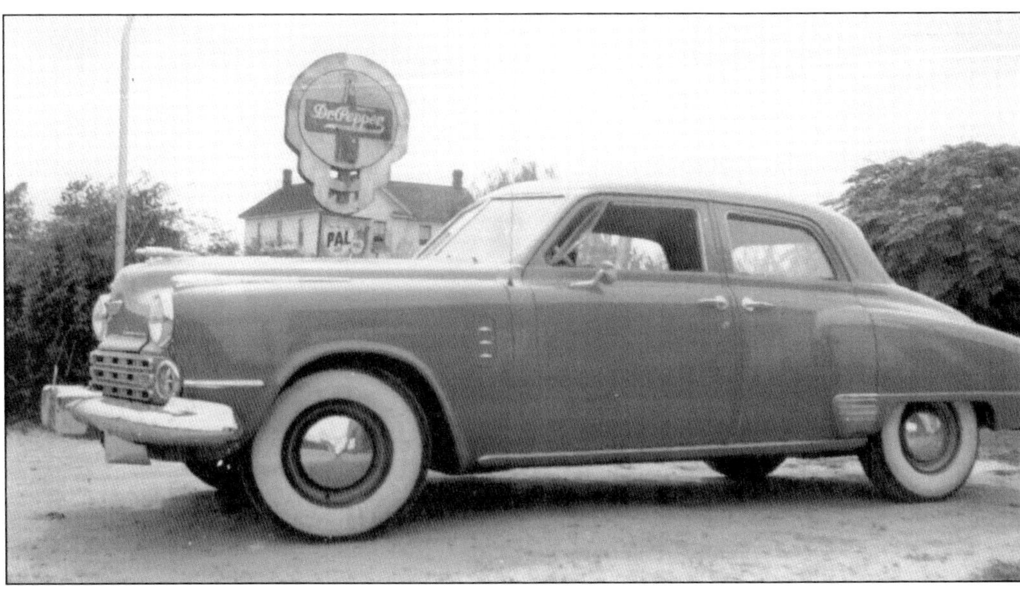

This sporty 1949 Studebaker Champion Land Cruiser four-door belonged to Essie Bartlett Sears Dough, who has it parked at the store on Trotman Road near where she lived. Notice the rear suicide doors, gangster whitewall tires, and half-moon chrome hubcaps. The styling of the car changed in 1950 with the introduction of the "bullet nose." (Courtesy of Doris Dough Forehand.)

Silas Berry Seymour was born in 1889 and his wife, Bettie Bartlett Seymour, was born in 1890. They reared eight children in a home in the heart of Camden County known as the Gatlin House. Here, they check the mail on the same road that was trampled by Union troops on their way from Chantilly. (Courtesy of Betty Brock.)

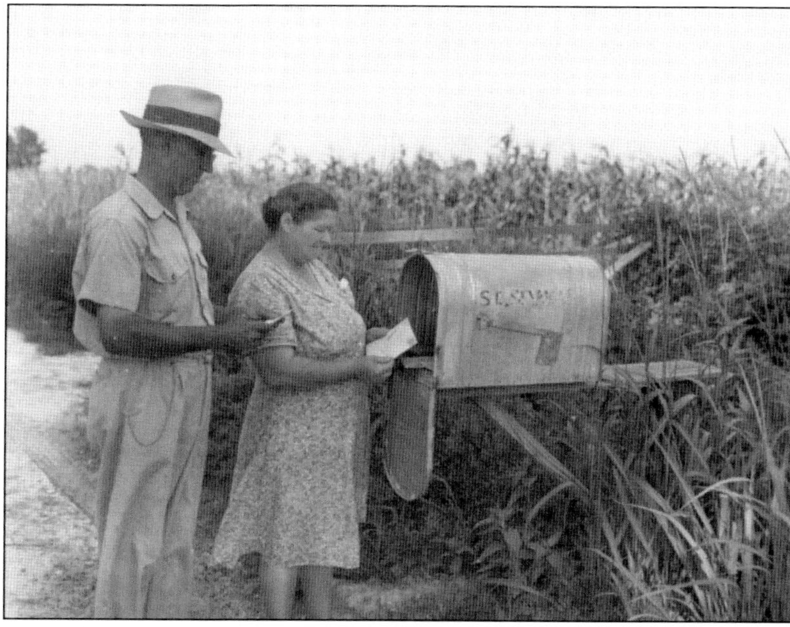

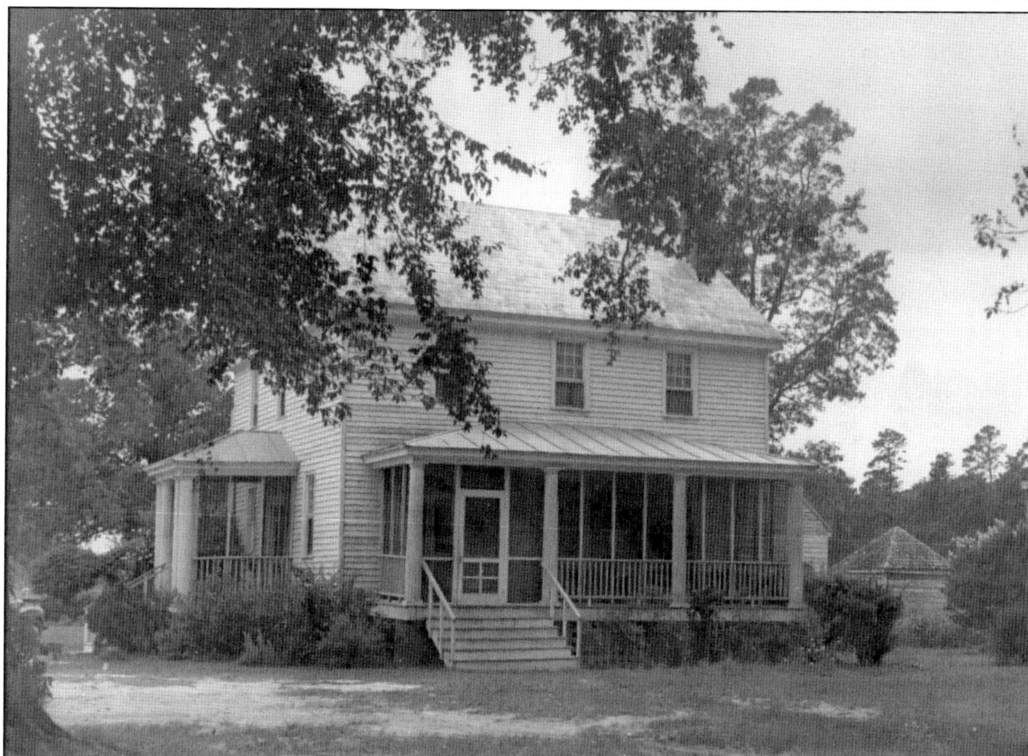

The construction of the Gatlin House began in 1823 when Alfred Moore Gatlin, who had been a resident of Chowan County, defeated Lemuel Sawyer for a seat in the lower house of Congress. Gatlin was not reelected and moved to Florida around 1835. Once Gatlin left the state, the property fell into local ownership and remains as a well-loved family home and landmark today. (Courtesy of Betty Brock.)

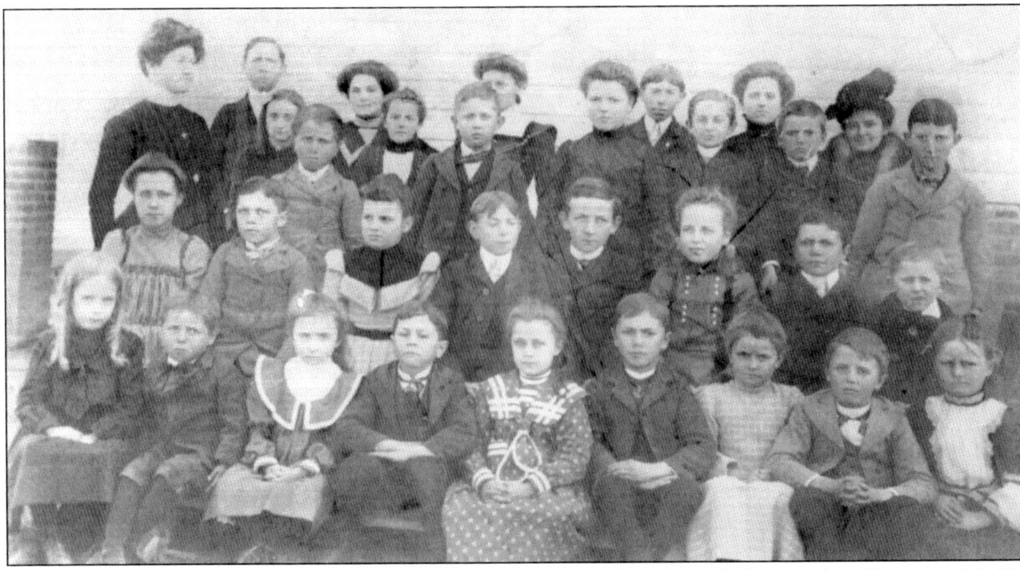

This picture of Camden School students of 1900 includes, from left to right, (first row) Lillie Bell, Charles Berry, Mary Ferebee, Howard Etheridge, Linda Mercer, Mack Stevens, Hattie Seymour, Robert Stevens, and Maude Upton; (second row) Camilla Berry, Caleb Etheridge, Ethel Midgett, Vincent Hughes, Joseph Upton, Annie Berry, Willie Stevens, and Oscar Sawyer; (third row) teacher Annie Boushell, Fred Upton, Cora Ferebee. Vance Berry, Jennie Midgett, Minnie Stevens, unidentified, Bettie Mercer, Ethel Upton, George Cox, unidentified, Eugene Midgett, Bell Midgett, Maude Midgett, and Silas Seymour. (Courtesy of Betty Brock.)

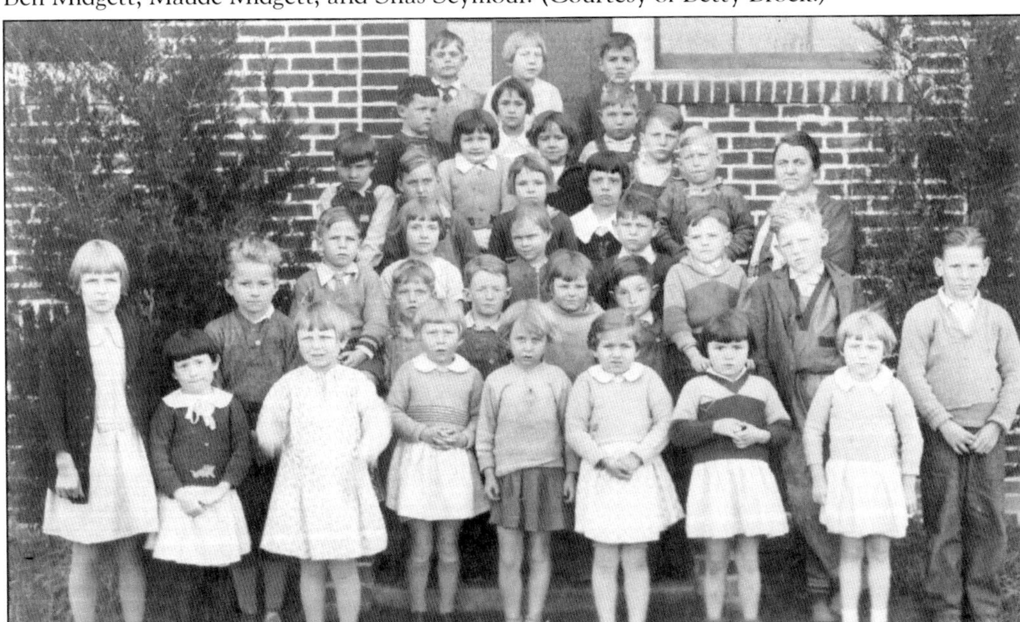

The class of 1933–1934 taught by Mary Whaley at Camden School is known to include Doris Cartwright, William Dobie, Lloyd Williams, Walter Kight, Willie Cuthrell, Ruby Midgett, Frank McPherson, G. T. Williams, ? Dough, Virginia Midgett, Isabelle Burgess, Ernest Dough, Virginia Bray, Eva Mansfield, Myrtle Edwards, and Alfred Sawyer. (Courtesy of Doris Dough Forehand.)

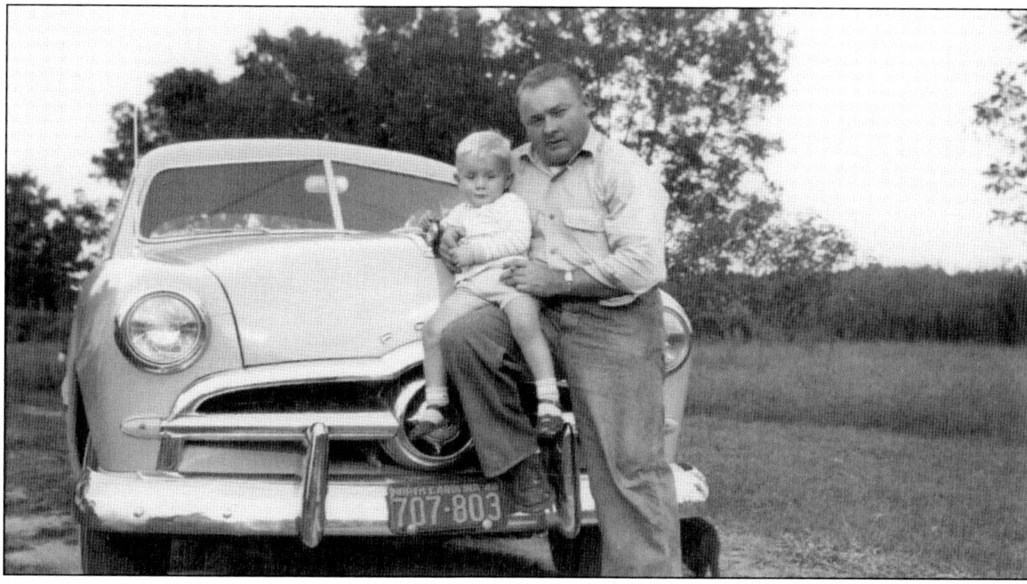

Terry Forehand sits on the knee of his father, Johnnie Paul Forehand, as he props on the hood of his 1948 Ford. The Forehands lived at Indiantown and often went fishing in Indiantown Creek. Terry graduated from North Carolina State University and came back home to teach at Camden County High School, where he was the advisor to the Future Farmers of America. (Courtesy Doris Dough Forehand.)

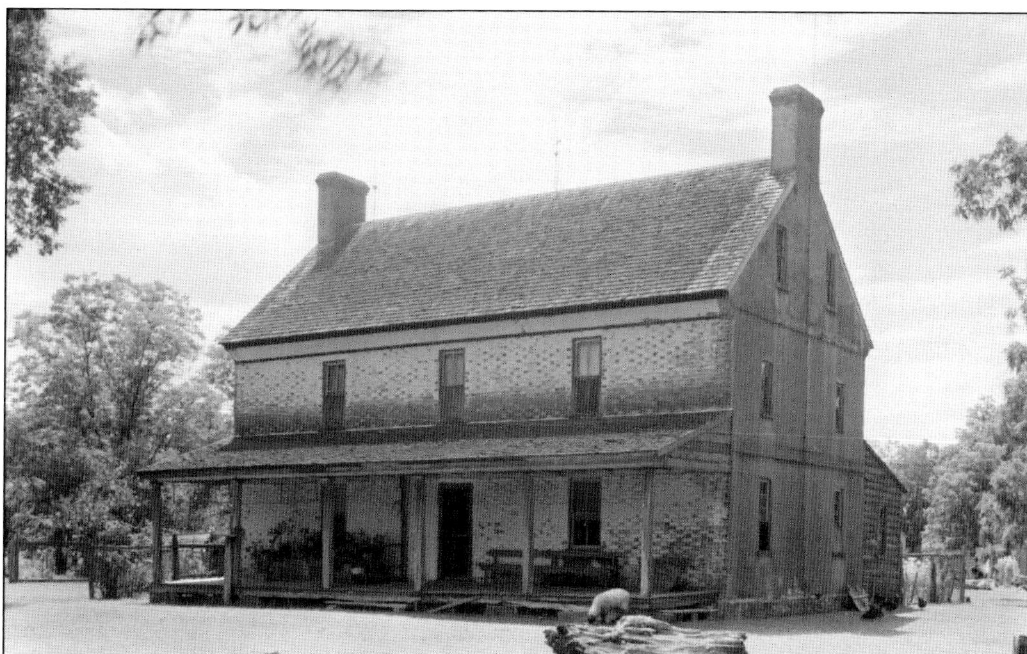

This front view of Milford shows some of the livestock needed on the farm. Horses and mules were used for transportation and pulling. Chickens and other poultry were needed for meat and eggs, and the pecking of the chickens around the foundations of buildings helped control termites. Sheep were used for wool and meat and kept the grass mowed. (Courtesy of the Library of Congress.)

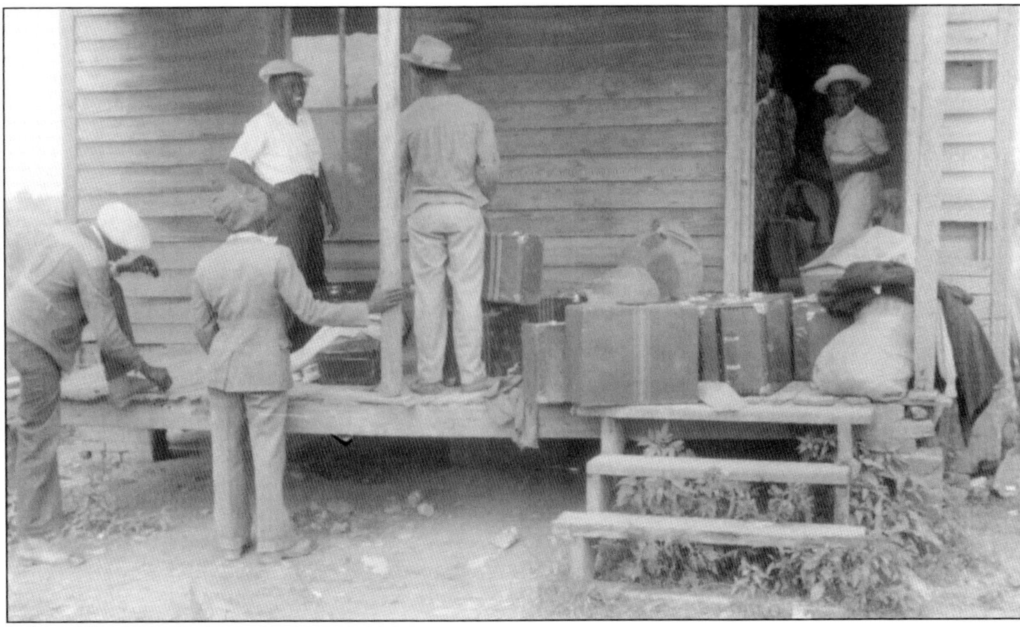

As early as the 1930s, migratory laborers would follow the agricultural harvests from Florida up the East Coast to earn a living and keep their families fed. This group of laborers is either coming or going in 1940. Migratory workers still come to work the potato season today, but working conditions, living quarters, and wages have improved since this photograph was taken. (Courtesy of the Library of Congress.)

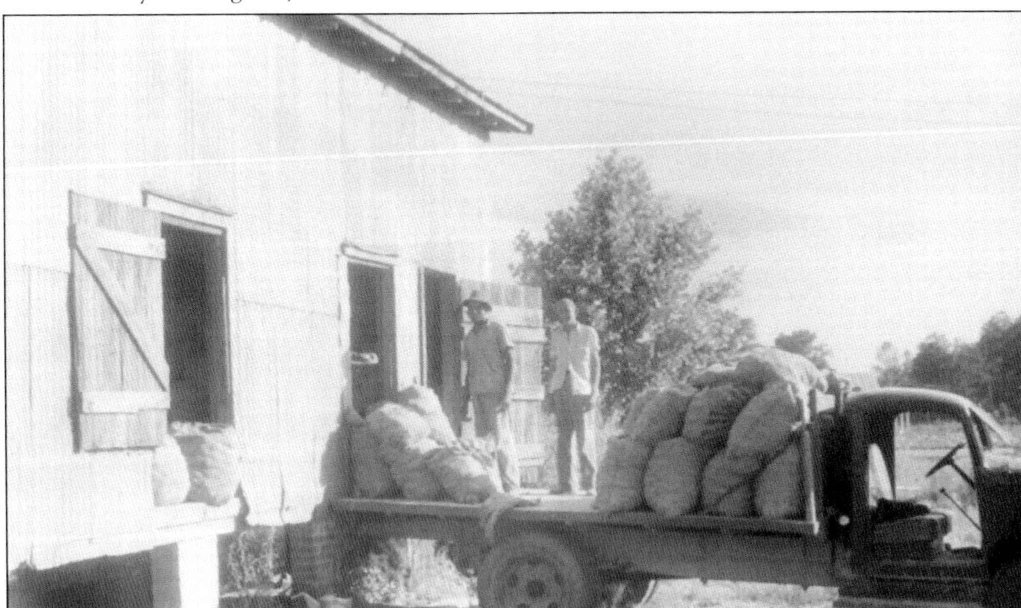

Bags of potatoes are being loaded onto a flatbed truck from the potato grader that was parallel to the railroad tracks at Belcross in 1940. Once potatoes were harvested, they were washed, graded, and bagged. The bags could then be loaded onto either trucks or boxcars directly from the grader. Graders were located on the tracks at Belcross and Camden. (Courtesy of the Library of Congress.)

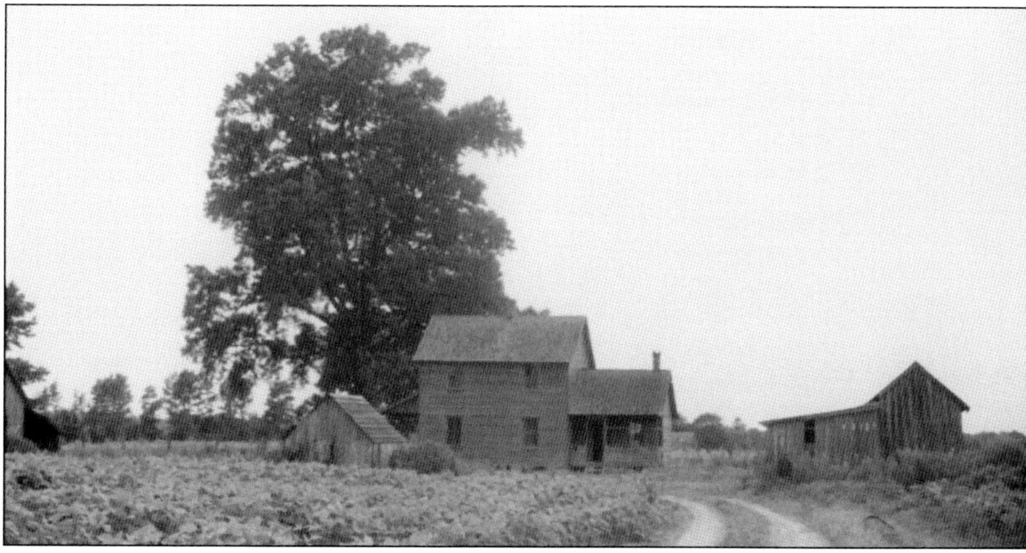

Abandoned farms like this one were common all over Camden County in 1940. Many families had lost their farms during the Great Depression, and young folks had to join the service or find employment in cities, leaving the old farmsteads vacant. Some of the old buildings housed migratory laborers in the summer, and some of the old houses were used for barns. (Courtesy of the Library of Congress.)

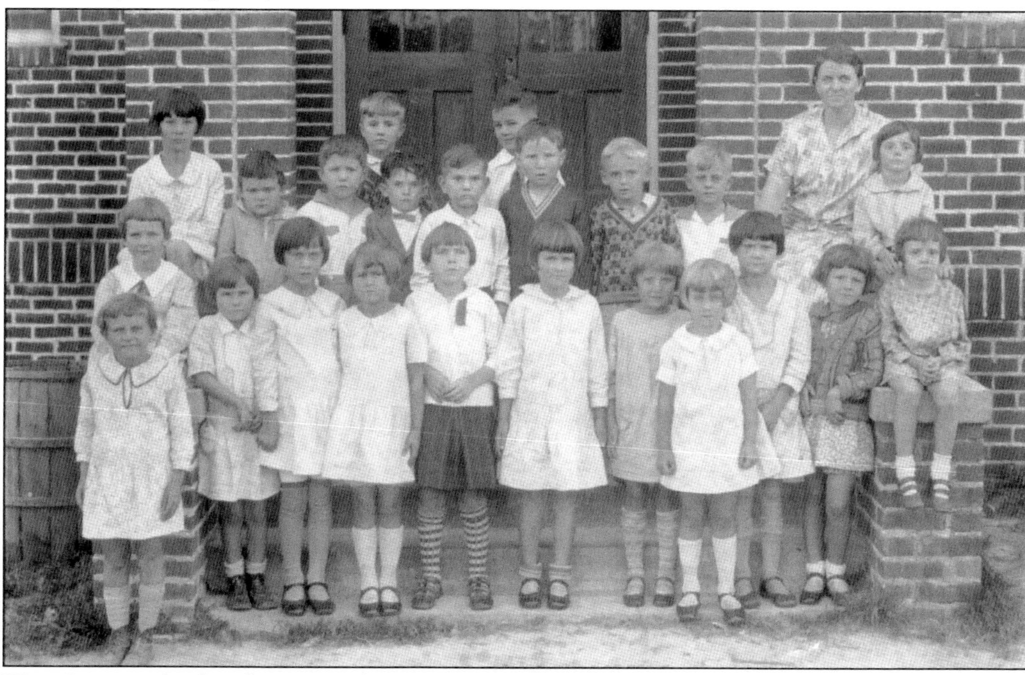

This photograph of students attending Camden School in the 1929–1930 school year includes, from left to right, (first row) unidentified, Marguerite Williams, unidentified, Ruby Lane, two unknown, Kathleen Bray, Audrey Seymour, Doris Dough, unidentified, Audrey Ward, and Aliene Stevens; (second row) three unidentified students, Aubrey Seymour, Tom Sawyer, Lloyd Williams, Tully Tarkington, Edwin Ferebee, Clayton Morrisette, teacher Mary Whaley, and Margaret Stanley; (third row) unidentified, Rupert Gregory, and F.P. Wood. (Courtesy of Doris Dough Forehand.)

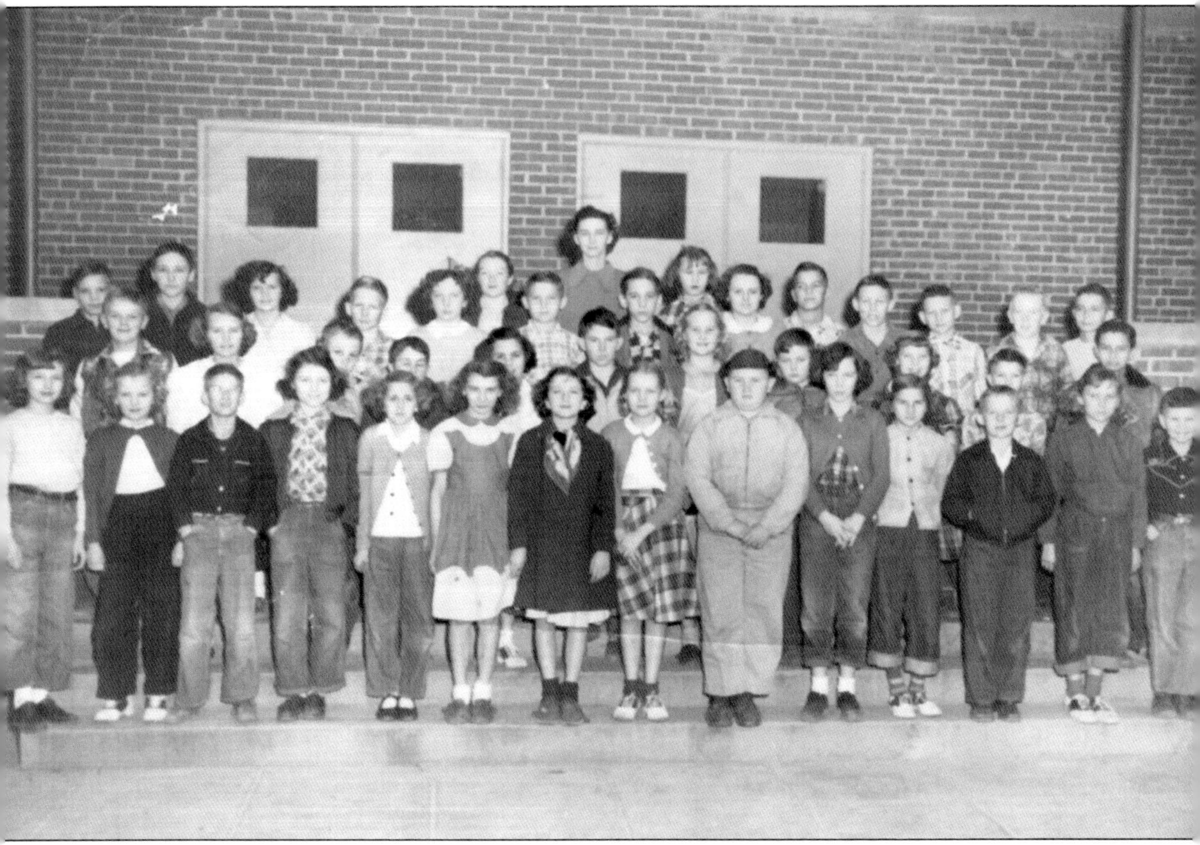

The Camden School fifth grade class picture in 1953–1954 (pictured) shows, from left to right, (first row) Edna Benton, Linda Riggs, Hersey Kight, Sylvia Godfrey, Dora Watkins, Janet McPherson, Lucy Simpson, Connie Burke, Ramona Heath, Carolyn Dozier, Glenn Roberts, Billie M. Sawyer, and Charles C. Williams; (second row) Staley Paul, Ora Lee Riggs, Edgar Lee Mitchell, Elvin Gregory, Linda Sue Lamb, Francis Pugh, Ginger Featherson, Vernon Squires, Dot Evans, Horace Wright, and Shelton Riggs; (third row) William Baily McPherson, Harry Coppersmith, Evelyn Needham, Joe Jones, Billie Faye Forehand, Beatrice Pugh, teacher Vera Garzeria, Pearl Faye Burgess, Bessie Voliva, Miford Jones, Lester Harrison, Gerald Berry, Carmen Guard, and Joe Forbes. (Courtesy of Linda Ann Mansfield.)

Four

Shiloh and the Old Trap

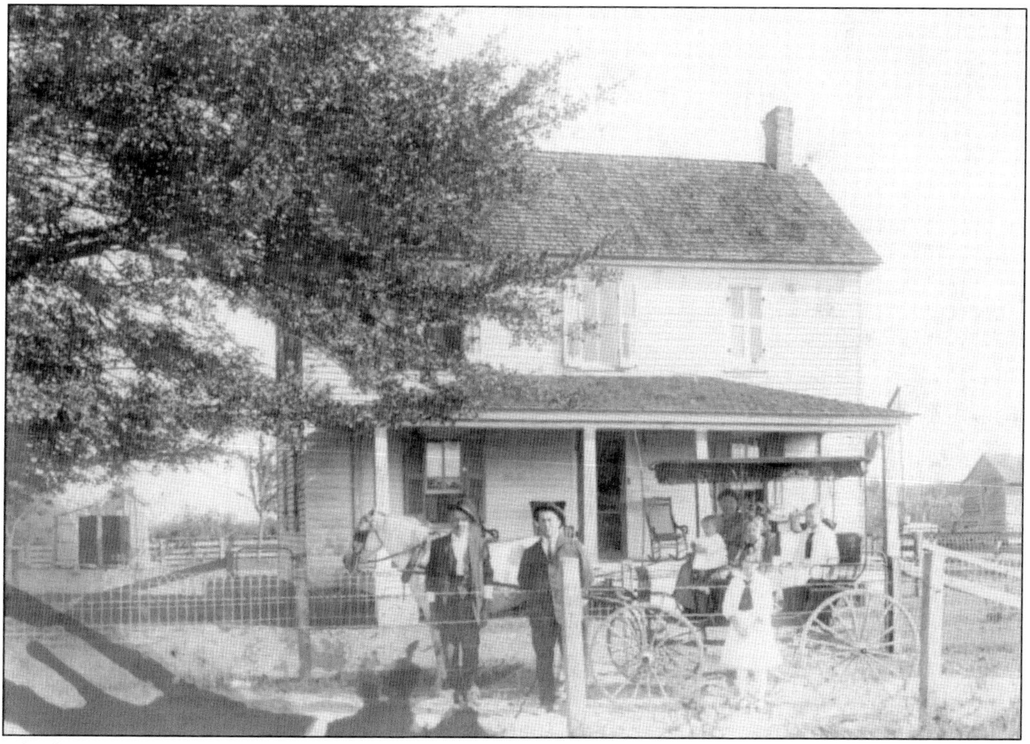

The home of Quinton Mitchell no longer exists but is very typical of the houses of this period in the Old Trap area. Pictured in 1914 are, from left to right, (first row) Quinton Mitchell, Jim Burgess, and Bertha Burgess; (second row, seated in surrey with fringe) Jobie Burgess holding son Waldorf Burgess, Claudie Burgess, and James Edward Burgess. (Courtesy of Alex Leary.)

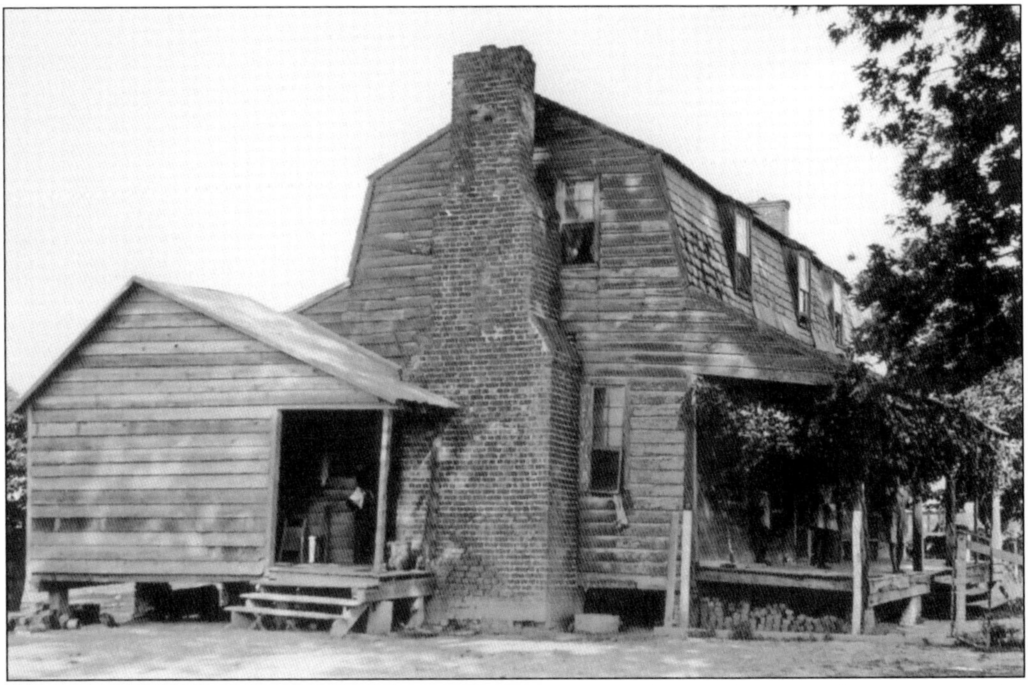

The Cartwright house, built by Samuel Williams in the 1740s on a 600-acre plantation was, for a brief period, the residence of Williams's daughter Rebecca and her husband, Capt. John Forbes, who was killed at Guilford Courthouse. Williams directs in his will that one of his slaves be freed and given 240 acres in Currituck County, the first known instance in the county of a slave receiving property. (Courtesy of the Library of Congress.)

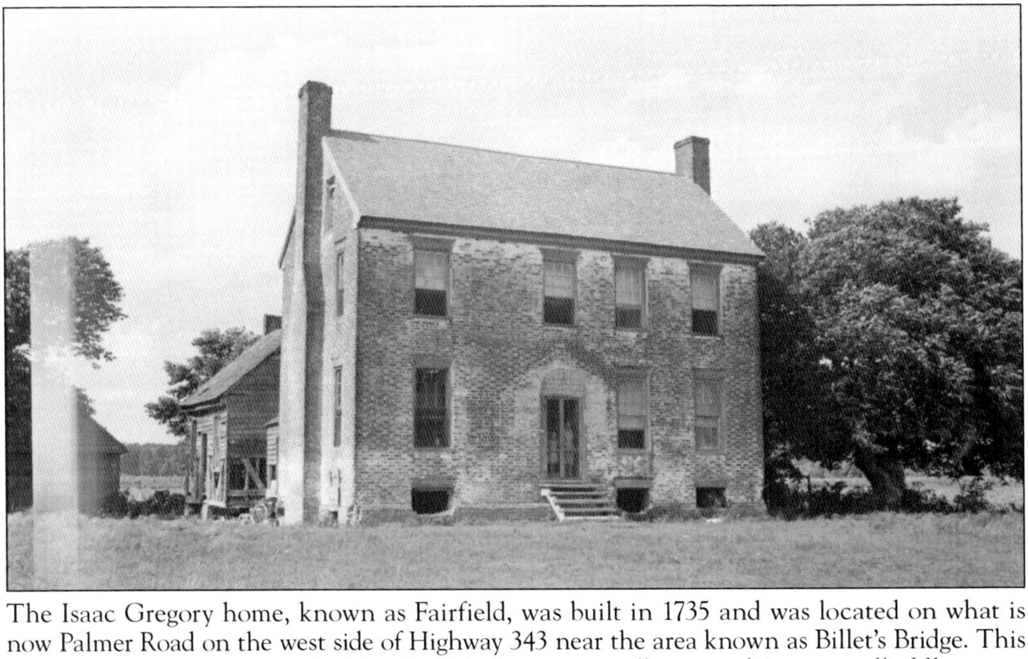

The Isaac Gregory home, known as Fairfield, was built in 1735 and was located on what is now Palmer Road on the west side of Highway 343 near the area known as Billet's Bridge. This photograph was made around 1940, when the house was still occupied. It eventually fell to ruin, but the site can still be identified. (Courtesy of the Library of Congress.)

Mary Clark Leary Burgess and Peter Tumbler Burgess are pictured on the road between Old Trap and Shiloh, taking grain to the mill. The Burgesses adopted and reared Cecil Walker. By this time, the last windmill was no longer operating and had been replaced by a more modern mill, but the trip on the cart remained the same as it had for over a century. (Courtesy of Wilse Burgess)

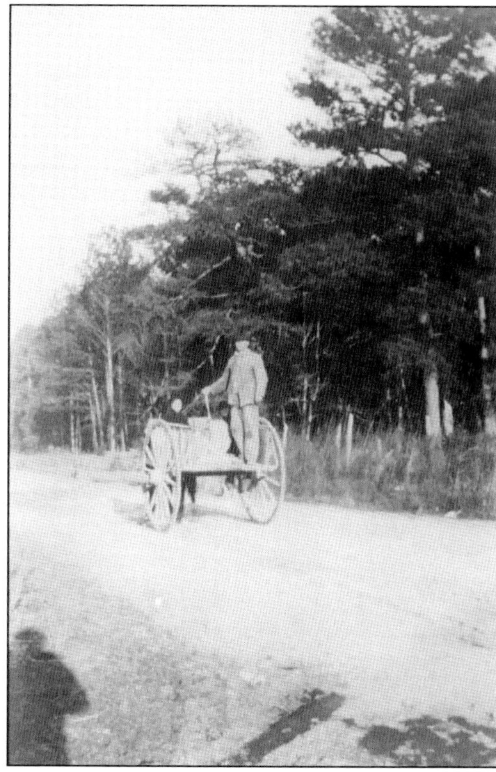

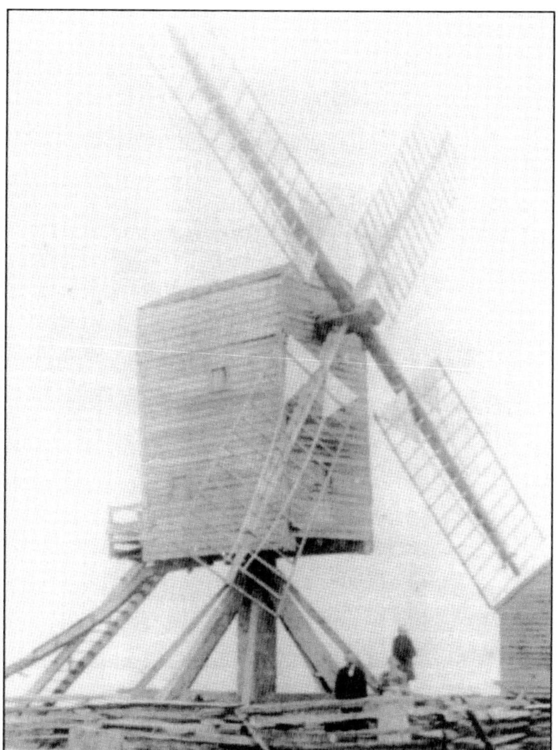

In the 1850s, five windmills operated in Shiloh, also know as Milltown, but most were destroyed by the 1880s hurricane. By the early 1900s, only this one windmill, built in 1895 and owned by Sylvester Forbes, remained. Earlier windmill owners included William Jones, John Bell, Jacob Bell, Noah Toxey, and Robert Gallop. Figures pictured in the foreground are, from left to right, Andrew Bell, Nannie Bell, and Ivey Bell. (Courtesy of Brian Forehand.)

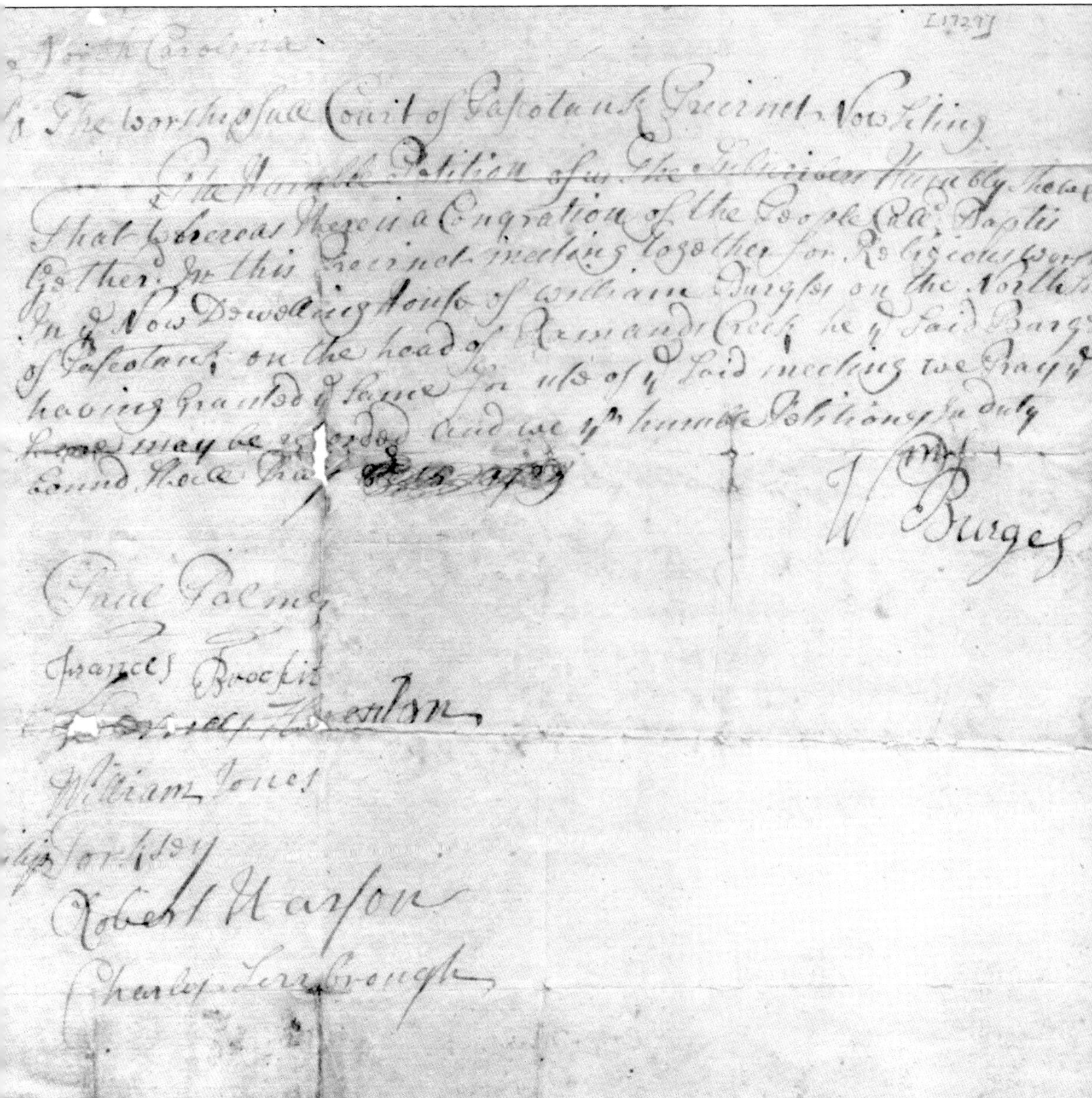

[1727]

North Carolina

To The worshipfull Court of Pasquotank Precinct Now Sitting

The Humble Petition of us The Subscribers Humbly Shew

That Whereas there is a Congregation of the People Call[ed] Baptis[ts]

Gather[ed] In this Precinct meeting together for Religious worship

In ye Now Dwelling House of William Burgess on the North[illegible]

of Pasquotank on the head of Raymonds Creek he ye said Burgess

having granted ye same for use of ye said meeting we Pray ye

same may be recorded and we ye humble Petitioners in duty

bound shall Pray [illegible]

W Burgess

Paul Palmer

Francis Brockit

[illegible]

William Jones

[illegible]

Robert [illegible]

Charles [illegible]

Shiloh Baptist Church is the oldest Baptist church in North Carolina. By 1727, people were worshiping in the home of pastor Rev. William Burgess. The number of worshipers grew, and in 1736, Reverend Burgess built a small church next to his home. The petition was made by the church to the king's court on September 5, 1729, for them to continue worshiping as they had been for years. (Courtesy of Wilson Library, University of North Carolina.)

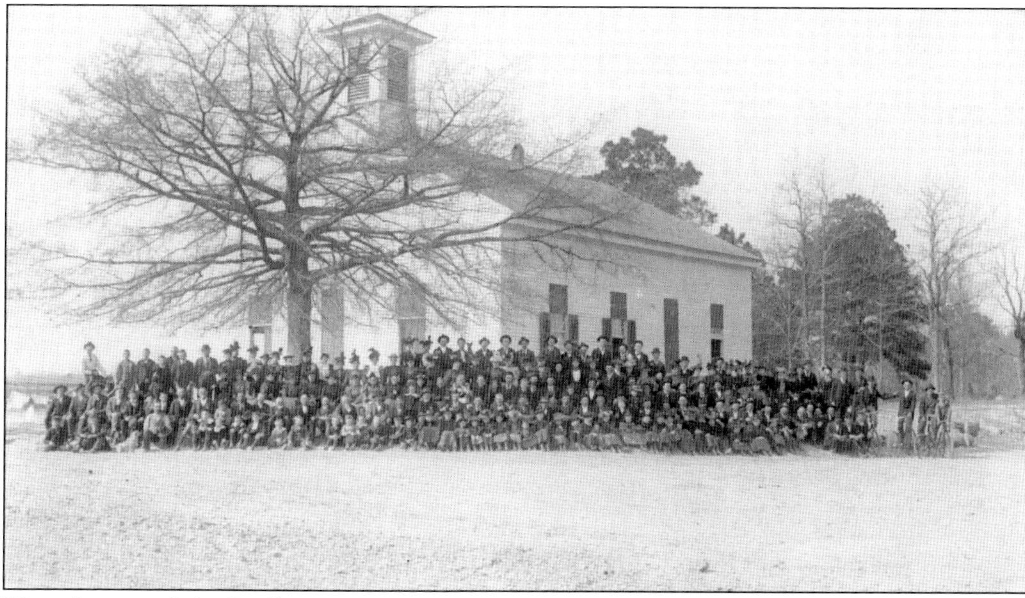

This photograph by Zoeller, Morgan Company around 1895 shows the congregation of Shiloh Baptist Church after the steeple was added to the building. Mary and Luke Stevens donated funds and labor to add the steeple in 1878. Luke died from flu and pneumonia on March 8, 1878, and Mary died from the flu 10 days later. (Courtesy of Linda Ann Mansfield.)

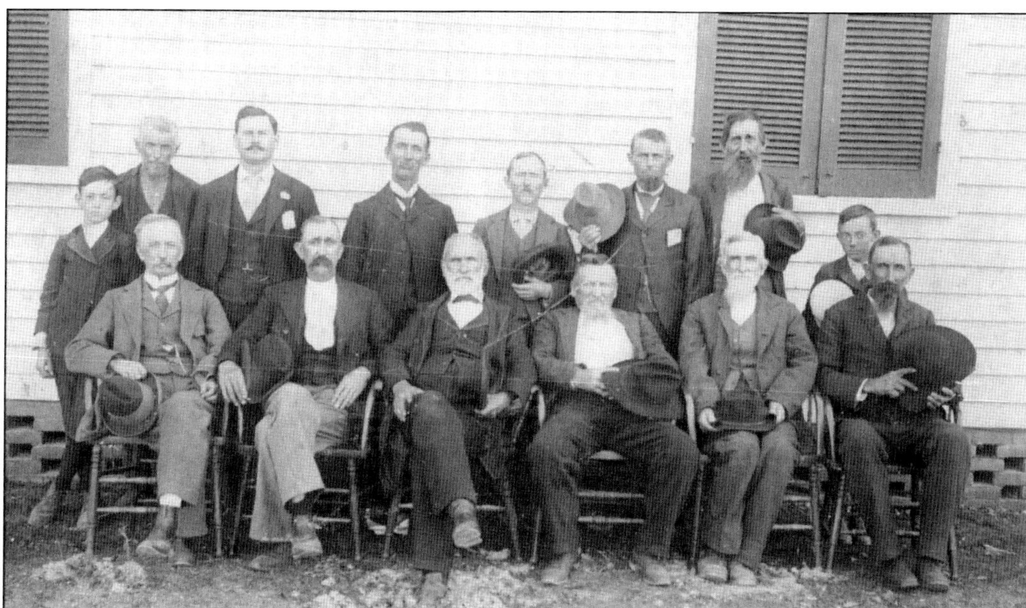

The deacons and pastor of Shiloh Baptist Church in 1895 are seated in chairs, two of which are displayed in the modern church. Pictured are, from left to right, (first row) Joseph Morrisette, Samuel G. Squires, pastor Rev. R.R. Overby, Nathan Stevens, Enoch Daily, and Billy Stevens; (second row) Herbert Morrisette, Elijah Staples, Charles Garrett, Charles Berry, John Godfrey, Marshall Toxey, Joseph Walston, and an unidentified boy. (Courtesy of Linda Ann Mansfield.)

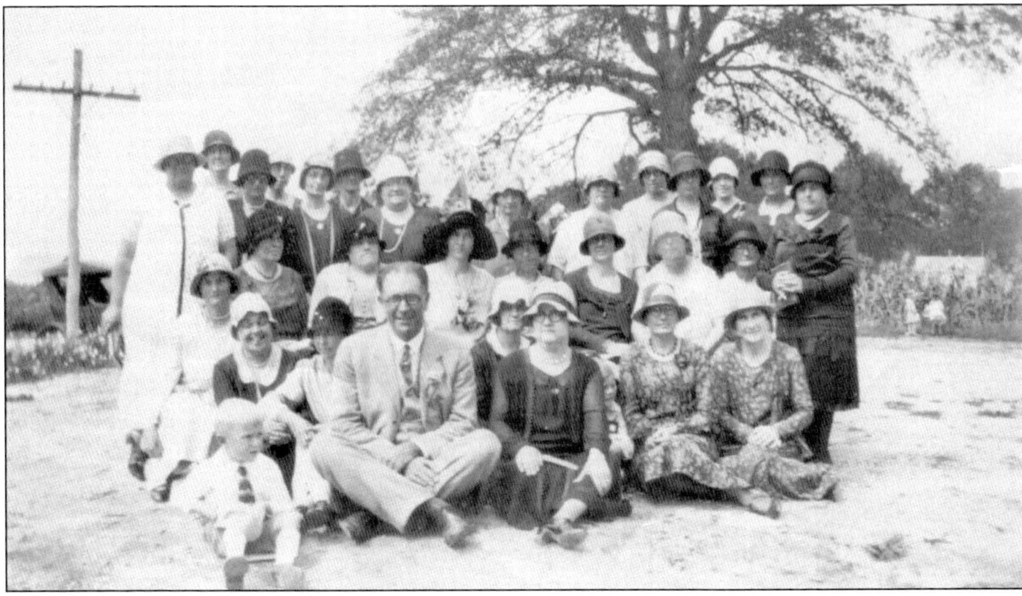

Rev. W.L. Barrs served as pastor of Shiloh Baptist Church from 1927 until 1928. Barrs and his wife returned to visit the Shiloh Baptist Church ladies, and this picture was taken at Elizabeth City Beach in 1929 during their reunion. The boy in the front left is Marvin Jordan. (Courtesy of Linda Ann Mansfield.)

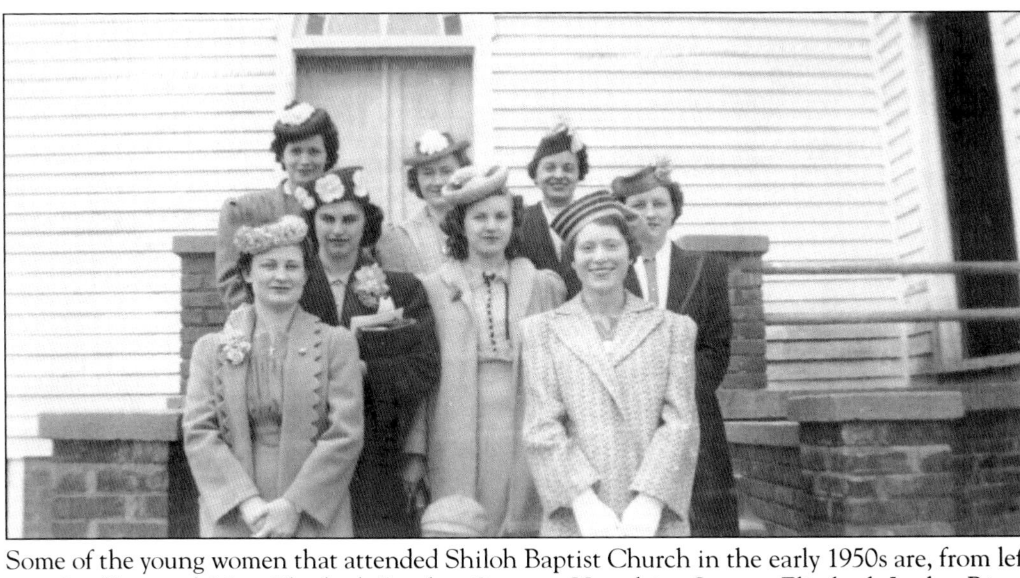

Some of the young women that attended Shiloh Baptist Church in the early 1950s are, from left to right, (first row) Mary Elizabeth Bartlett Gregory, Hasseltine Sawyer, Elizabeth Jordan Riggs, and Nellie Cartwright Berry; (second row) Laura Lee Davenport, Mary Elizabeth Mercer, Mary C. Sawyer, and Florence Walston. The photograph was taken before the church was bricked. (Courtesy of Linda Ann Mansfield.)

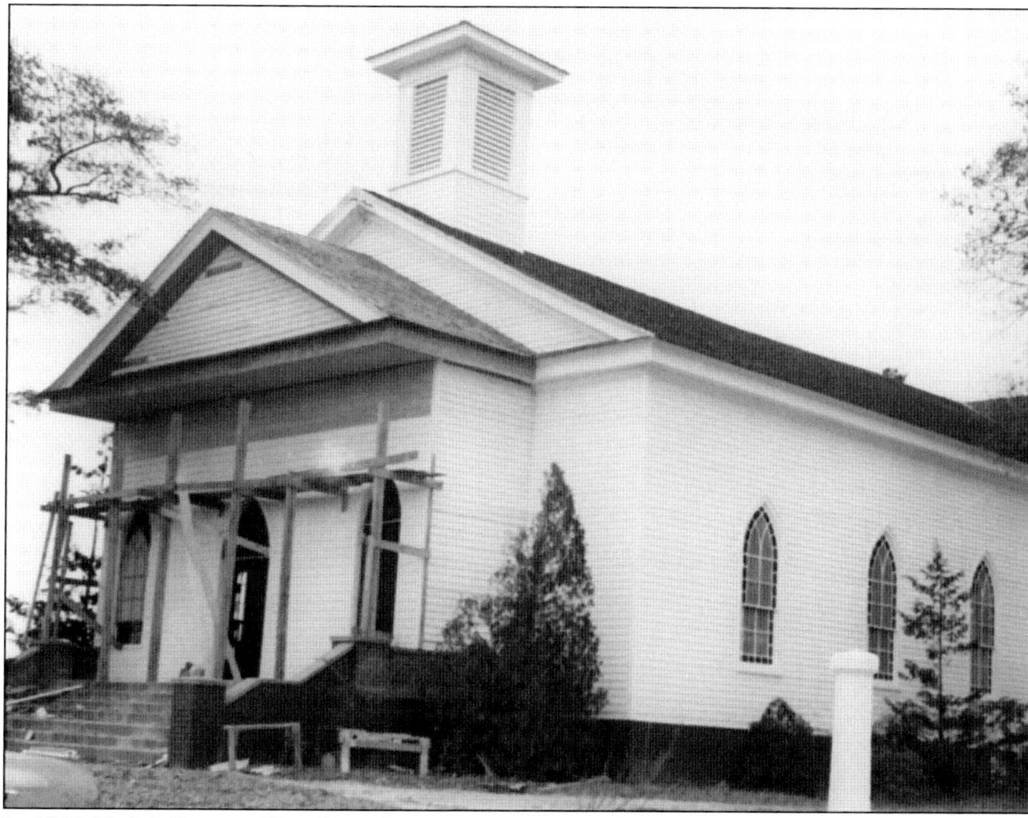

In 1947, Shiloh Baptist Church underwent a major remodeling that involved replacing two front doors with windows and the single central window with a double door. Under the influence and guidance of Paul Palmer and William Burgess, the Shiloh Baptist Church congregation began to continually serve the community of Shiloh since 1727, making it the oldest known Baptist church in North Carolina. (Courtesy of the Outer Banks History Center, David Stick Collection.)

The children of Geneva Hughes and William "Billie" Forehand, Brian (left) and his sister, Billie Faye, are ready to celebrate Christmas in 1950. The Forehand family lived directly across the road from Shiloh Baptist Church. The Mary and Dennis Bartlett home can be seen in the background. (Courtesy of Anita Whitehurst.)

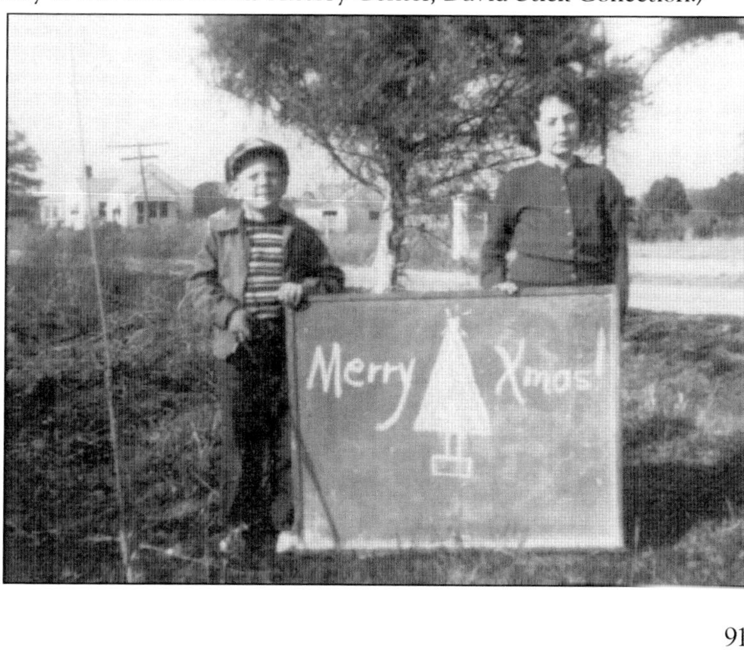

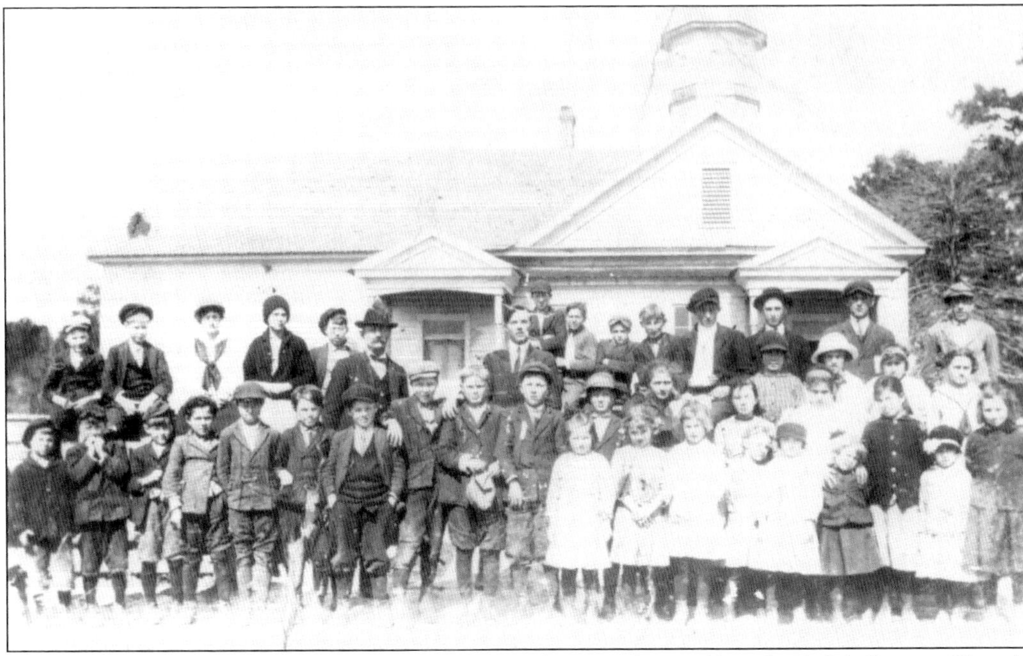

This Shiloh School, built in 1908 by Dennis F. Bartlett, was located beside Shiloh Baptist Church. This photograph was taken in 1912 when the church next door was also used for some classes and Willie J. Burgess was a teacher. Shiloh students attended this school until 1923, when they moved into the newly built Shiloh High School. (Courtesy of the Family Research Society of Northeastern North Carolina, Inc.)

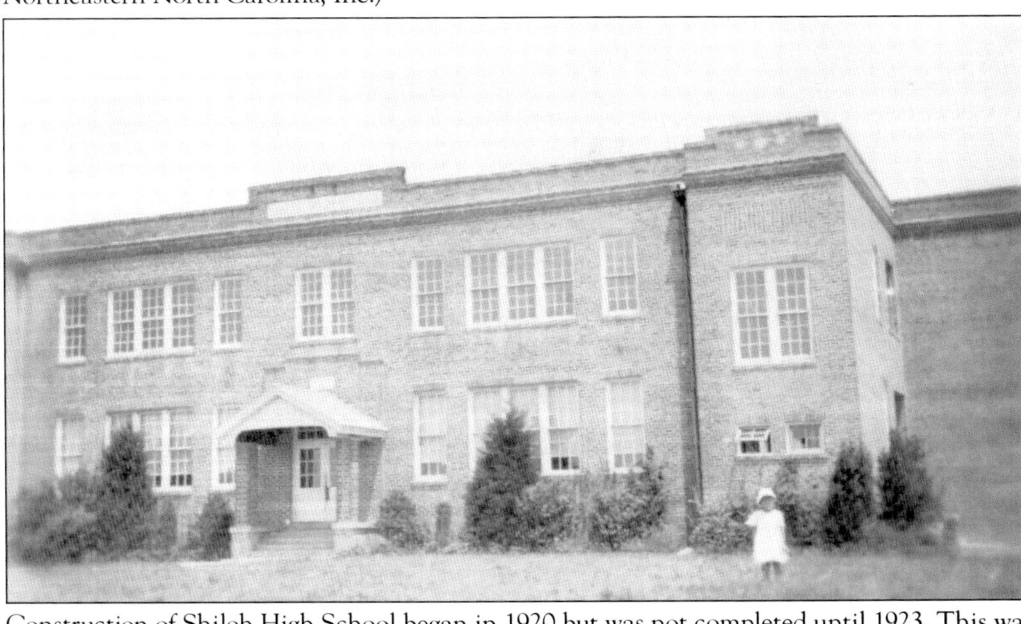

Construction of Shiloh High School began in 1920 but was not completed until 1923. This was the first state-funded school building in Camden County. High school students from Old Trap began riding a bus to Shiloh High School in 1928. By 1945, all high school students attended Elizabeth City High School. The Shiloh school closed in 1952 and was later converted into a store. (Courtesy of Anita Whitehurst.)

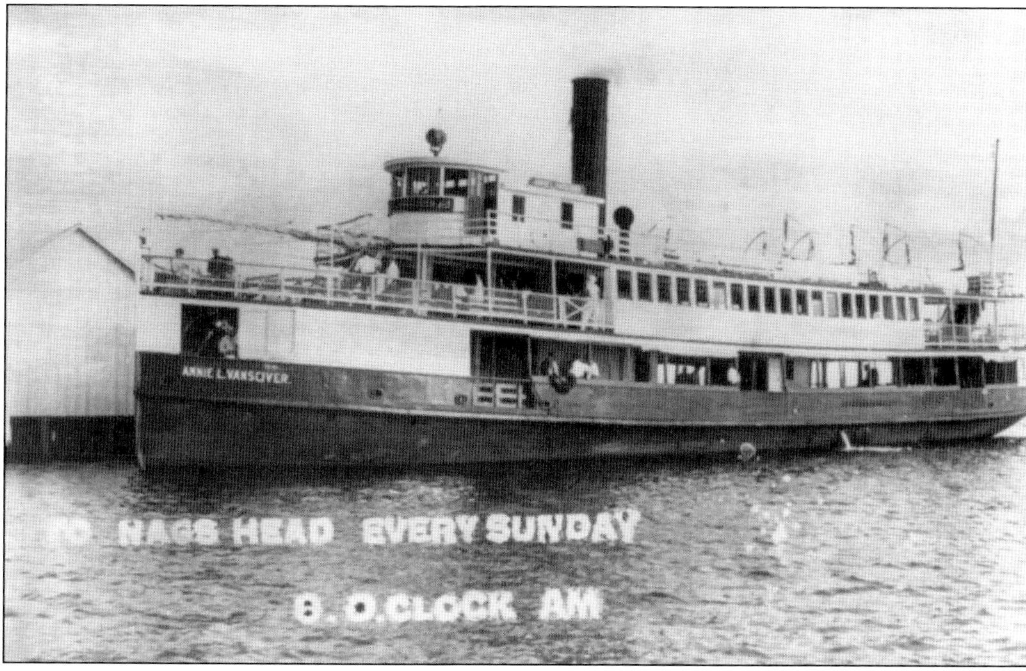

The *Annie L. Vansciver* was probably the most popular of the many boats that traveled the Pasquotank River on regular passenger and cargo runs. Capt. James M. Richardson blew the whistle and left Elizabeth City punctually at 2:00 p.m. to regularly scheduled stops at Shiloh, Old Trap, Newbern's Landing, Jarvisburg, and Barnett's Creek. (Courtesy of Thelma Naomi Sawyer Forbes.)

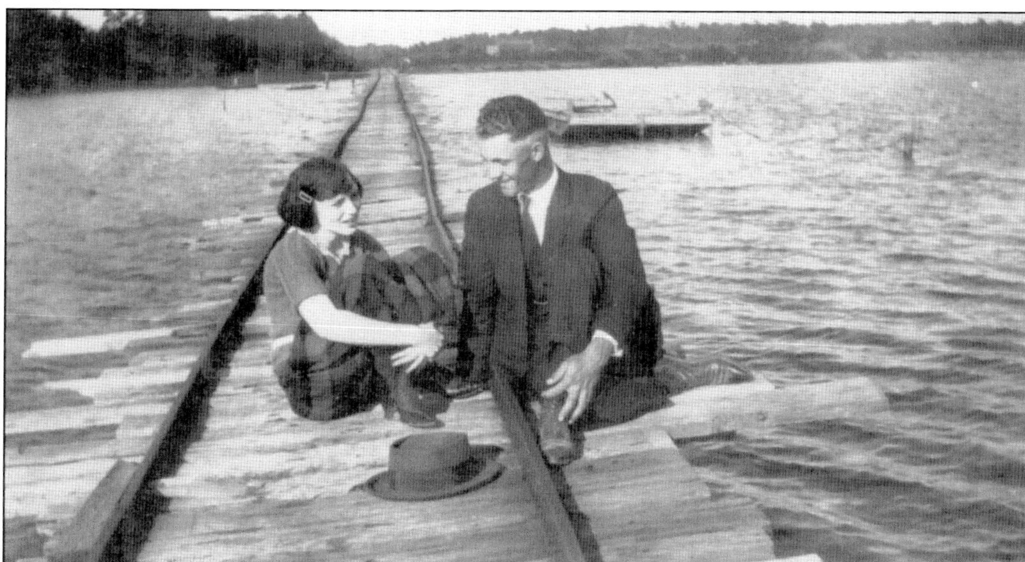

Around 1910, W. Cowell and S.W. Gregory had a narrow-gauge railroad built, stretching from the village of Shiloh at Gregory's General Store to the 600-foot-long Cowell's Pier that accommodated the docking of steamships on the Pasquotank River. The original pier was destroyed in the big freeze of 1917–1918 and had to be rebuilt at a cost of $50,000. Florence Walston and Robert Old are pictured on the pier. (Courtesy of Anita Whitehurst.)

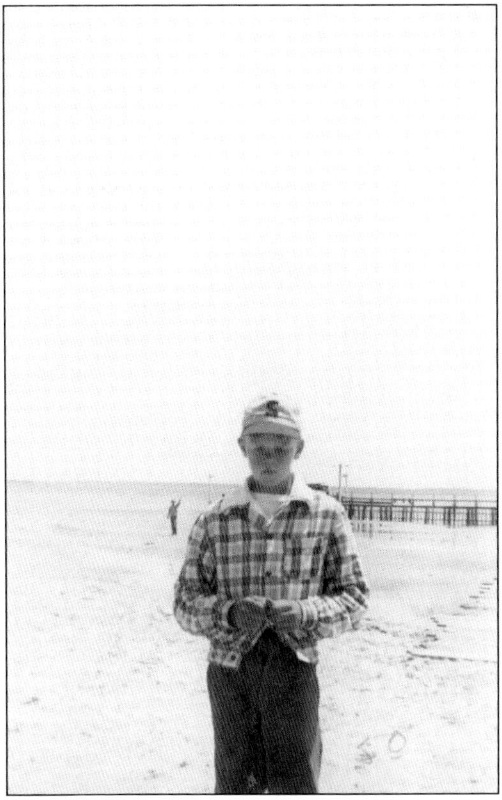

Larry Paul is standing in front of the pier that extended into the Pasquotank River at the end of Milltown Road in Shiloh. Depending upon the time, the area has been known as Milltown, Elizabeth City Beach, and Texaco Beach. Slightly to the right out of this picture was the blimp hangar, which burned in 1995. The glow of the fire could be seen for many miles that night and destroyed all but the huge concrete pillars that framed the hangar doors. The four columns still stand as a monument and can be seen across the river. The US Navy built 17 of these hangars to the same plan, and they were among the largest wooden structures in the world. Of the original 17, only seven have survived. (Courtesy of Anna Cahoon Boyce.)

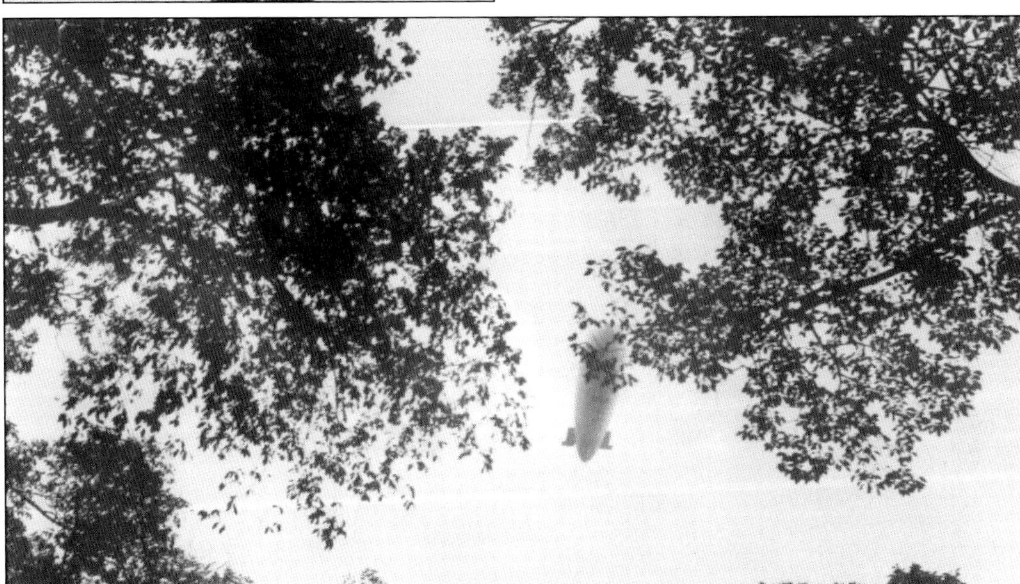

In 1941 the US Navy needed a way to patrol enemy submarines off the coast. Before blimps patrolled, German submarines were destroying vessels every other day. After the Navy dispatched a blimp squadron from its Weeksville Naval Air Station, which operated from June 8, 1942 until June 30, 1957, the number dropped to one every 75 days. Patrolling blimps were a reassuring sight. (Courtesy of the Outer Banks History Center, D. Victor Meekins Collection.)

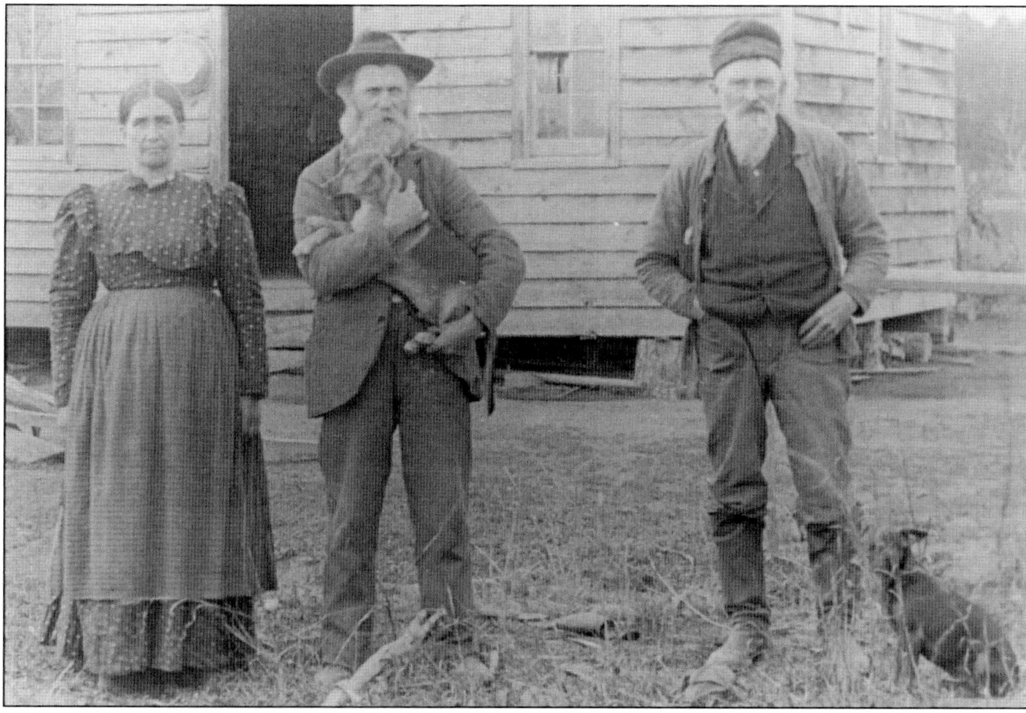

Thomas B. Jones (right) was a private in the Confederate army. He told Quinton Mitchell, "I know I am going to die but I have done some terrible things in the Civil War and I am scared to be buried under the ground. Would you please make sure that I am buried on top of the ground?" His request was honored. (Courtesy of Thelma Naomi Sawyer Forbes.)

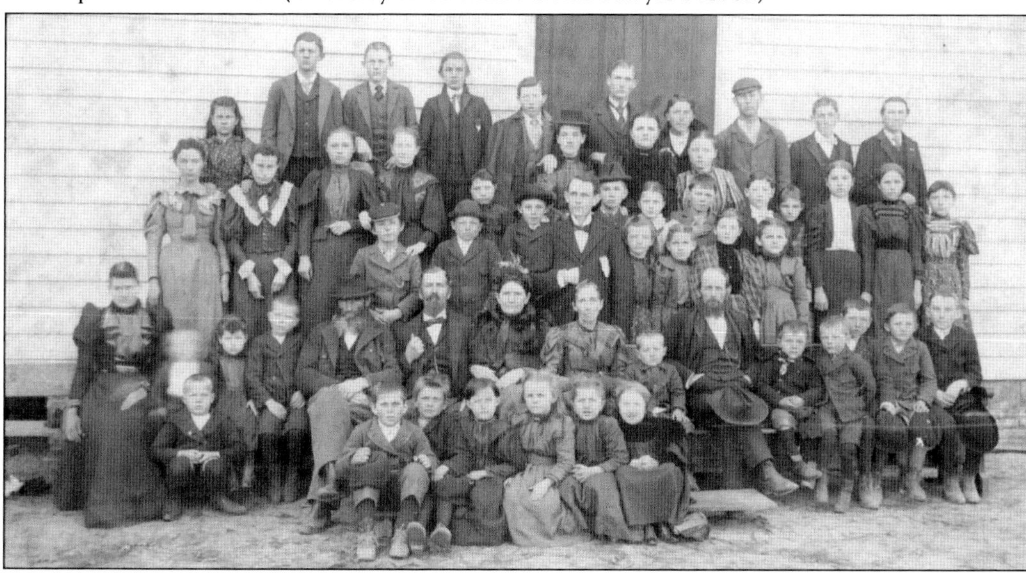

Oak Ridge School was located in the Bray's Corner section of the Riddle community. This photograph, taken in 1896, shows nearby residents as well as students. During the late 1800s, there were 29 schools in Camden because they had to be within walking distance of the students' homes. School buses did not come into use until the late 1920s. (Courtesy of the Family Research Society of Northeastern North Carolina, Inc.)

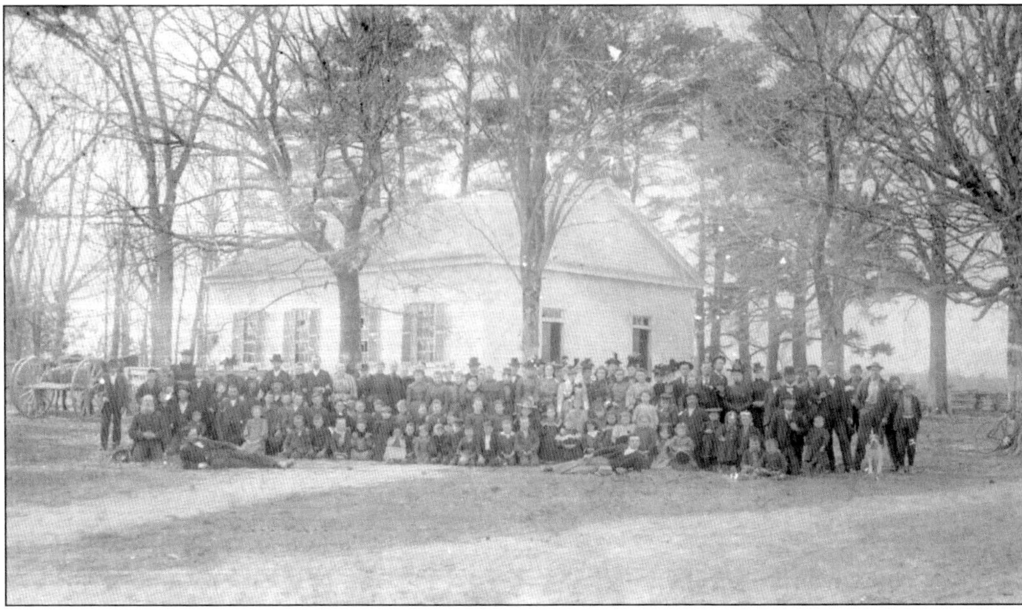

The Wesley Methodist Episcopal Church in Old Trap was organized by Rev. Samuel Ferebee Jr., and the congregation began meeting in a brush arbor in 1834. The first church structure was also built in 1834. By 1857, when it was replaced with the building pictured in this Zoeller, Morgan Company photograph taken around 1895, it had become known as Wesley Methodist Episcopal Church South. (Courtesy of Alex Leary.)

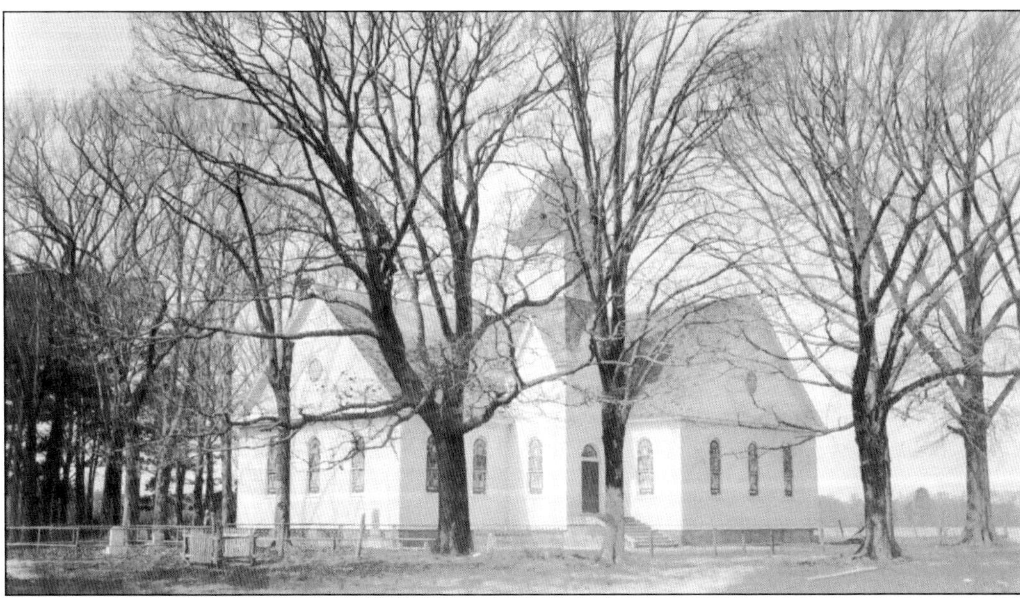

In 1917, a new Wesley Methodist Episcopal Church South was constructed on the same site as the 1857 church. By comparing this photograph made around 1930 with the earlier photograph taken around 1895, one can match the growth pattern of the trees to determine without doubt that this third building is on the same site as the previous church. (Courtesy of the Outer Banks History Center, D. Victor Meekins Collection.)

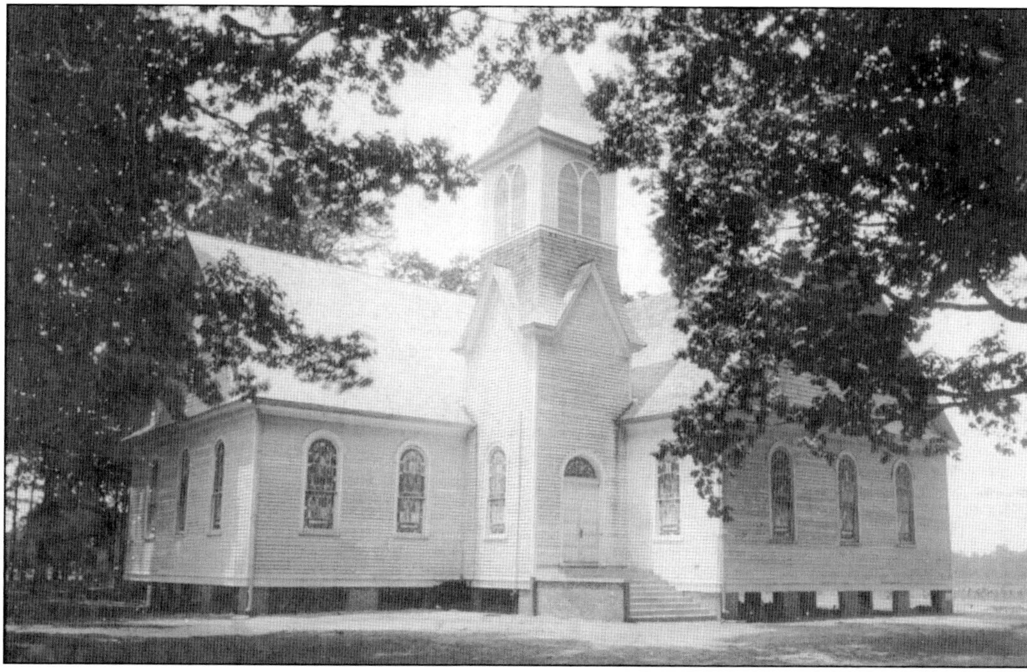

On a Sunday afternoon on February 9, 1947, the Wesley United Methodist Church burned to the ground. Some of those who witnessed the terrible fire that day were Rev. A.L.G. Stephenson, Horace Burgess, Henry Burgess, Ambrose Staples, Abner Staples, Elroy Pugh, Charlie Riggs, Ira Topping, and Roosevelt Topping. A few items, including a Bible, a picture of Christ, pulpit furniture, piano, and a few pews, were saved. (Courtesy of Betty Brock.)

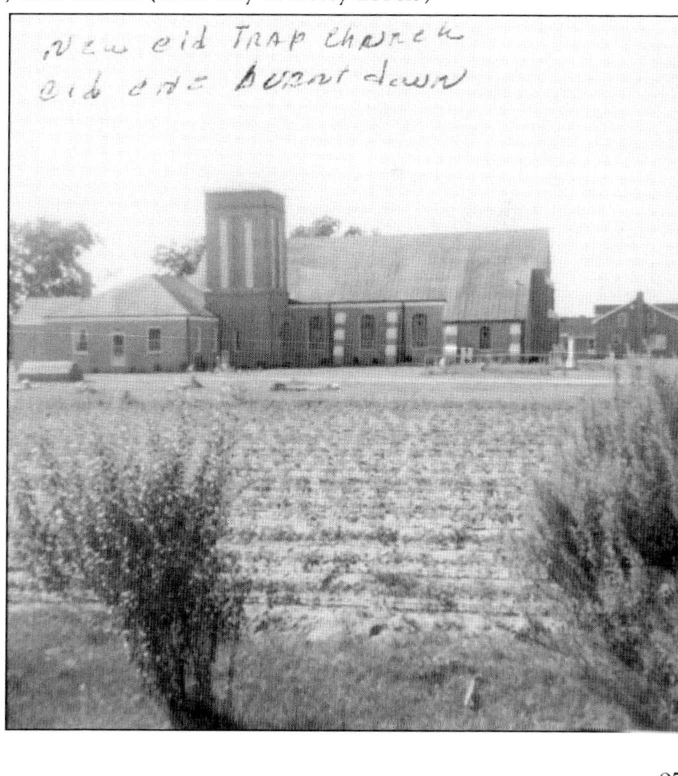

After the 1947 fire, the Wesley Methodist Church met in the former dance hall at the Roy Forbes store and at the Old Trap Community Building. Plans for the fourth and present building, seen here, were bought 10 months after the fire and the building is constructed with around 150,000 gray bricks. On April 19, 1953, Sunday school was held in the present church. With the uniting of the Methodists and the United Bretheren Churches in 1968, this church is now known as Wesley United Methodist Church. (Courtesy of Joyce Mitchell Cuthrell.)

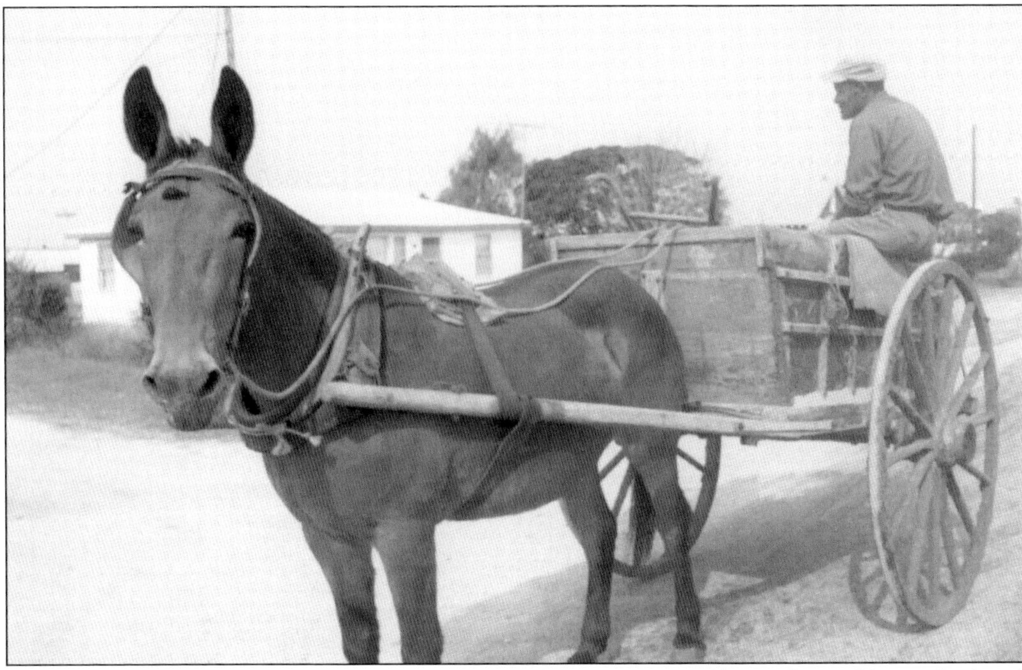

Jordan Jones was remembered as being a wonderful person. He and his wife would give the locals rides on the cart up and down the road between stores and homes. Jones would ride in the cart many times when he would cut the hedgerows on the farms. The horse or mule cart was reliable transportation. (Courtesy of Thelma Naomi Sawyer Forbes.)

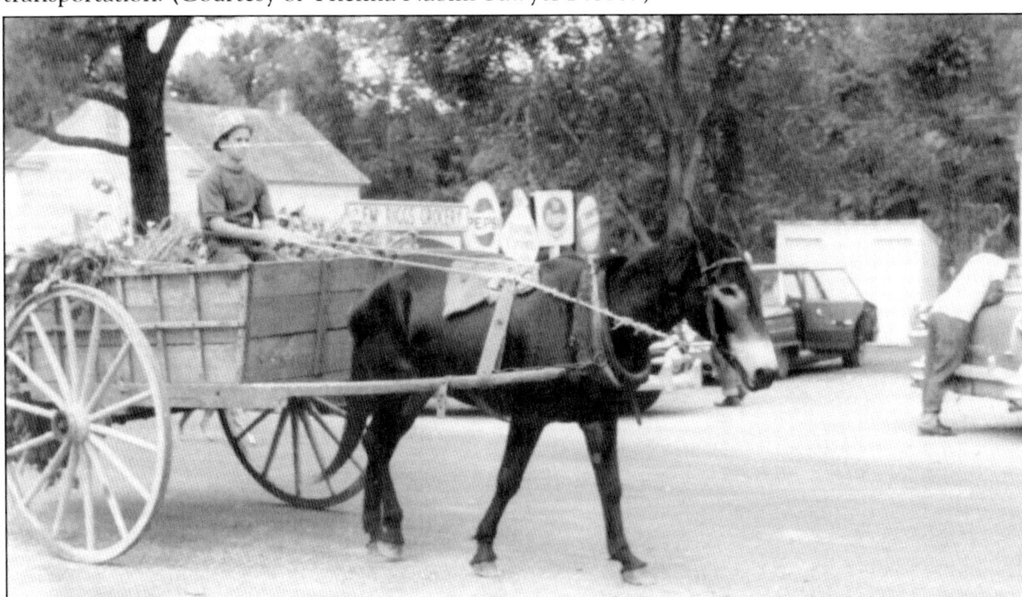

Ronald Scheibach drives a cart pulled by a mule named Sally in front of the Lem Riggs Grocery Store, formerly the Roy Forbes Store, at the intersection of Texas and One Mill Roads in Old Trap during the 1960s. Addie and Sanford Harris were running the store when it burned in the late 1960s. The store warehouse escaped the fire and was moved in 1995. (Courtesy of Thelma Naomi Sawyer Forbes.)

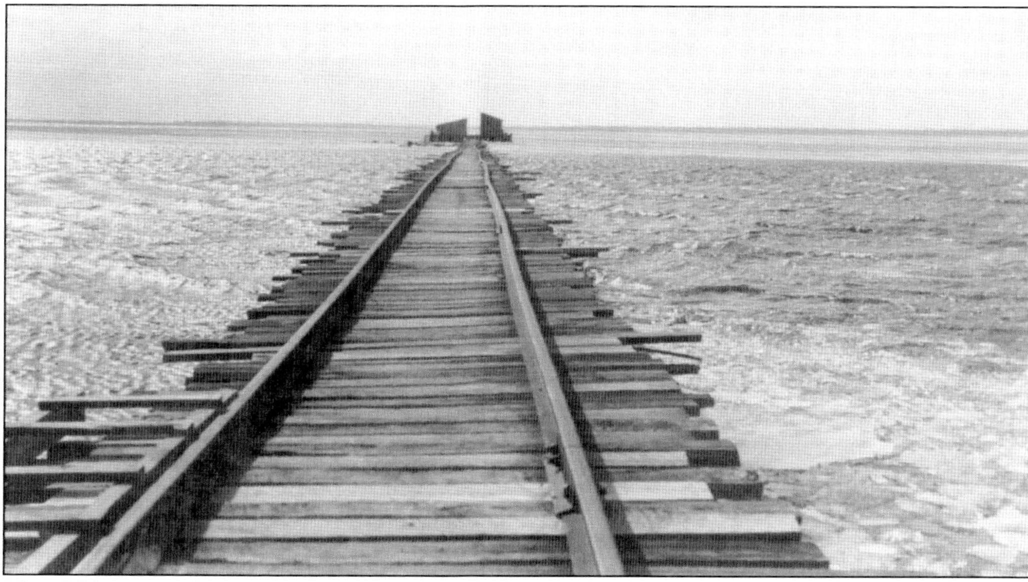

The Old Trap Wharf, owned by James Edward Burgess and later by his son Jim Burgess, was the lifeline of the people of Old Trap. All transportation of people and goods was by way of the Pasquotank River, which necessitated a long pier to cross shallow water to the channel. In this image, the wharf is paralyzed by an unusual winter freeze. (Courtesy of Joyce Mitchell Cuthrell.)

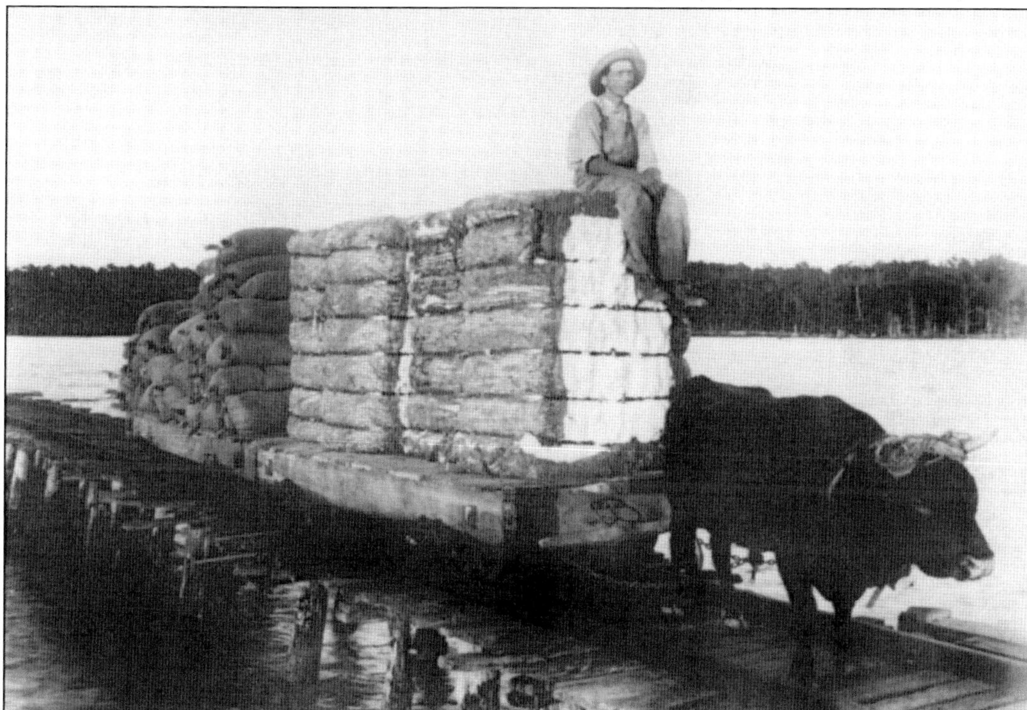

Gideon Needham sits on truckload of baled cotton followed by a truckload of sacks of soybeans. Needham drives an ox down the rails of the pier of the Old Trap Wharf. The trucks were too long to turn around, so the ox would be unhitched from one end and re-hitched to the other end to make the return trip to the warehouse. (Courtesy of Betty Brock.)

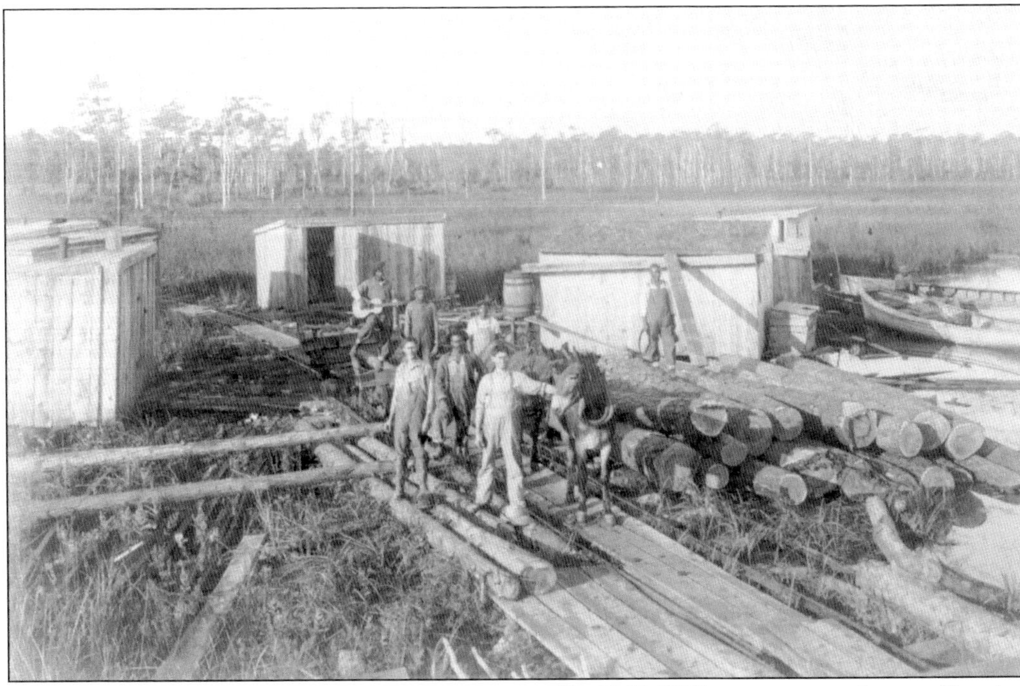

Employees of Buck Island Logging Company, owned by D. E. Williams, are seen here pulling logs out of the swamp around the North River in 1914. The two men standing in front are Will Dean (left) and John Leary (holding the mule). The men behind them are unidentified. The logs were dragged out of the swamp with teams of mules. Logs would be rafted and pulled out by tugboats. (Courtesy of Alex Leary.)

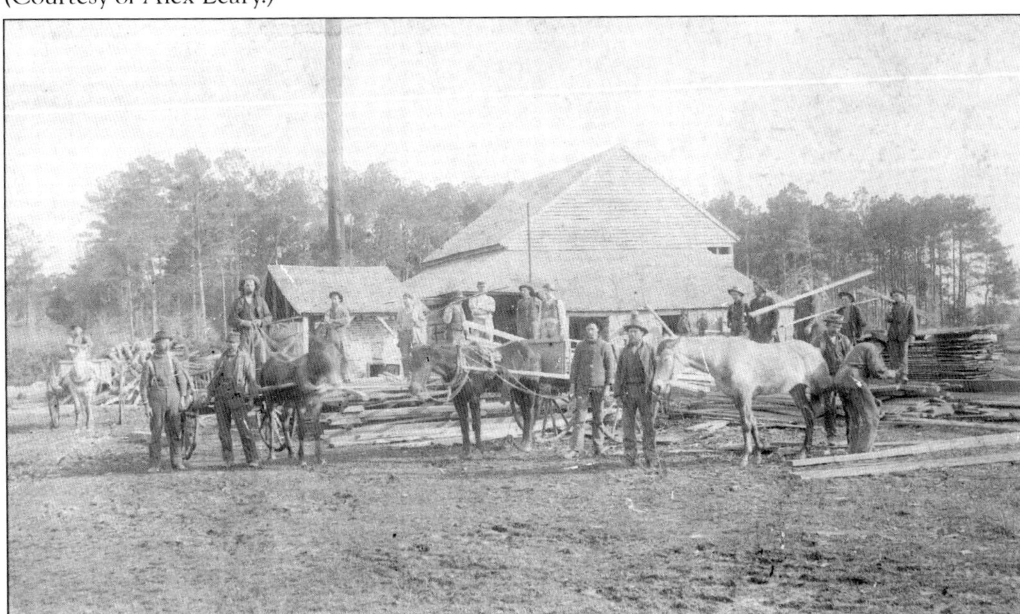

Around 1900, mule teams were used to pull logs up from the river to this sawmill at Old Trap. Sawmills provided year-round employment for local men who were otherwise relying mostly on farming and fishing to generate income. (Courtesy of Alex Leary.)

Wade Point Lighthouse, located at the mouth of the Pasquotank River, was one of two screw-pile lighthouses operated by the US Life-Saving Service in the waters off the shores of Camden County. The North River Lighthouse, built to the same plan, was damaged in the big freeze in 1917–1918, salvaged in 1920, and moved to Rodanthe. (Courtesy of the Outer Banks History Center, River Lights of North Carolina Collection.)

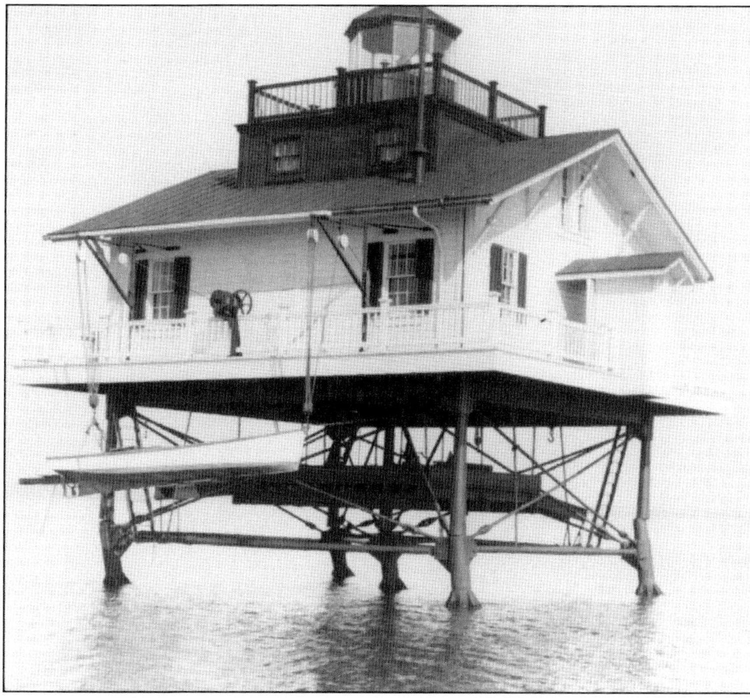

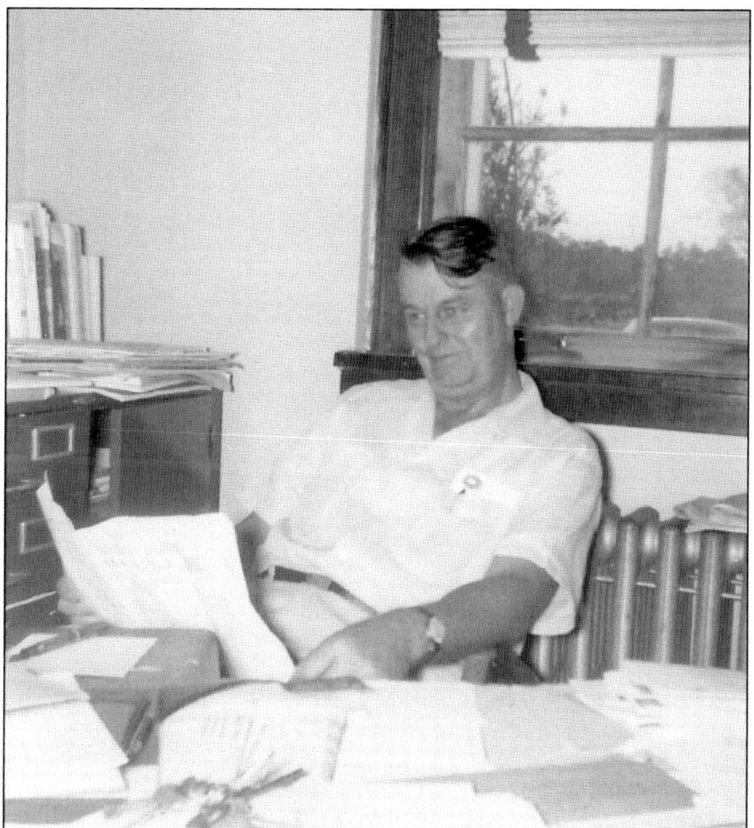

Camden County native and Wake Forest graduate Dempsey B. Burgess was an eighth-grade teacher and principal at Shiloh High School from 1946 until 1952 and superintendent of Camden County Schools from 1959 until the early 1970s. He loved Camden County history and enjoyed challenging young people to grow, advising them, "Don't say you can't. Give it your best. You might be surprised, but I won't." (Courtesy of the author.)

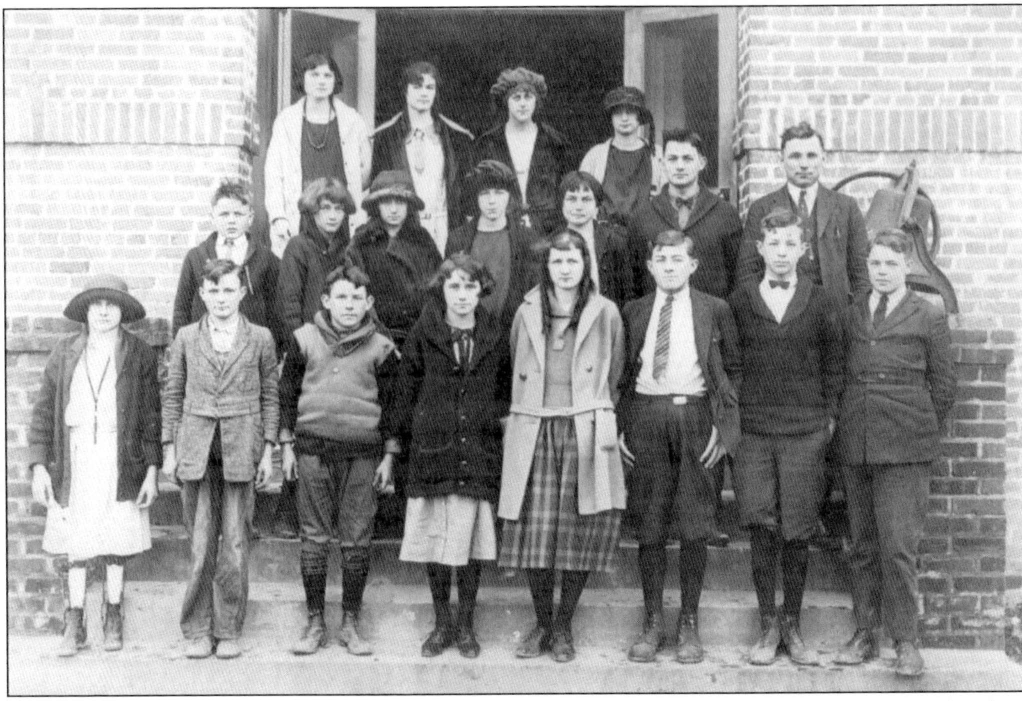

This photograph of Old Trap High School's eighth and ninth grades of 1924–1925 includes, from left to right, (first row) Elsie Leary, La Salle Leary, Sammie Leary, Marguerite Pugh, Florence Pugh, Walter Burgess, Vincent Leary, and Bryce Salyer; (second row) Randolph Burgess, Nellie Wilson, Pattie Sawyer, Bessie Salyer, Margaret Leary, Vernon Burgess, and Elroy Pugh; (third row) teacher Mary Francis Sawyer, Idella Wilson, Polly Burgess, and Emma Whitehurst. (Courtesy of Alex Leary.)

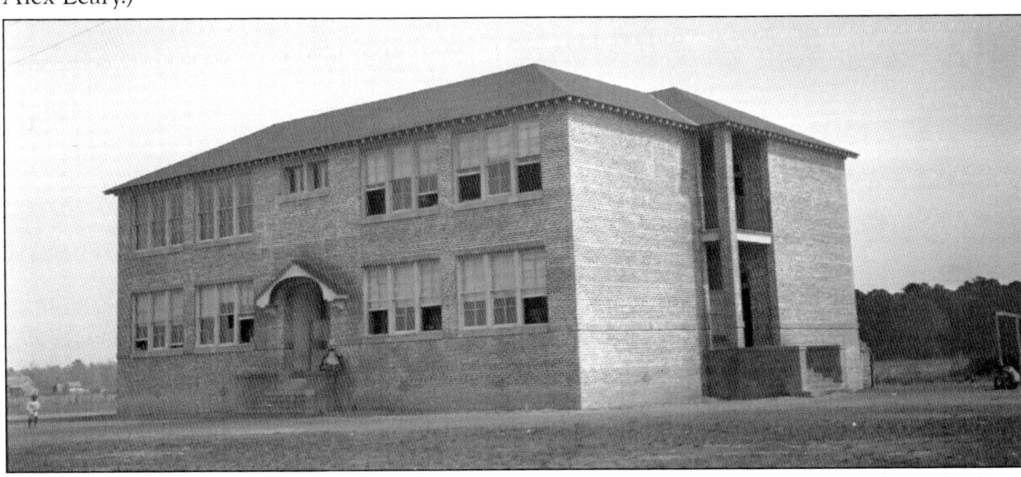

Old Trap High School was built with community funding and housed grades one through eleven until 1928, when grades eight through eleven began riding a bus to Shiloh. There were four classrooms downstairs and an auditorium and two classrooms upstairs. Effie Hoffler was the principal when the school closed in 1931. The structure was destroyed by fire in the late 1930s. Later, when the boys' brick outhouse began to crumble, Willard Forbes rebuilt it. Forbes and Alvin Staples saw to it that a historical marker for Old Trap High School was put in place before they both passed away. (Courtesy of the Outer Banks History Center, D. Victor Meekins Collection.)

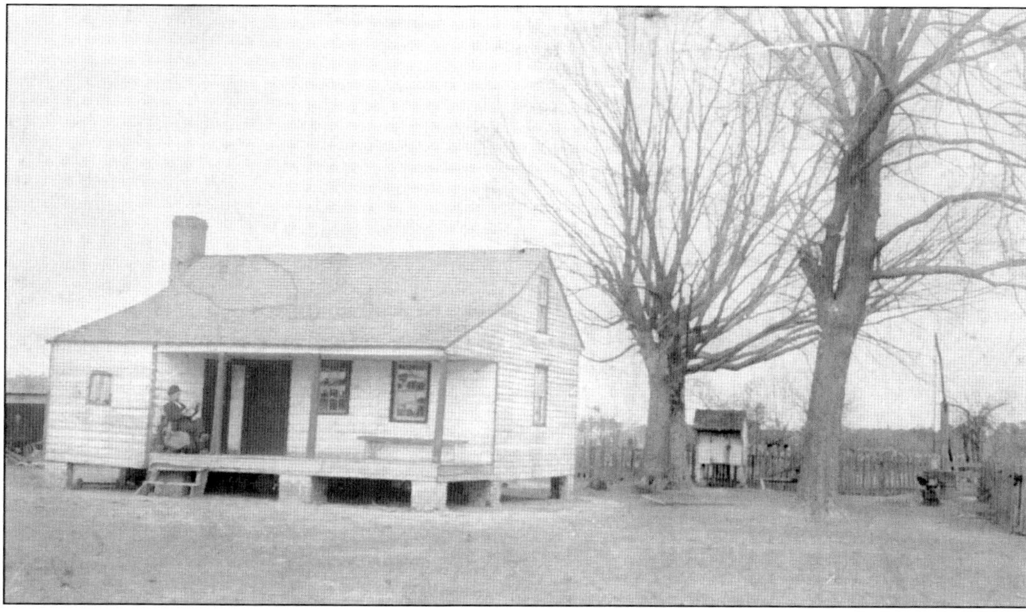

This unidentified home in Old Trap is a good example of the sorts of dwellings that were common in the area around 1900. The woodshed is to the left, with the milk house on the right. Water was drawn up from the well in a bucket extended from the well sweep with a rope. (Courtesy of Joyce Mitchell Cuthrell)

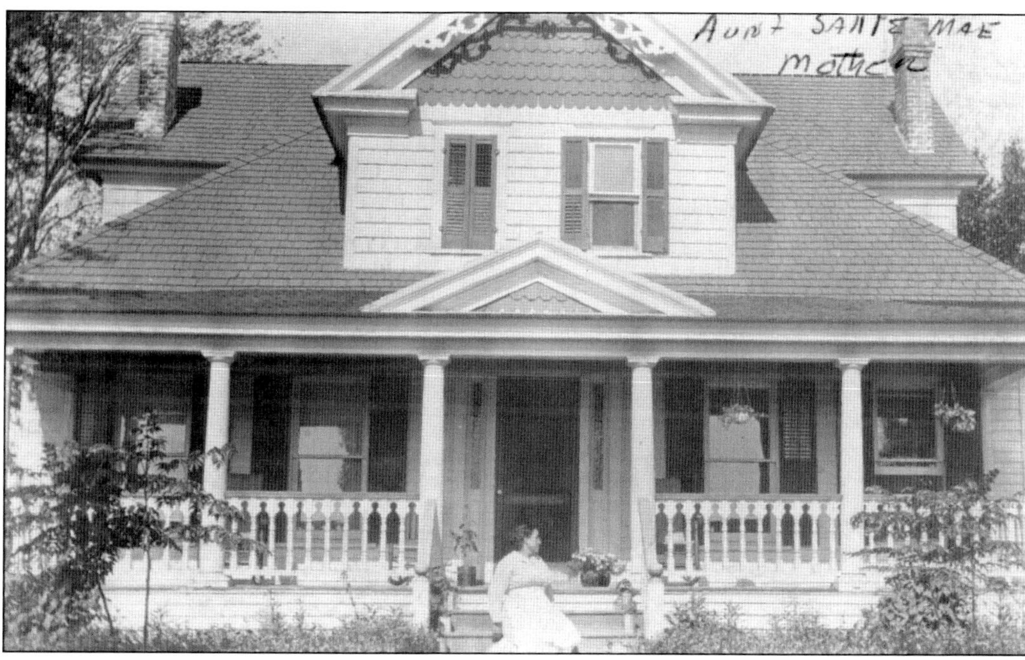

George K. Burgess, born in 1866, and his wife, Elizabeth (also known as "Bettie"), lived in this lovely Victorian-style home across the road from the Old Trap High School. They had six daughters—Hattie, Lillian, Clara, Abbie, Jennie, and Mary. After George died, his widow married Lemuel T. Turner, and they lived in the home. (Courtesy of Joyce Mitchell Cuthrell.)

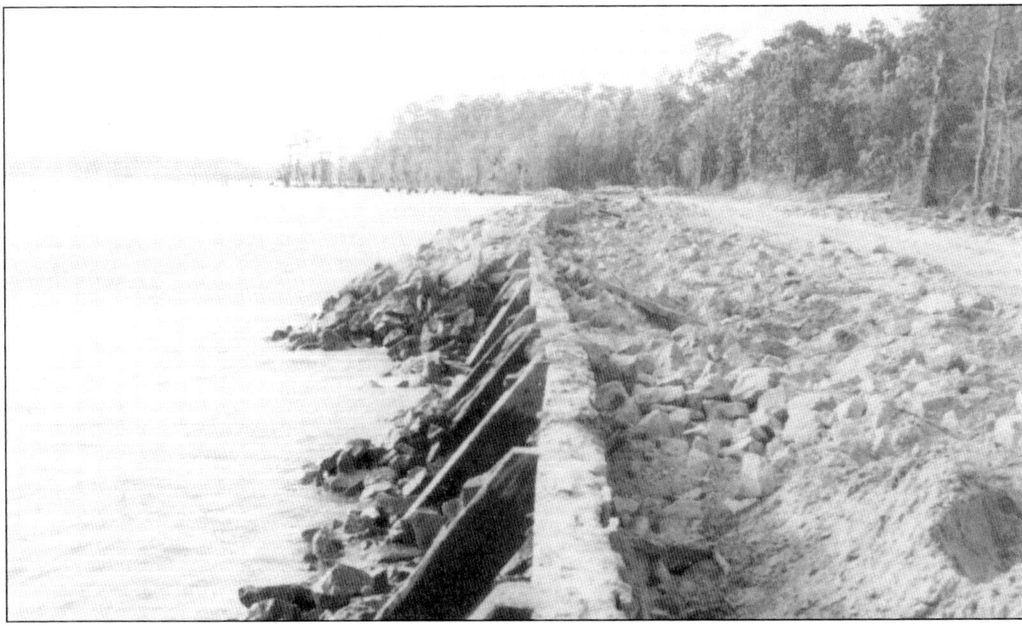

In the mid-1960s, Willard Forbes built a bulkhead at his family farm at Thomas Point to prevent the loss of more land to the erosion by the Pasquotank River. This view looks from south to north toward the cabin in 1966, soon after the bulkhead was constructed. This same bulkhead is still in place today. (Courtesy of Thelma Naomi Sawyer Forbes.)

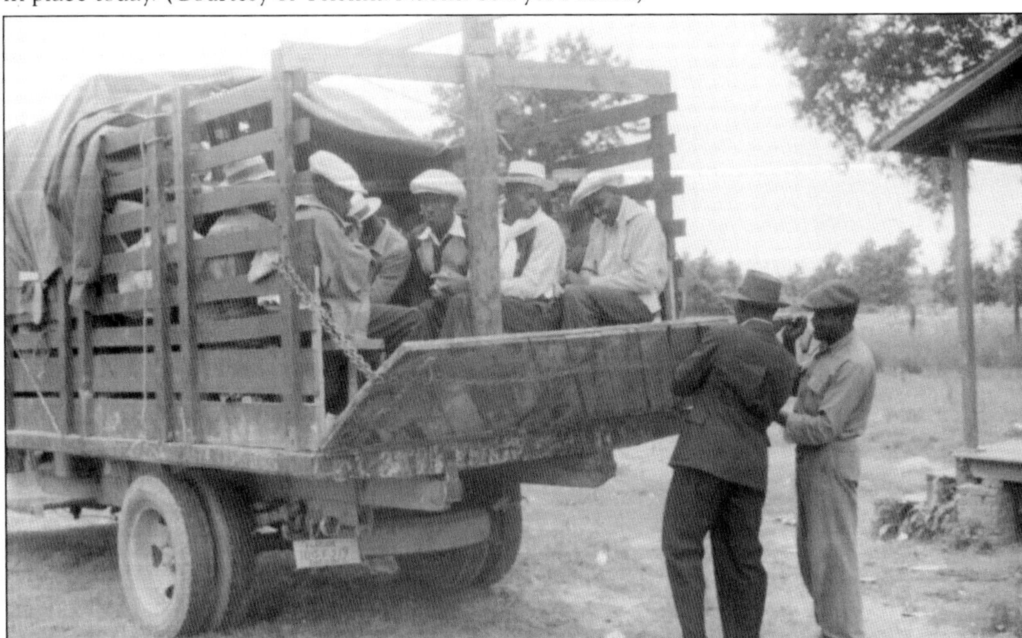

In the summer of 1940, with the addition of a couple of long planks in the bed, this farm truck became a bus. These migratory laborers have cleaned off the dirt of working in the potato fields of Old Trap and wear their traveling clothes. The Florida license tag on the truck indicates they have had a long, hard ride. (Courtesy of the Library of Congress.)

Five

Fun and Games

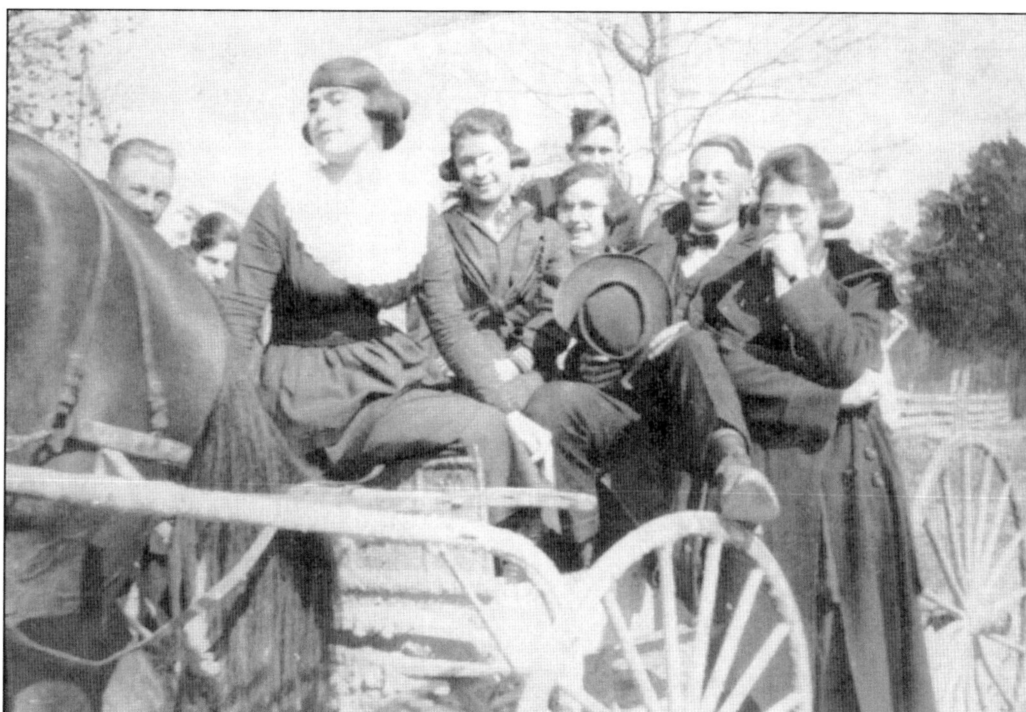

Until automobiles became common, the young people had to do their sporting with buggies or wagons. There were few opportunities to take in professional entertainment, so they made do with a ride with conversation and cutting up. Known to be among those in this sporting crowd are Louise Bartlett, Essie Bartlett, Eula Holmes, Vernon Duncan, and Dennis Bartlett. (Courtesy of Doris Dough Forehand.)

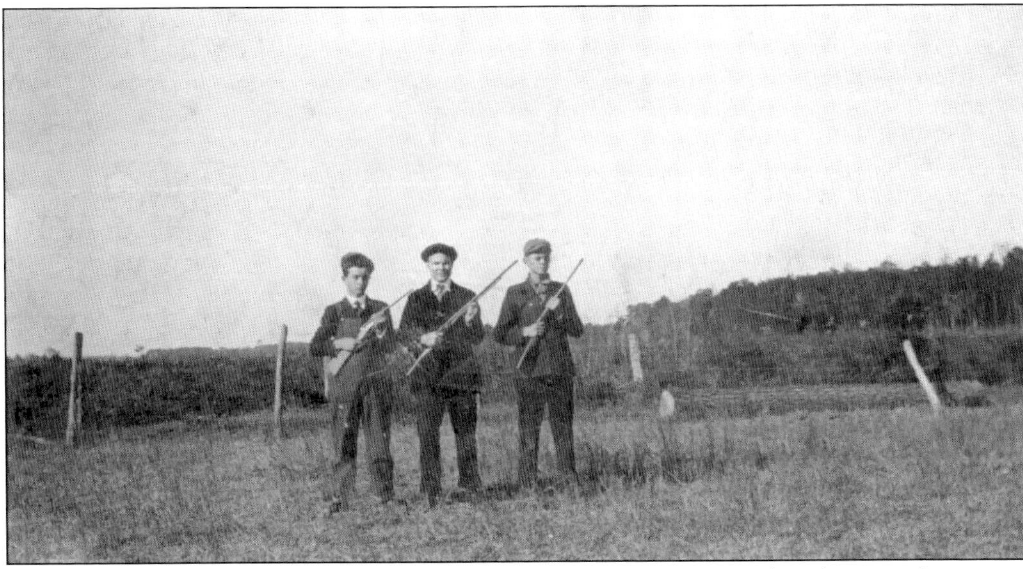

John Beale (left), Elton Burgess (center), and Eddie Pugh are prepared to do some shooting in Old Trap. Good marksmanship was a valuable skill, and young men would compete for bragging rights. Ammunition had to be bought in order to put game on the table. These boys look ready to shoot bottles, rabbits, or squirrels. (Courtesy of Joyce Mitchell Cuthrell.)

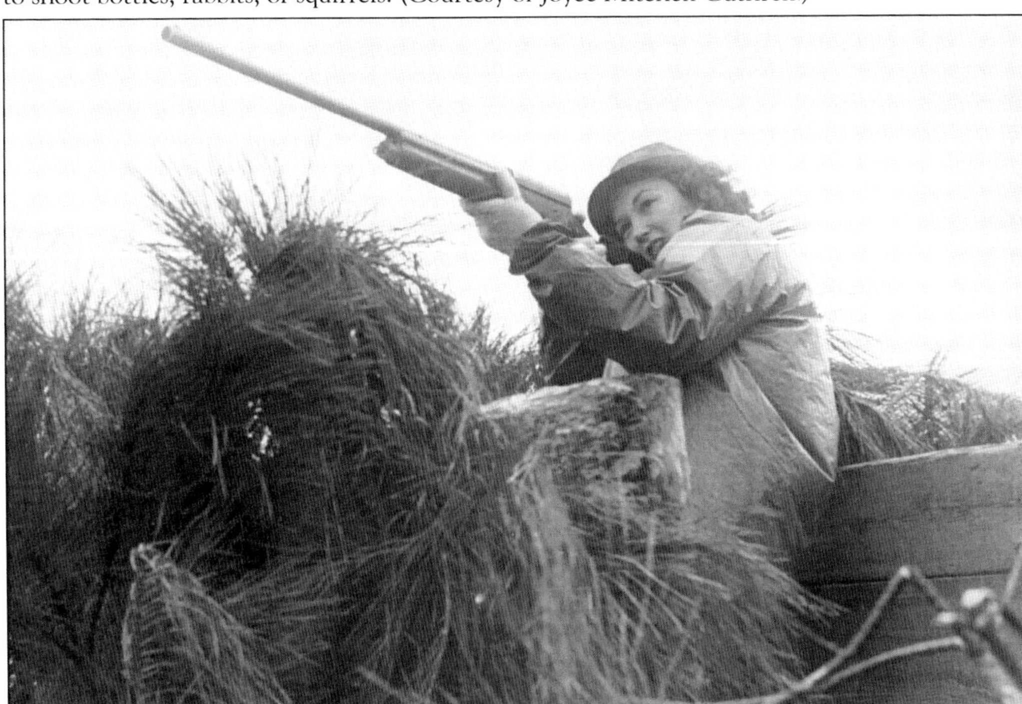

Violet Cahoon demonstrates the use of an old Browning automatic 12-gauge shotgun from within a blind camouflaged with pine branches, a technique used for hunting wild waterfowl. This model of shotgun was designed to hold five shells, but hunters would be cited for a violation if the game warden caught them hunting without a plug in the gun, so only three shells could be loaded at a time. (Courtesy of the Outer Banks History Center, D. Victor Meekins Collection.)

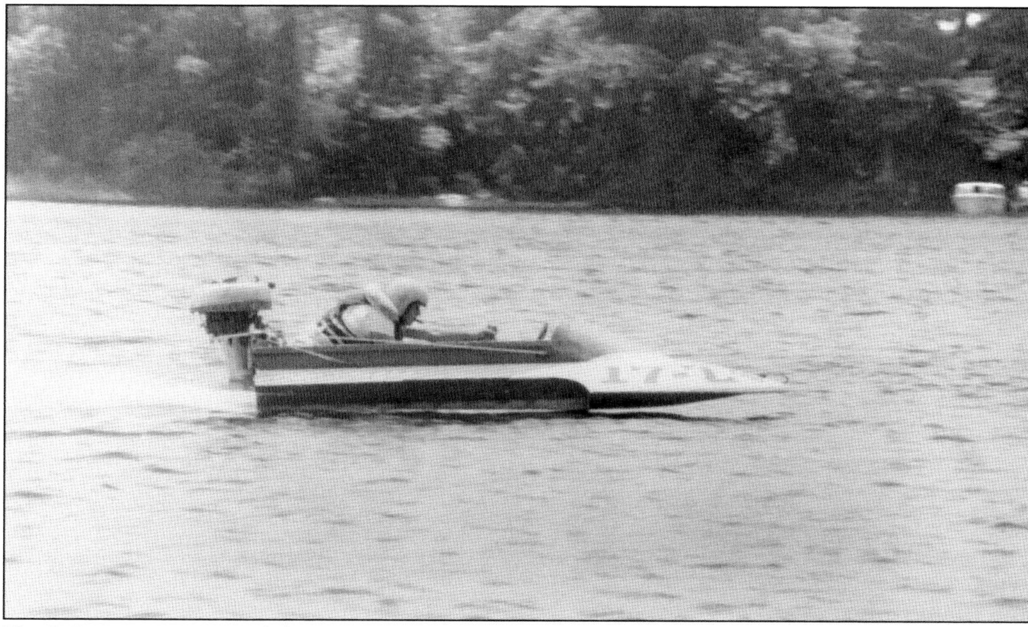

Floid Owens was one of the entrants in the 1966 Labor Day two-day, 16-heat powerboat races sponsored by the Pasquotank River Yacht Club. Owens is seen here on the Pasquotank River in his 16-horsepower class B racer on a one-and-two-thirds-mile-long course in front of Bogue's Beach. Admission to the beach was 50¢ for adults and 25¢ for children. (Courtesy of Kitty Owens Games.)

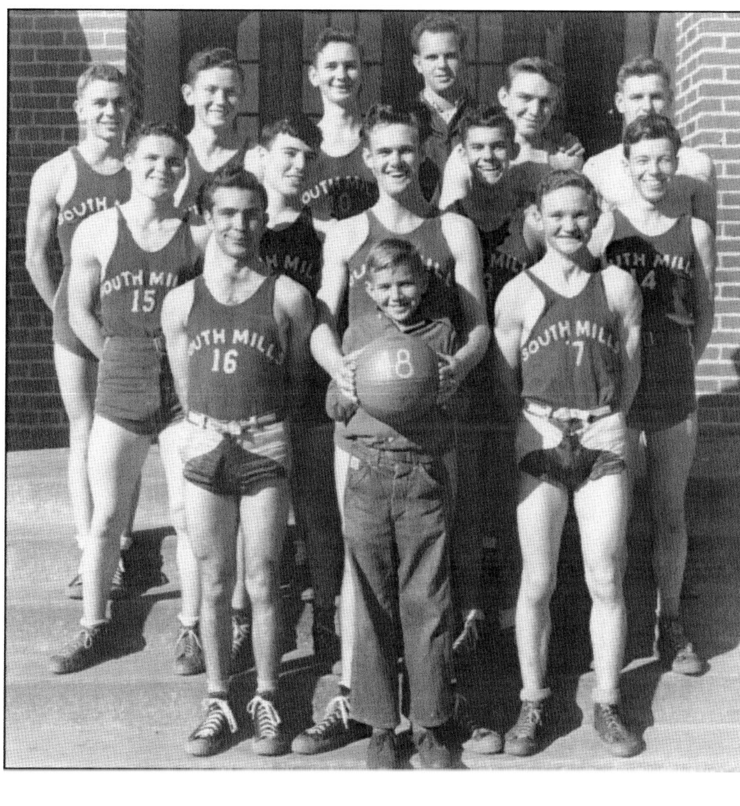

Basketball did not become an official event at the Olympics until the 1936 Games in Berlin. By this time, Camden County had several basketball teams for boys and girls at both Shiloh High School and South Mills High School. Here are members of the South Mills High School boys' basketball team of 1948. (Courtesy of Alex Leary.)

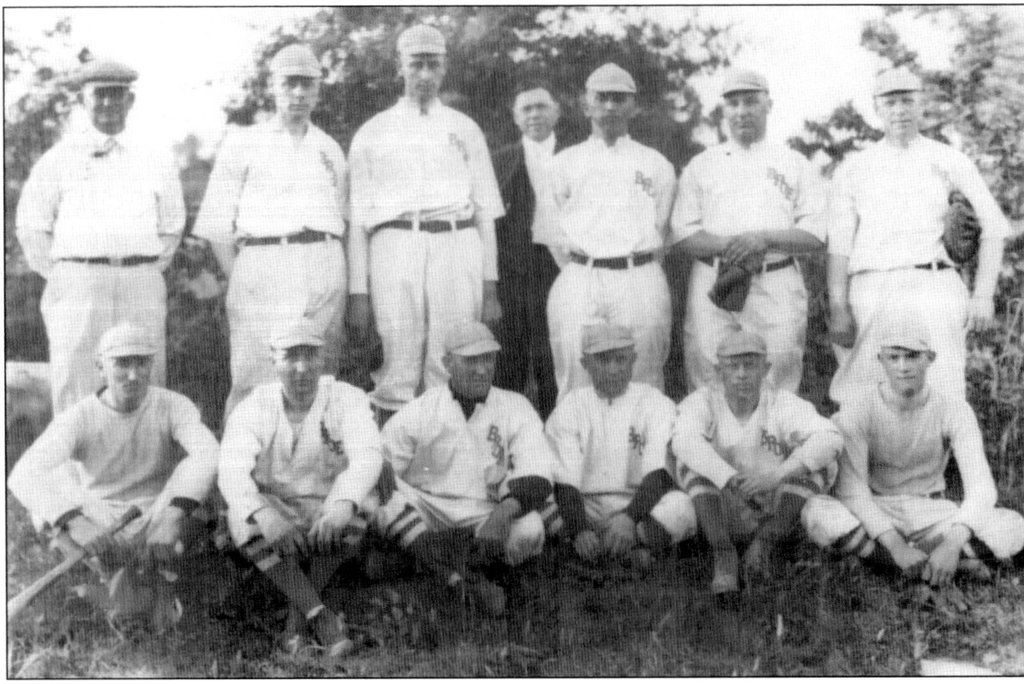

Regular baseball games were played at Elizabeth City Beach in Shiloh during the 1930s. Pictured is the visiting Elks Club team that had come to play at the baseball field, part of a family-oriented recreational area on the river. The baseball field, located near the end of Milltown Road, was close to the Elizabeth City Beach Club. (Courtesy of Alex Leary.)

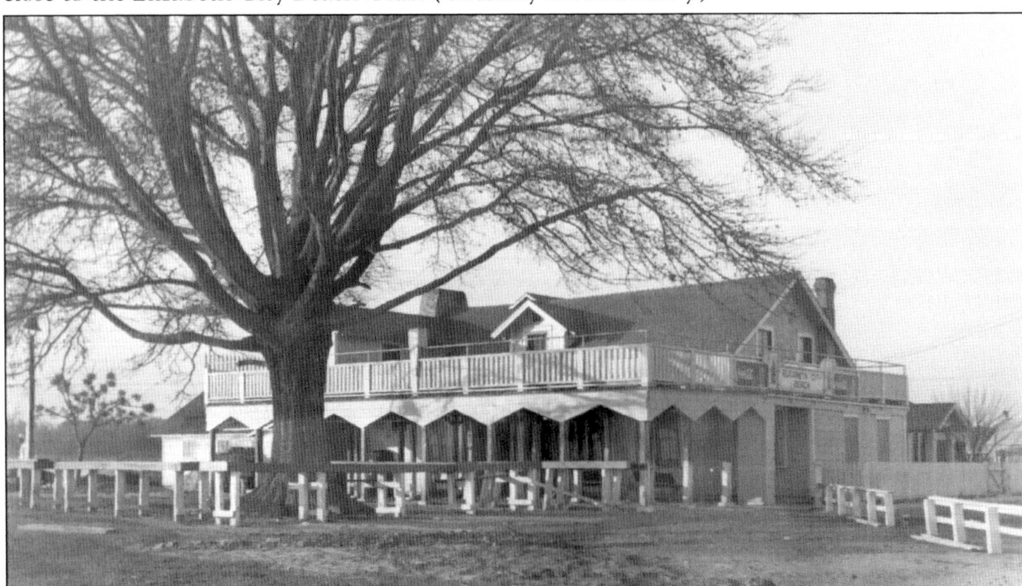

The club and restaurant were built at the end of Milltown Road in Shiloh by the Cuthrell family as a place to come for entertainment on weekends. It was convenient to cross the Pasquotank River and dock at the public landing. This building eventually burned down, and nothing was left but the large chimney. (Courtesy of the Family Research Society of Northeastern North Carolina, Inc.)

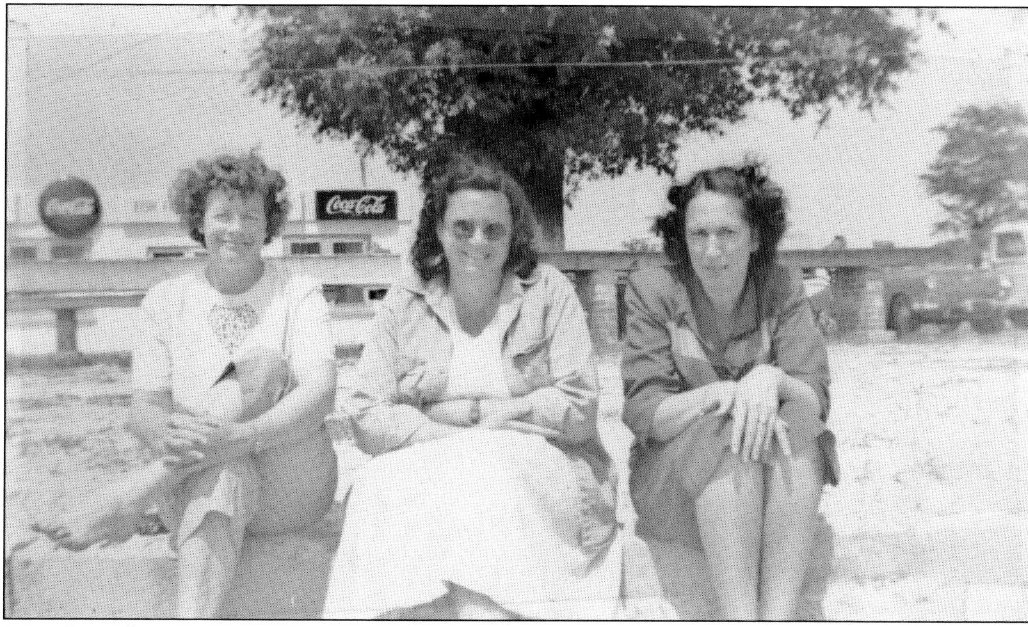

In 1950, a class picnic was held at Elizabeth City Beach, also known as Texaco Beach. From left to right are Mary Leary, Jeannie Raper, and Geneva Hughes Forehand. The Coca-Cola signs in the background are on the Elizabeth City Beach Club building, which extends out over the Pasquotank River and was accessible by a pier. (Courtesy of Anna Cahoon Boyce.)

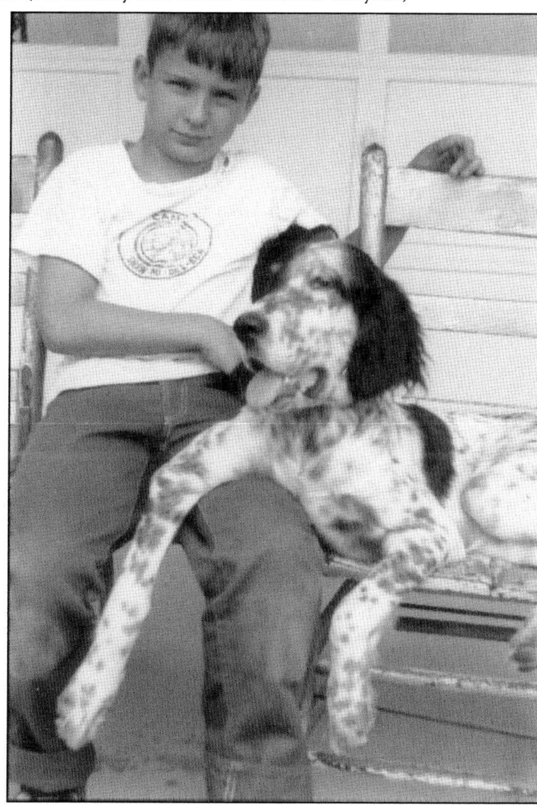

Terry Forbes is enjoying some quality time with his beautiful bird dog in 1966. The bird dogs could flush and retrieve birds in marshy and grassy areas. What would have been difficult for their human companions was fun and frolic for these intelligent, graceful dogs with keen instincts and senses. (Courtesy of Thelma Naomi Sawyer Forbes.)

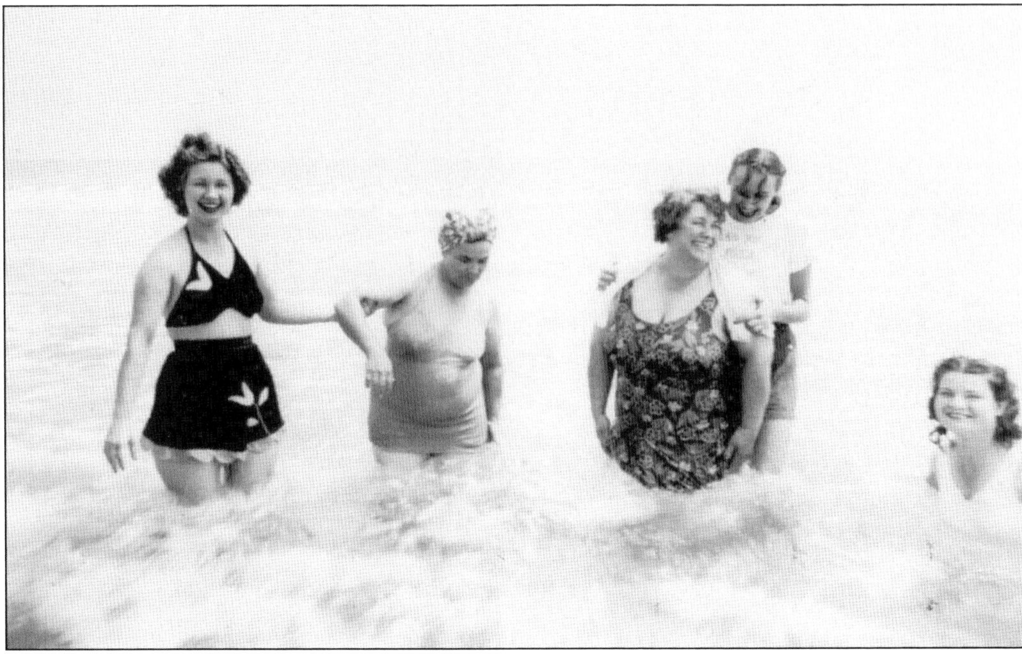

Swimming has always been a popular way to relax and have fun, whether in the river or at the beach. Here, from left to right, Doris Dough Forehand, Lena Forehand, Essie Dough, Delores Dough, and Ruth McPherson are having a nice swim. They are all smiles on this sunny day. (Courtesy of Doris Dough Forehand.)

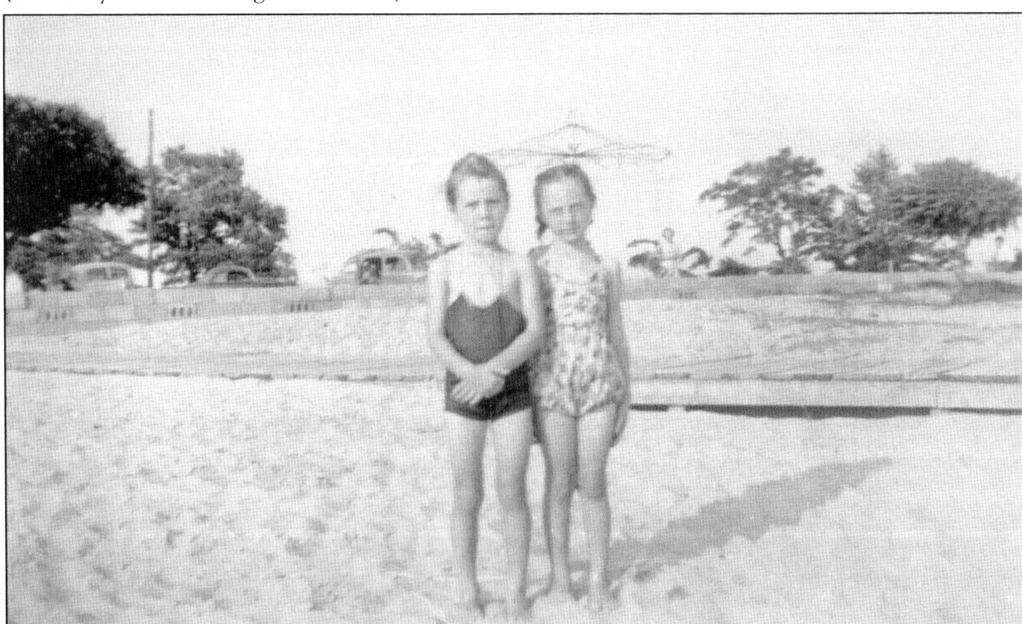

Joyce Walston (left) and Billie Forehand are enjoying a day at Elizabeth City Beach in Shiloh in 1948. Note the sandy beach, the boardwalk leading to the river, and the cars and people along the cinder block wall. Behind the girls, the top of the swinging merry-go-round that was part of the playground and amusements can be seen. (Courtesy of Brian Forehand.)

The George Wood Memorial Park, dedicated in memory of George Wood, a lifelong resident of Camden County, is located along Highway 158 on the Camden Causeway. A boardwalk, pier, and two gazebos extend into the Pasquotank River. Here, an unidentified gentleman enjoys fishing, and the Camden Causeway and the long Pasquotank River Shore of Camden County extend to the horizon on the left of side of the river. (Courtesy of the Outer Banks History Center, Fred Fearing Scrapbook Collection.)

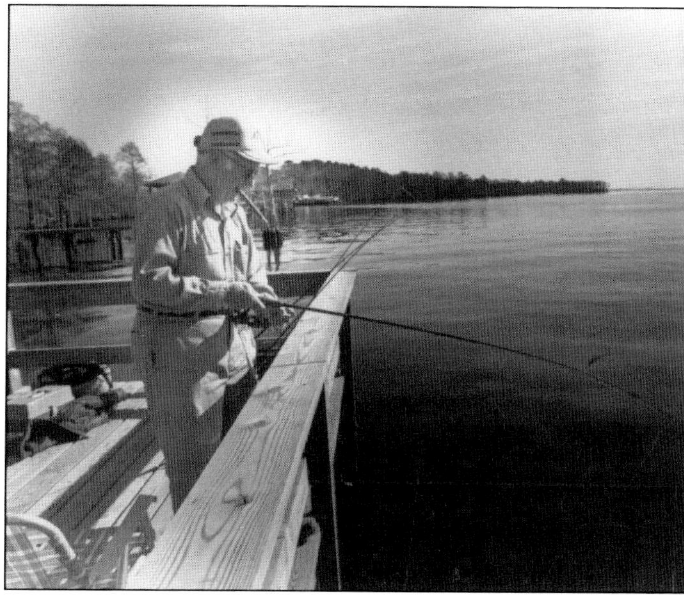

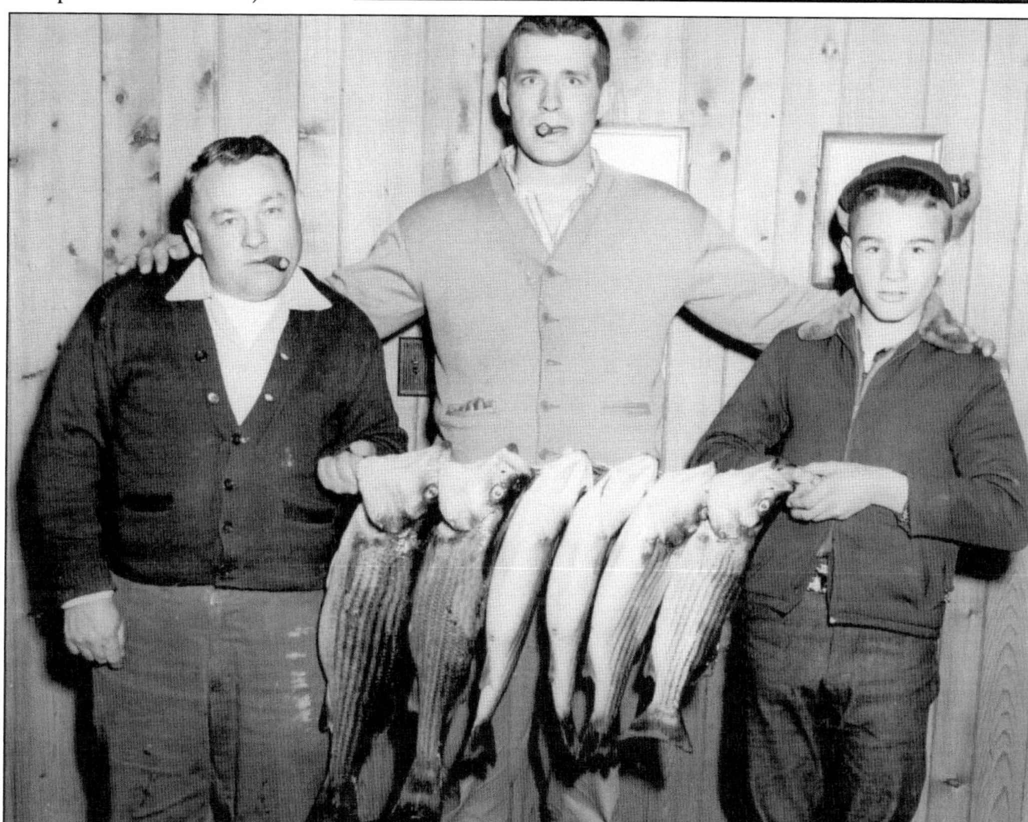

From left to right, J.P. Forehand, Alton Dough, and Terry Forehand show off a nice catch of striped bass, known locally as rockfish or simply "rock." The "stripers" can grow to in excess of 60 pounds and measure over 50 inches in length. A popular main course is the fish baked with onions, potatoes, and lemon slices. (Courtesy of Doris Dough Forehand.)

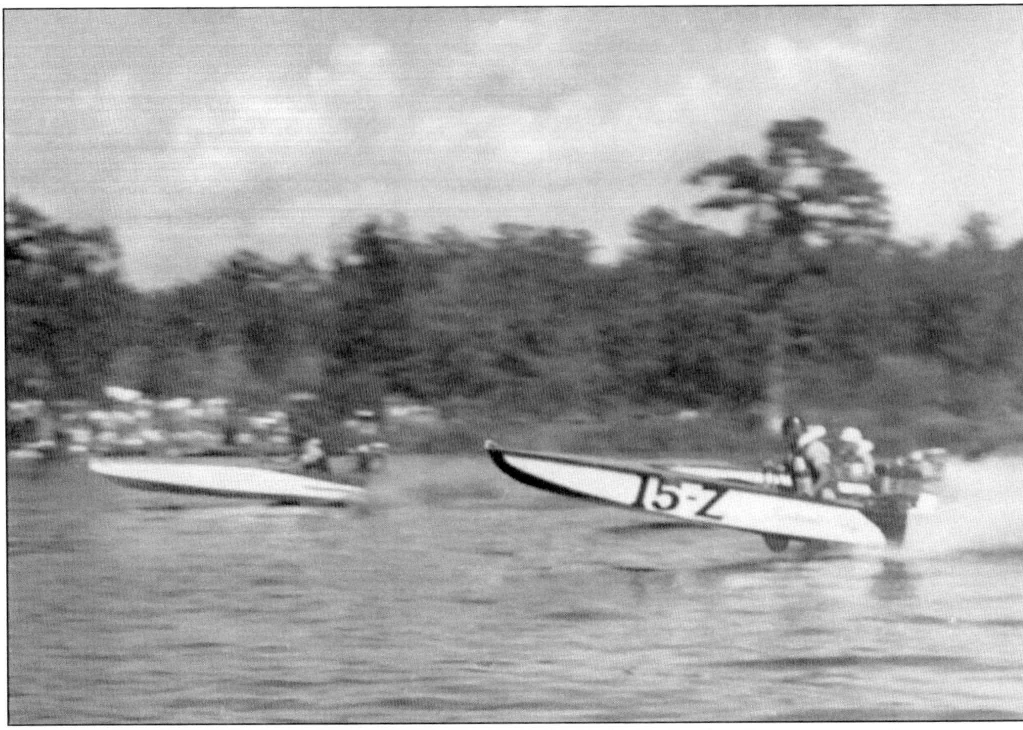

Sportsmen from Camden and surrounding areas have been hydroplaning powerboats up and down the Pasquotank River off the Camden County shore for decades. On October 5, 1958, the Pasquotank River Yacht Club held its 25th Annual International Cup Regatta, racing hydroplane powerboats. Six world records were set that day. (Courtesy of Doris Dough Forehand.)

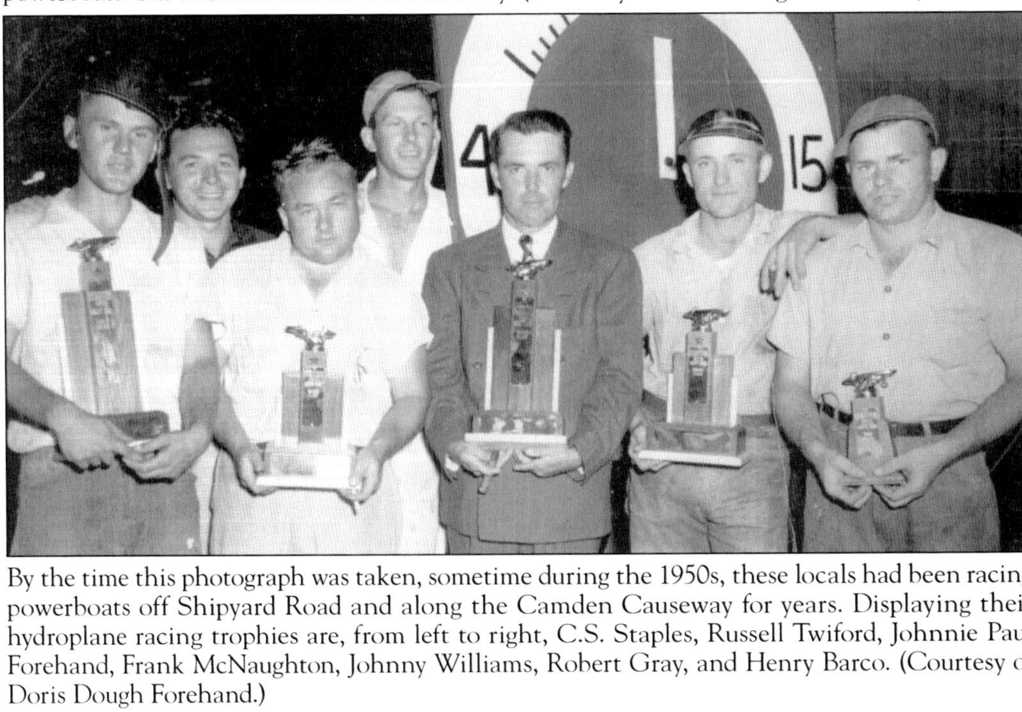

By the time this photograph was taken, sometime during the 1950s, these locals had been racing powerboats off Shipyard Road and along the Camden Causeway for years. Displaying their hydroplane racing trophies are, from left to right, C.S. Staples, Russell Twiford, Johnnie Paul Forehand, Frank McNaughton, Johnny Williams, Robert Gray, and Henry Barco. (Courtesy of Doris Dough Forehand.)

Henry Bartlett is shown here with one of his harness racing horses. In harness racing, the horse is harnessed to a cart, or sulky, and the jockey drives the horse from the lightweight cart rather than riding on the horse. Elwyn Leary was the owner of a top-earning horse named Camden Adios, who raced at Rockingham Park in 1964. (Courtesy of Betty Brock.)

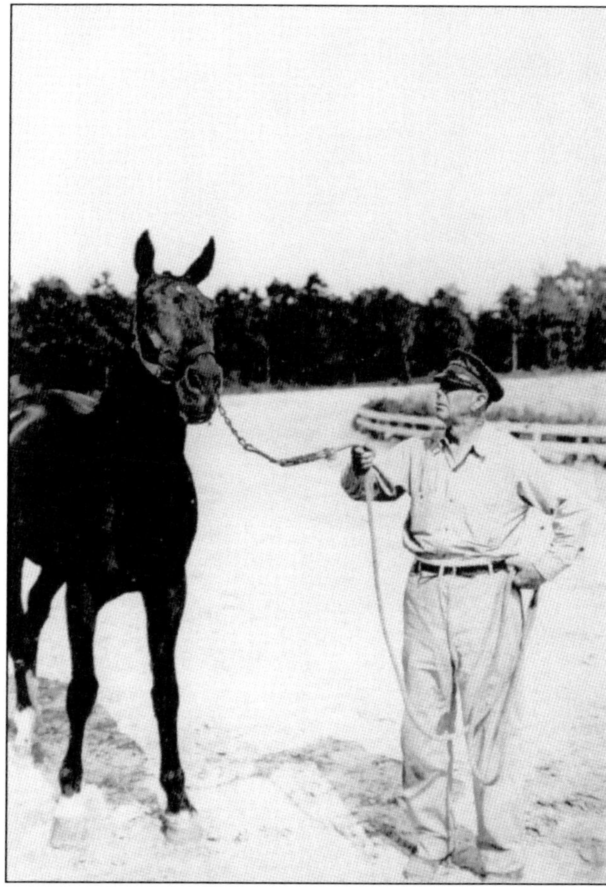

Breeding and training harness racing horses in Camden County produced the famous horse Forrest Skipper, owned by Forrest Bartlett of Shiloh. Trained by Marc Fontaine and driven by Lucien Fontaine, he won 15 consecutive races and 12 of them in 1 minute and 54 seconds or better. Forrest Skipper set 10 track records and was voted the 1986 Horse of the Year by the United States Trotting Association. (Courtesy of Anita Whitehurst.)

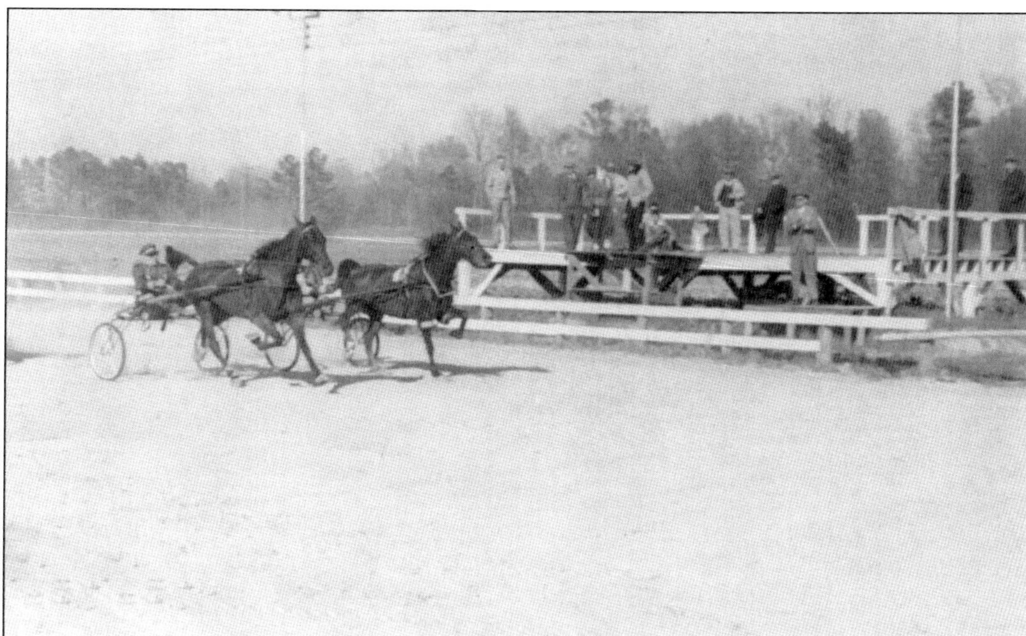

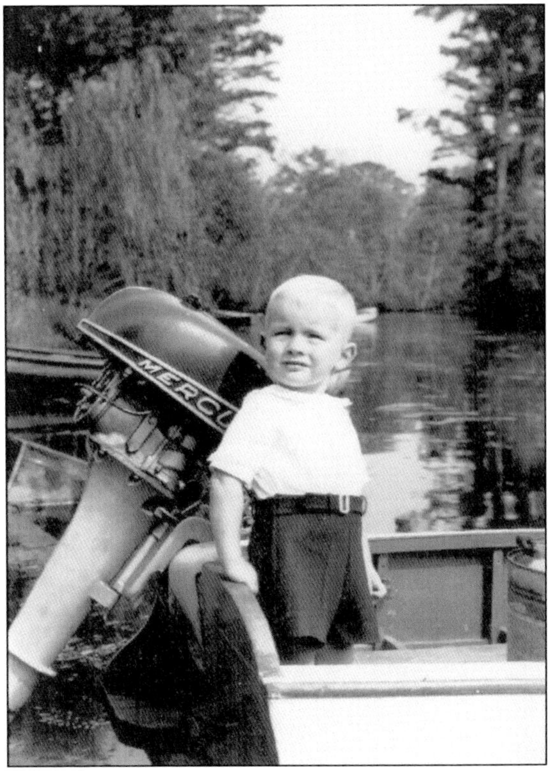

Terry Forehand stands in the boat belonging to his father, Johnnie Paul Forehand, at the landing on Indiantown Creek, a port of entry and McKnight's Shipyard during the Colonial period. The Mercury Lightning outboard motor is seven-and-one-half horsepower, with the fuel tank on top. This motor was designed by Carl Kiekhaefer and was introduced as the first four-cylinder outboard motor in 1947. (Courtesy of Doris Dough Forehand.)

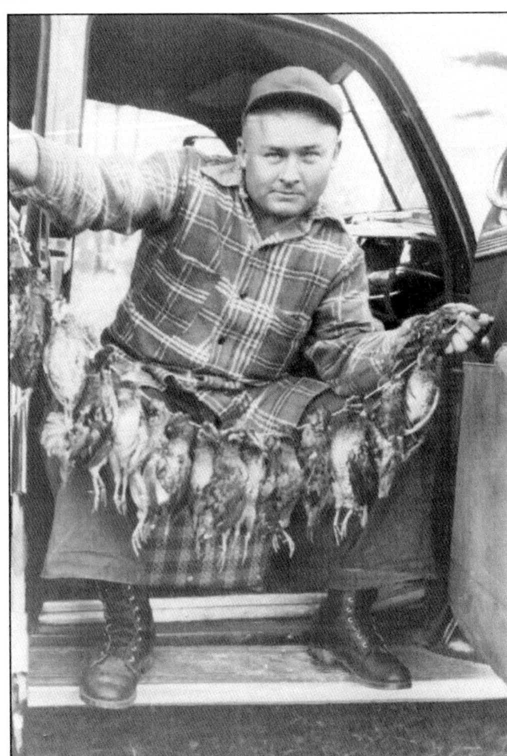

Here is Johnnie Paul Forehand with a nice stringer of quail. He seems to have bagged his limit, and there will be some good eating later. Quail is a popular game bird with large white breasts. Some people believe they are the best tasting of all of the local game birds. (Courtesy of Doris Dough Forehand.)

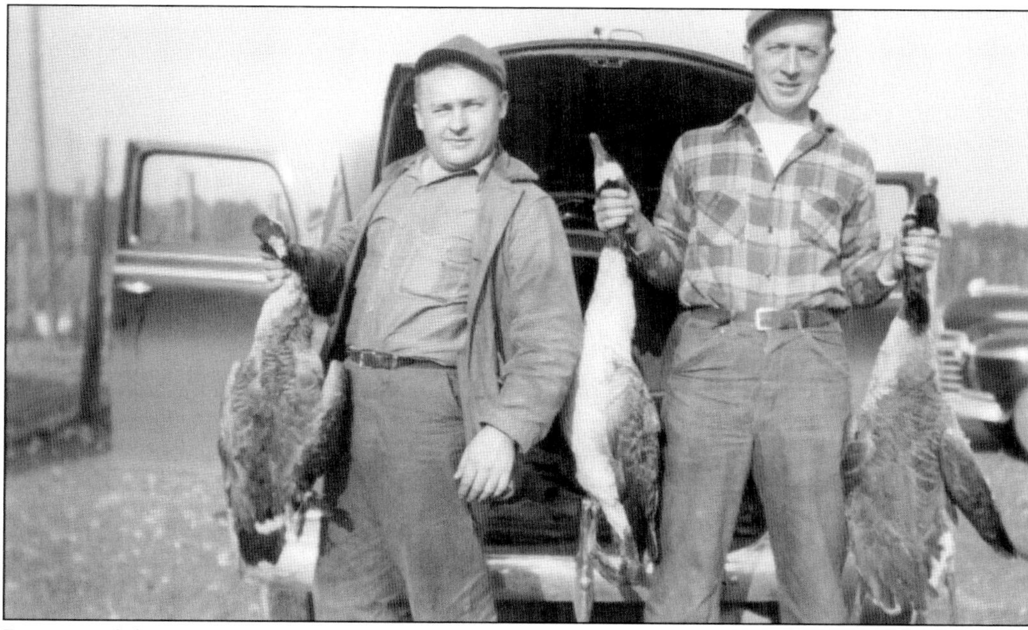

Because of the rural nature and common occupations of farming, fishing, and logging in Camden County, hunting has been a popular activity during the autumn and winter months. Johnnie Paul Forehand (left) and John Duncan have returned from a successful hunt with three Canada geese sometime in the 1950s. One goose would have provided enough meat for an ample family meal. (Courtesy of Doris Dough Forehand.)

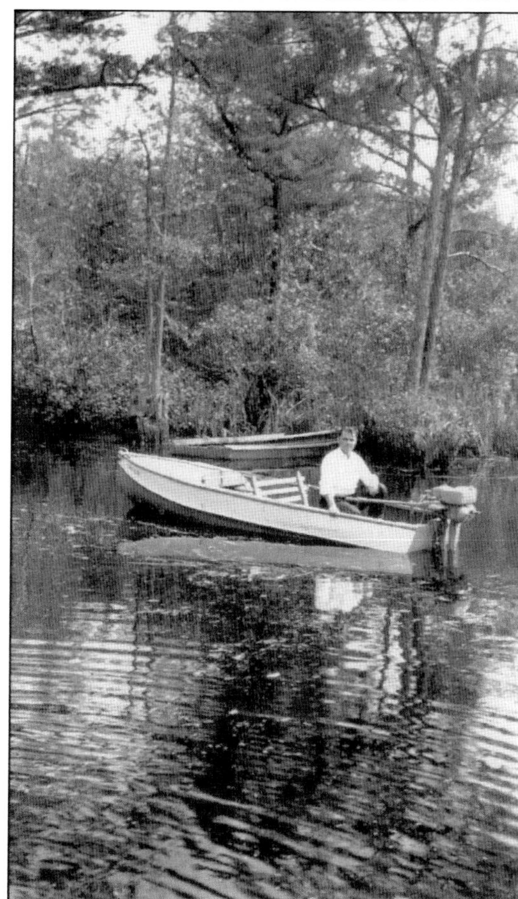

The boat landing at Indiantown Creek, situated on the border of Camden and Currituck Counties, has been the starting and ending point for many fishing trips. Tommy Gregory appears to be heading out in his outboard-equipped johnboat. With the exception of the new bridge, the landing at Indiantown looks the same today as it did more than 50 years ago. (Courtesy of Doris Dough Forehand.)

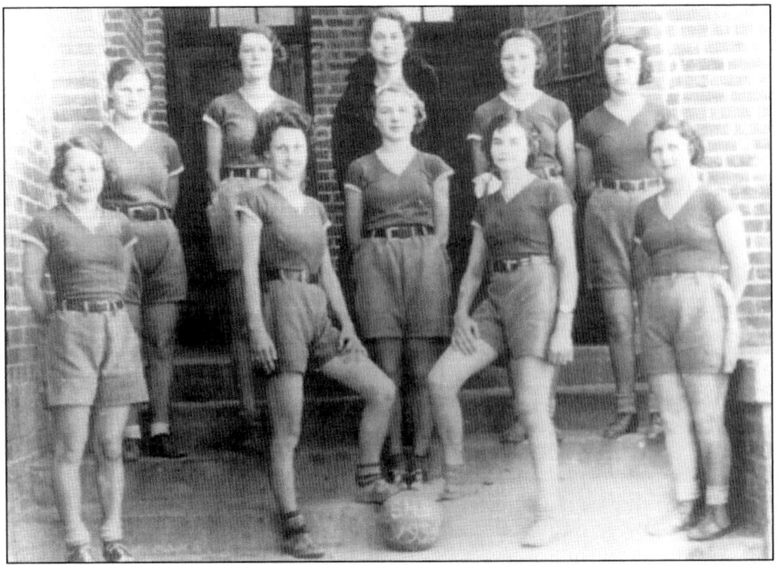

This photograph of the Shiloh High School basketball team of 1934 includes, from left to right, (first row) Mary C. Burgess Sawyer, Henrietta Brockett, Emily Sawyer, Elizabeth Ivey, and Mavie Staples; (second row) Emily Forbes, Laura Lee Davenport, Ruby Adams (coach), Sarah Wilson, and Ida Mae Staples. (Courtesy of Brian Forehand.)

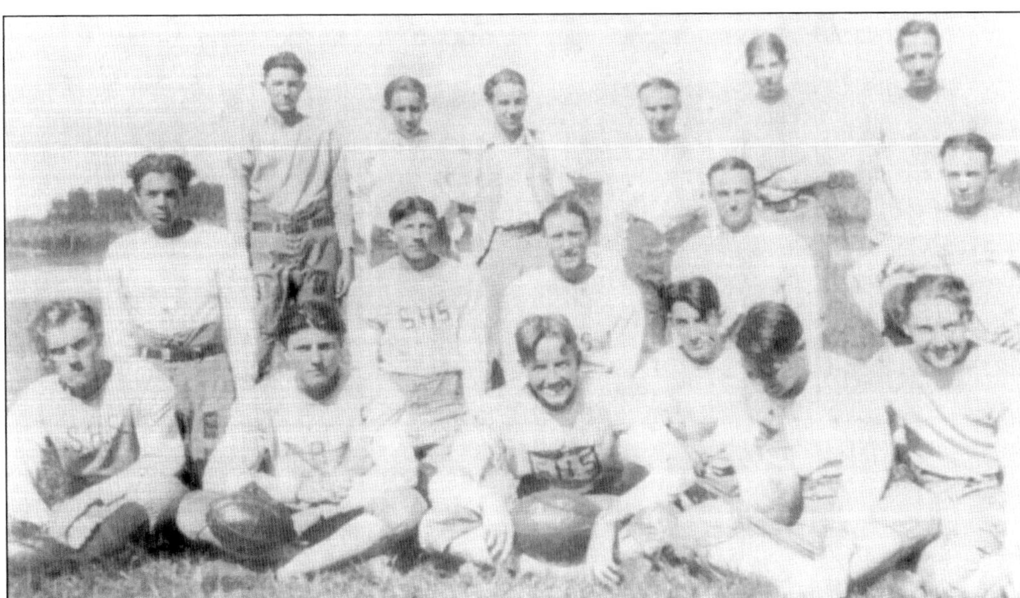

The Shiloh High School football team was known as the Wildcats. This 1928 team picture includes, from left to right, (first row) Frank Burgess, Worth Williams, J. V. Hoyle, Winfred McPherson, Dallas Swindell, and Jethro Jordan; (second row) Ashburn Leary, Hallet Owens, Gordan Burgess, Roy Brockett, and Horace Ferrell; (third row) Max Cox, Waldorf Burgess, Elbert Burgess, Elton Forbes, William Whaley, and teacher and coach C.C. Carter. (Courtesy of Alex Leary.)

Brother and sister Walter and Marjorie Barnard use their imaginations to cut up for the camera. Country kids stayed in good shape, doing chores on the farm and playing outdoors after school. The Barnard kids probably never saw a gymnastics meet, but it looks like Walter is ready to compete in one. (Courtesy of Anita Whitehurst.)

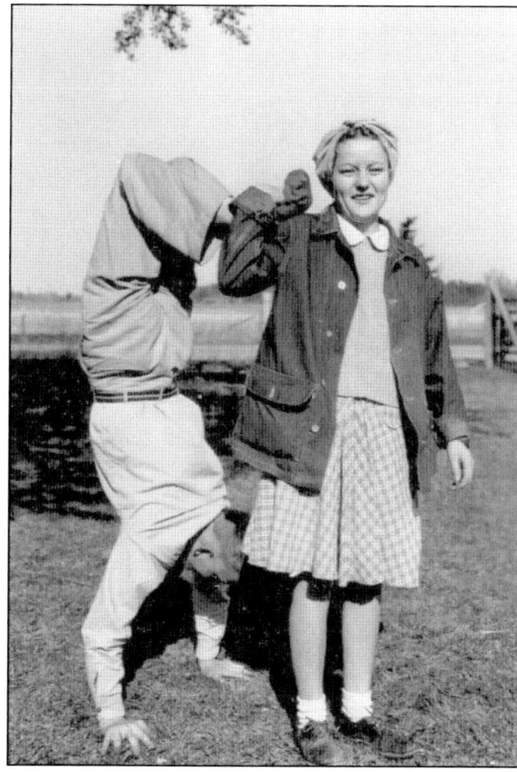

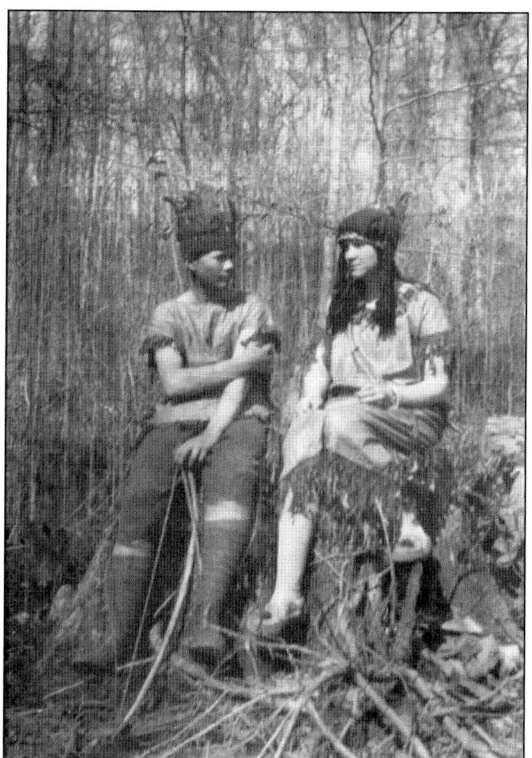

In 1931, Andrew and Edna Pearce are dressed up like Indians and play in the woods. Television was still not available, and radio drama was king of the airwaves. Staged plays were the theatrics of the day, so if children wanted to entertain themselves with drama, they could dress up like characters and act out their own plays. (Courtesy of Martha Ann.)

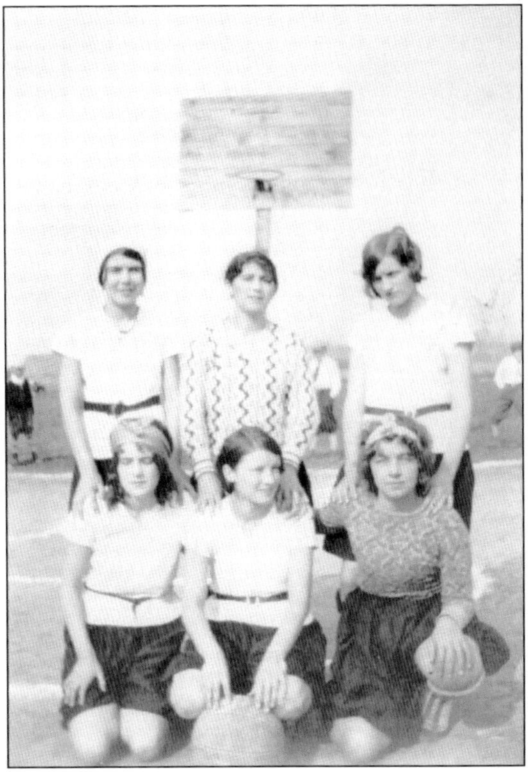

The first Camden County girls' basketball team at Shiloh is made up of, from left to right, (first row) Maxine Walston, Betty Gregory, and Elizabeth Mansfield; (second row) Jenny Seymour, Mable Seymour, and Ida Lee Games. Although she is not included in this picture, Fannie Seymour was the first team captain during the only year that she attended Shiloh High School. (Courtesy of Betty Brock.)

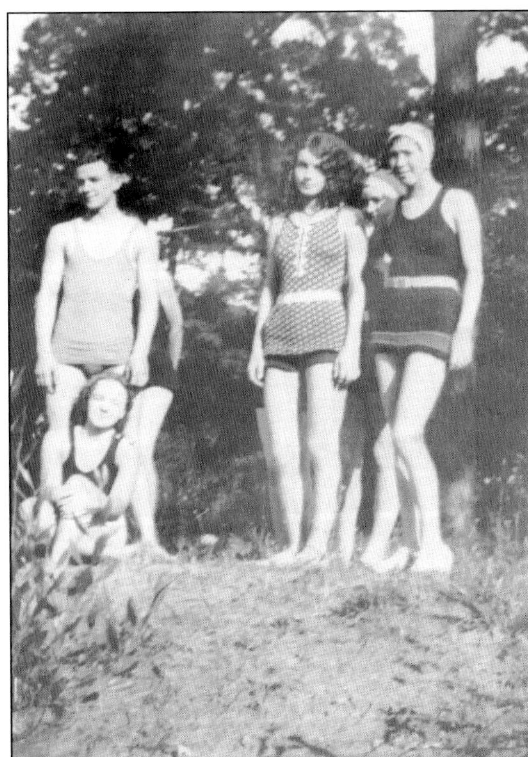

Ready to go swimming in the river in the 1930s are, from left to right, Oakley Mansfield, who is standing over his sister Elizabeth Mansfield, Virginia Meiggs, and Fannie Louise Seymour. Seymour, born in 1912, was one of eight children born to Bettie Bartlett Seymour and Silas Berry Seymour. She married Wilse Leary, who became a successful businessman in Camden County. (Courtesy of Betty Brock.)

Willie Henry Burgess was born in 1886 in Old Trap and spent his entire life there, working as a storekeeper and postmaster. He married Eva Belle Leary, and she and Willie had five children. Music brought a welcome lilt to everyday life, and here, Burgess can be seen playing his fiddle next to the gas pump at one of several stores in Old Trap. (Courtesy of Vernon Burgess Jr.)

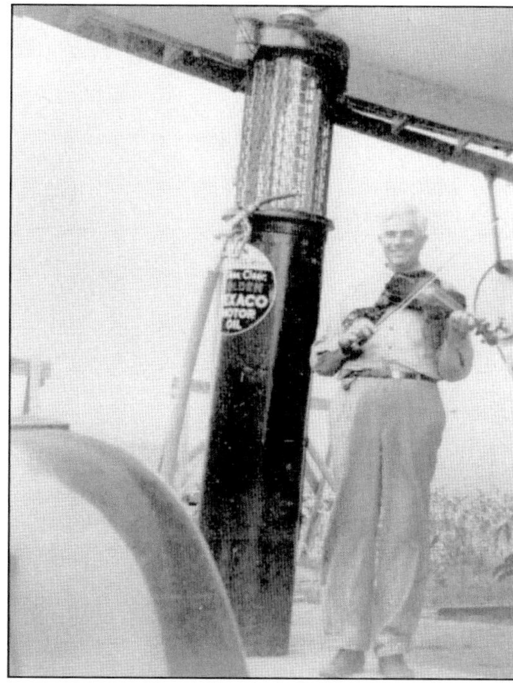

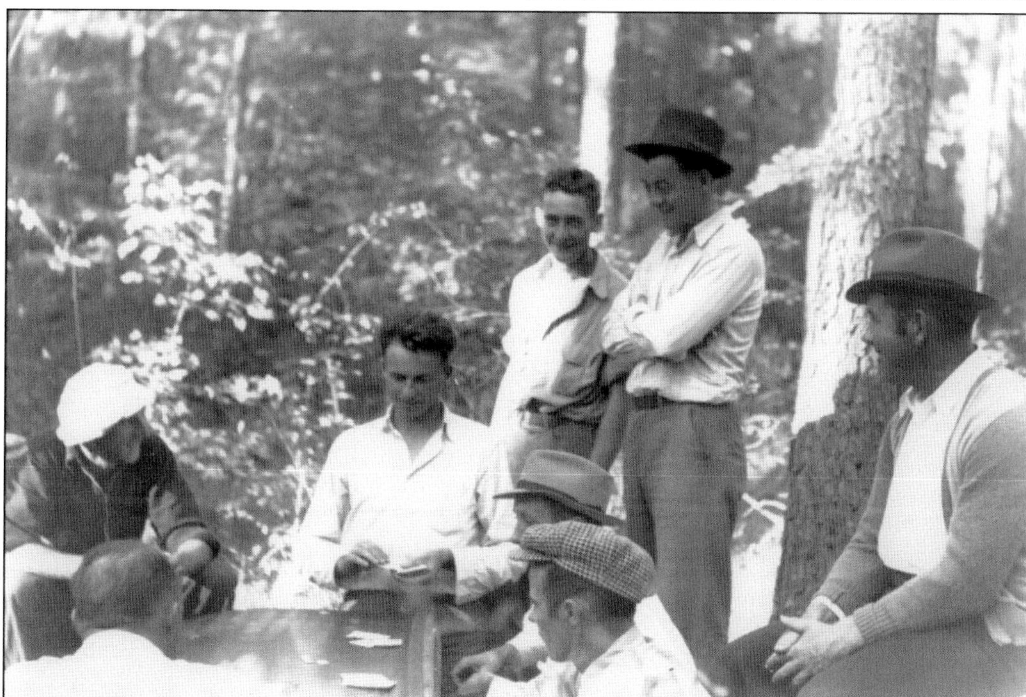

Men of southern Camden County sometimes enjoyed a game of poker in the woods at Goose Creek. Facing forward are, from left to right, Curtis Sawyer, Wilse Forbes, Calvin Forbes, Kenneth Wilson, and George Davis. Perhaps, by slipping off to the woods, they could enjoy their game and escape the attention of those who might have disapproved of their activities. (Courtesy of Thelma Naomi Sawyer Forbes.)

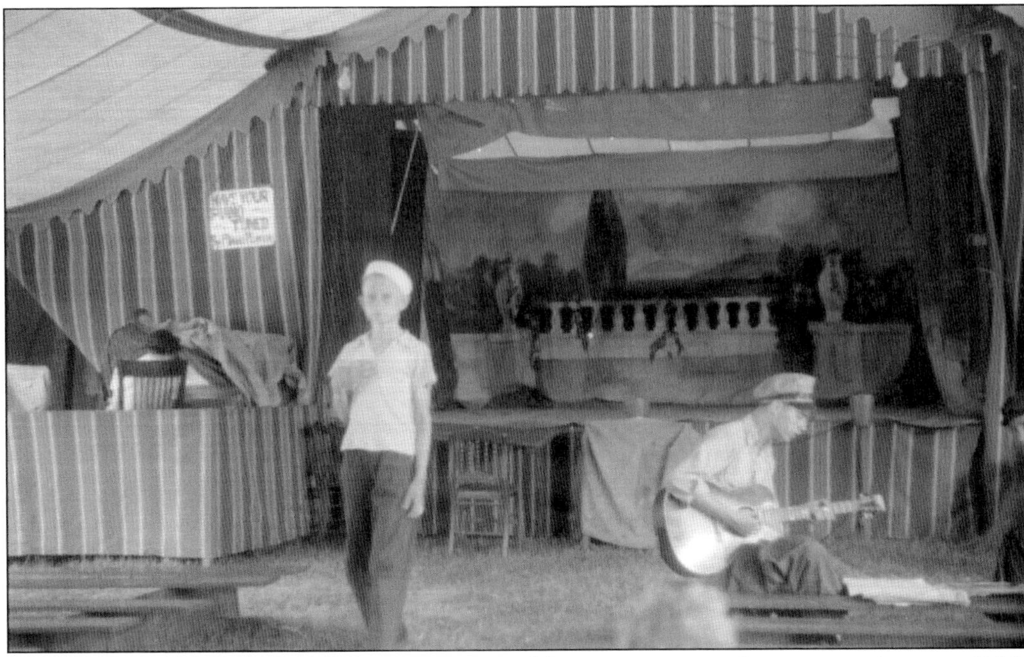

Some of the farmworkers' seasonal income was used for entertainment that was not always available. If there were a large enough group of laborers and locals, a traveling carnival would set up a tent. This photograph was taken in Old Trap in 1940 and shows the interior stage and backdrop of the performance tent of a such a carnival. (Courtesy of the Library of Congress.)

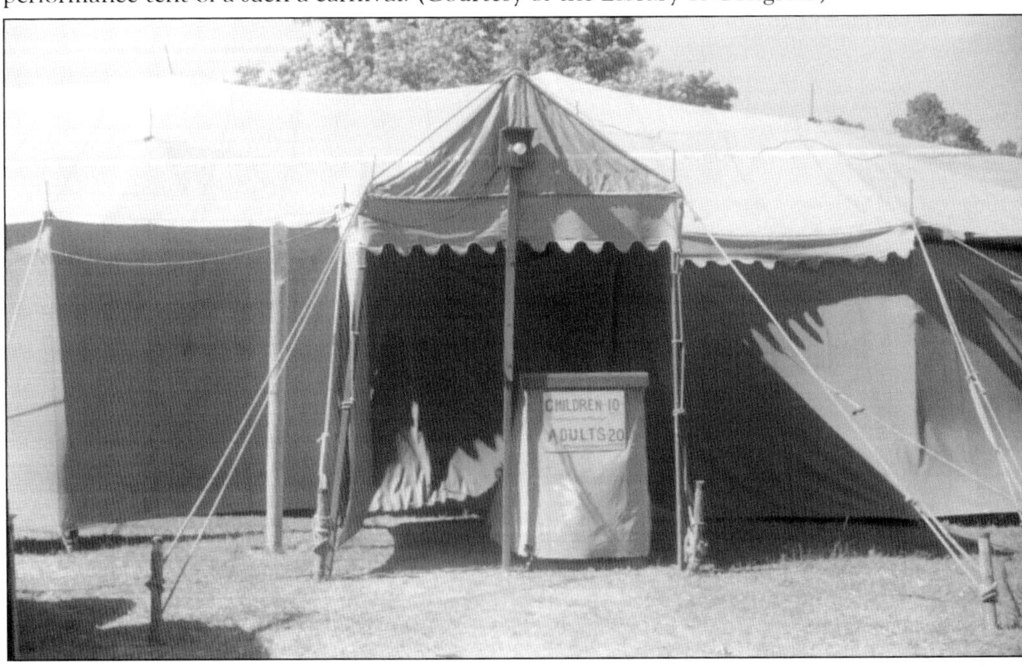

This tent was erected in Old Trap in 1940, during the time that migratory workers were there. Admission was 10¢ for children and 20¢ for adults. Movies were shown, and popcorn was sold. There were prizes for the children, and each box of popcorn had a small toy at the bottom. (Courtesy of the Library of Congress.)

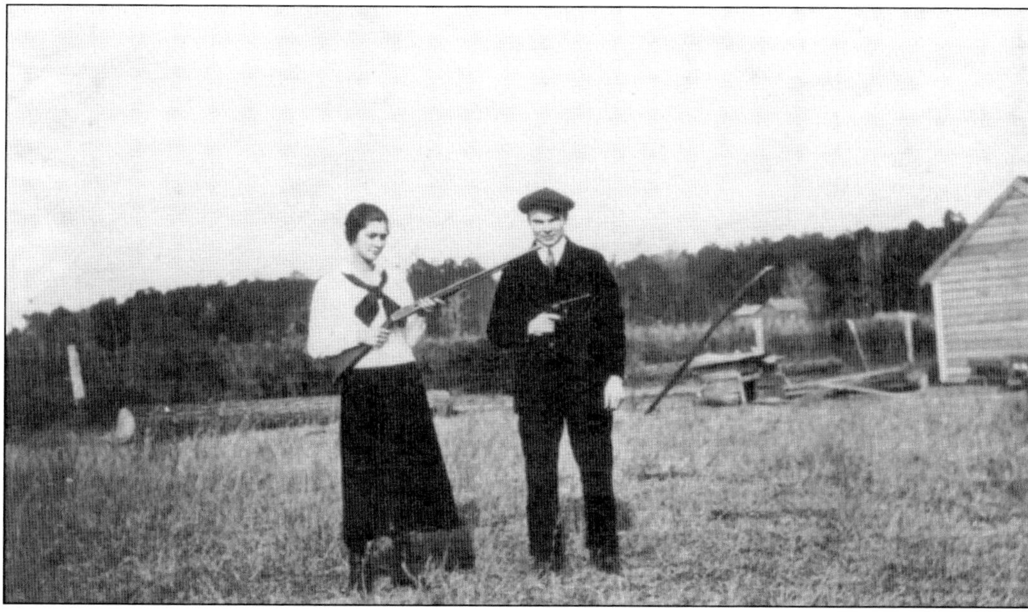

Bertie and Mack Sanderlin look like Bonnie Parker and Clyde Barrow in this staged photograph taken in Old Trap. Bertie and Mack were born around 1900, and both were still alive in Old Trap when the census taker came around in 1930, so they did not shoot each other, as might be implied by the theatrics in this photograph. (Courtesy of Joyce Mitchell Cuthrell.)

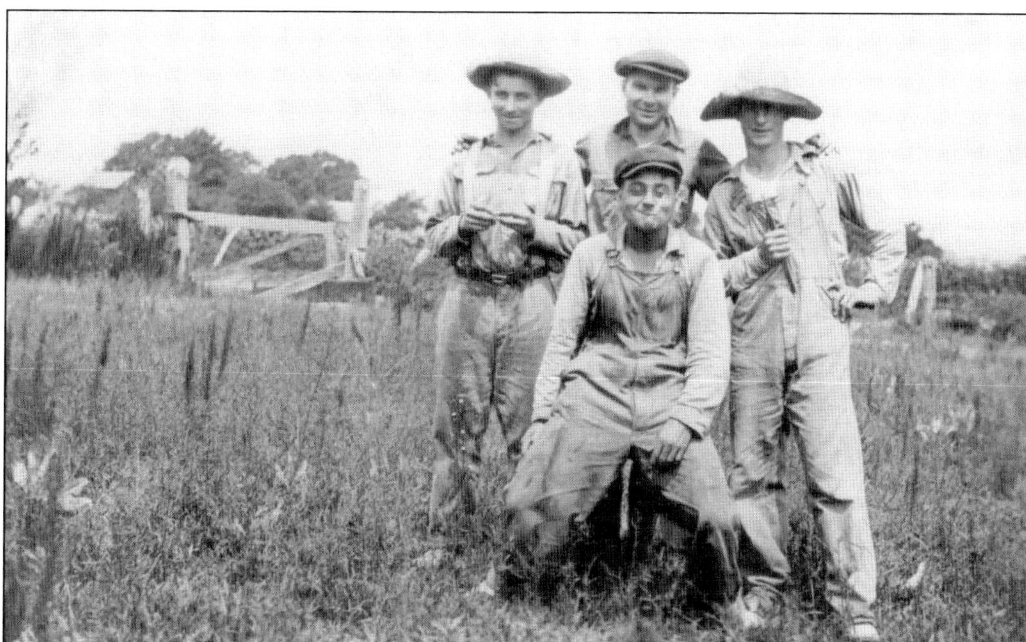

The farms of Camden County did not provide a wealth of opportunities for entertainment, and this group from Old Trap appears to be clowning around for the camera. Cameras and the means to develop the film were not readily available, and these fellows certainly did not miss the opportunity to make this frame count. (Courtesy of Joyce Mitchell Cuthrell.)

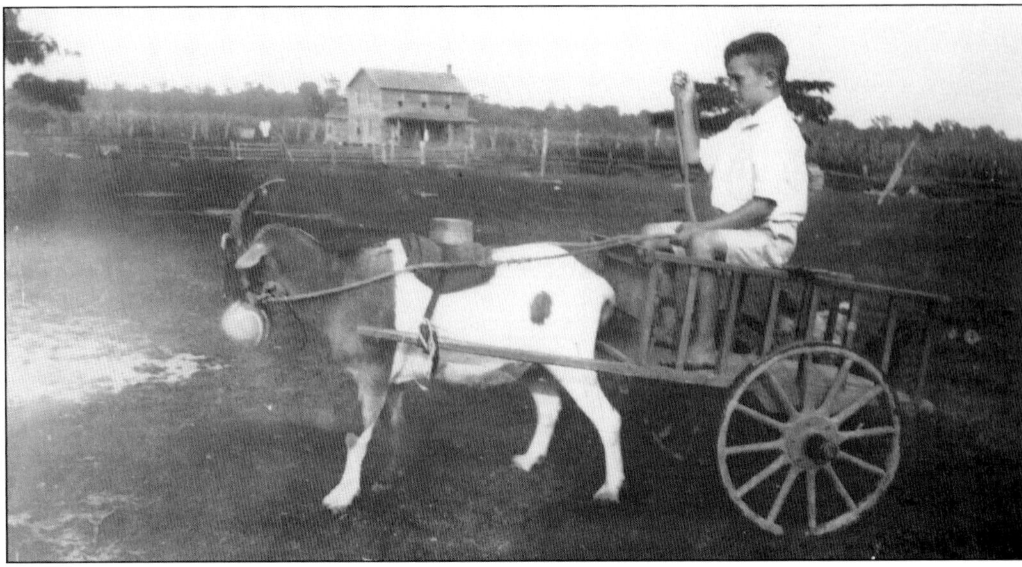

Willard Forbes's grandfather Joseph Mercer made him a goat cart with discarded wheels from the first car in Old Trap—a Maxwell—and Willard said this picture was "a fake" because the goat was not harnessed. The goat ate soybean shells, which killed him. Willard's father remarked, "You didn't play with him no way," to which Willard cried, "But, daddy, the goat didn't have to die! I loved my goat!" (Courtesy of Thelma Naomi Sawyer Forbes.)

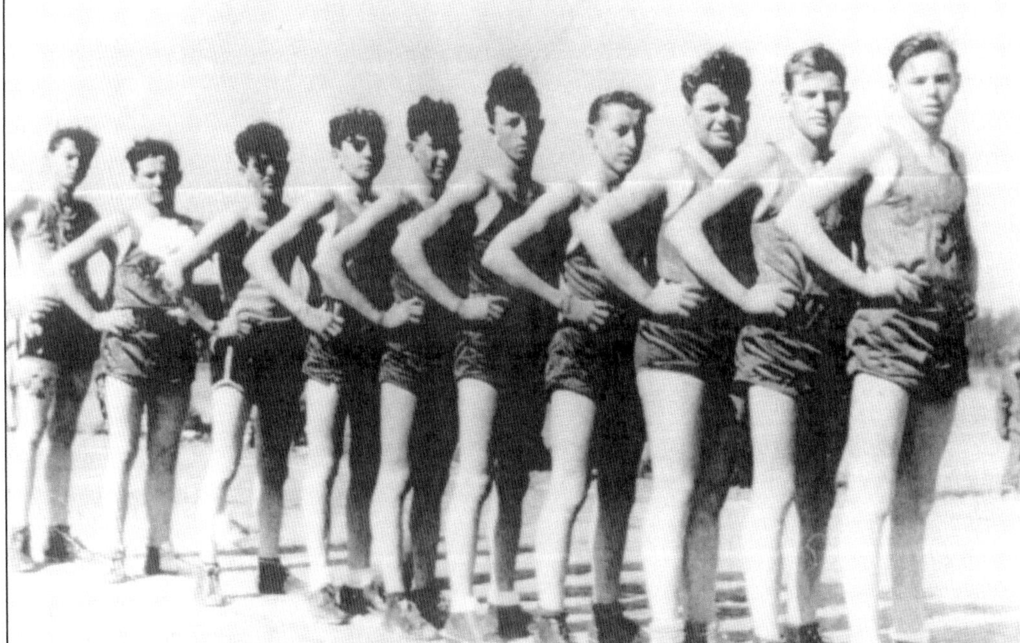

The last Shiloh High School basketball season was 1945. From left to right, the members of that last team are, Gid Forbes, William Sawyer, Nolan Riggs, Garland Pugh, McClellan Burgess, Jack Leary, Wilse Burgess, Daniel Forbes, Harvey Gregory Jr., and William Wilson. After 1945, high school students who had attended Shiloh High School went to Elizabeth City High School. (Courtesy of Alex Leary.)

Charles Tabb Hodges found this bear when it was tiny and brought it home. Hodges's daughter, Gertie, carried it in her apron pocket, and together, they raised Teddy. After he got too big, Hodges took him to the zoo in Norfolk. Gertie went to the zoo see him one Sunday, and after she left, he lay down, stopped eating, and died. Perhaps he grieved for her. (Courtesy of Anita Whitehurst.)

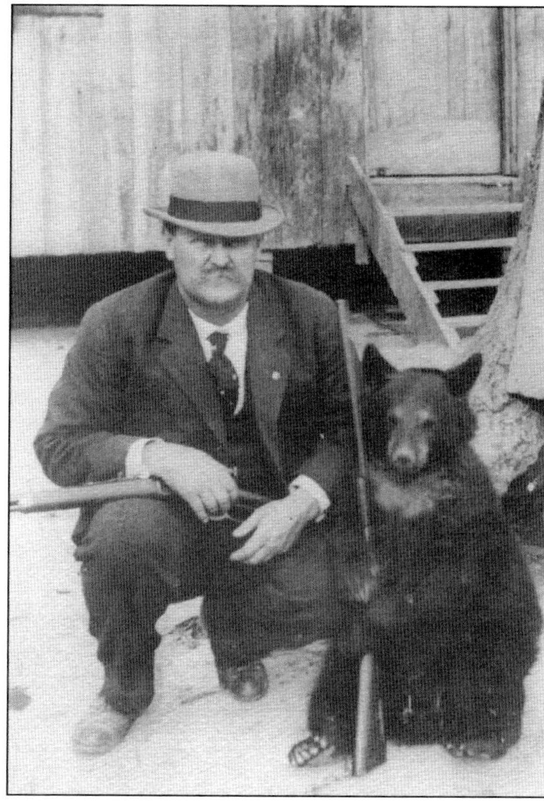

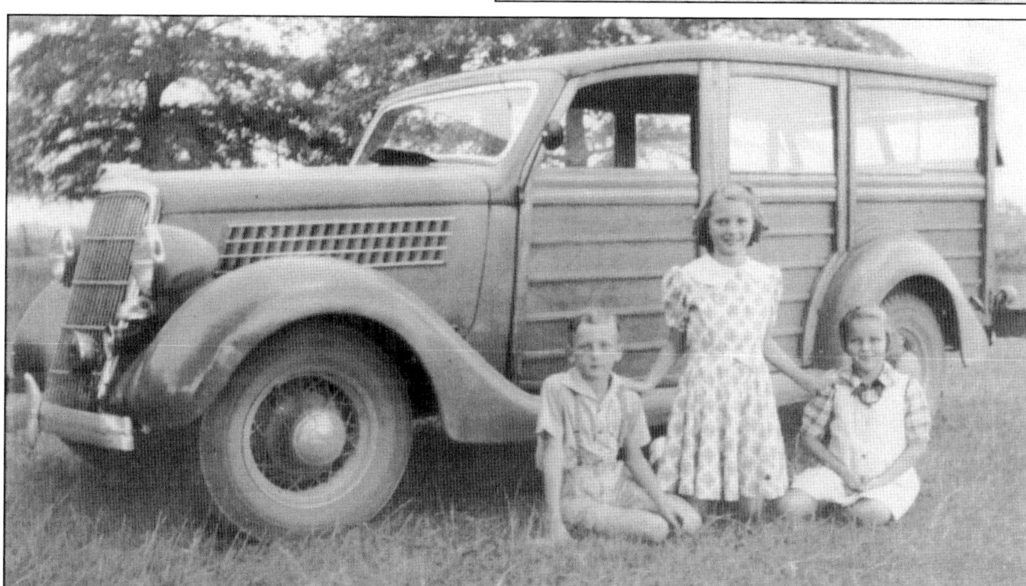

Taking a drive to picnic, fish, or visit friends and family was a good way to spend a Sunday afternoon. There is quite a distance between Old Trap and South Mills when traveling on unpaved roads, and opposite ends of the long narrow county were said to be like different countries. Pictured, from left to right, are Walter Barnard, Naomi Pugh, and Marjorie Barnard with Walter Pugh's car. (Courtesy of Anita Whitehurst.)

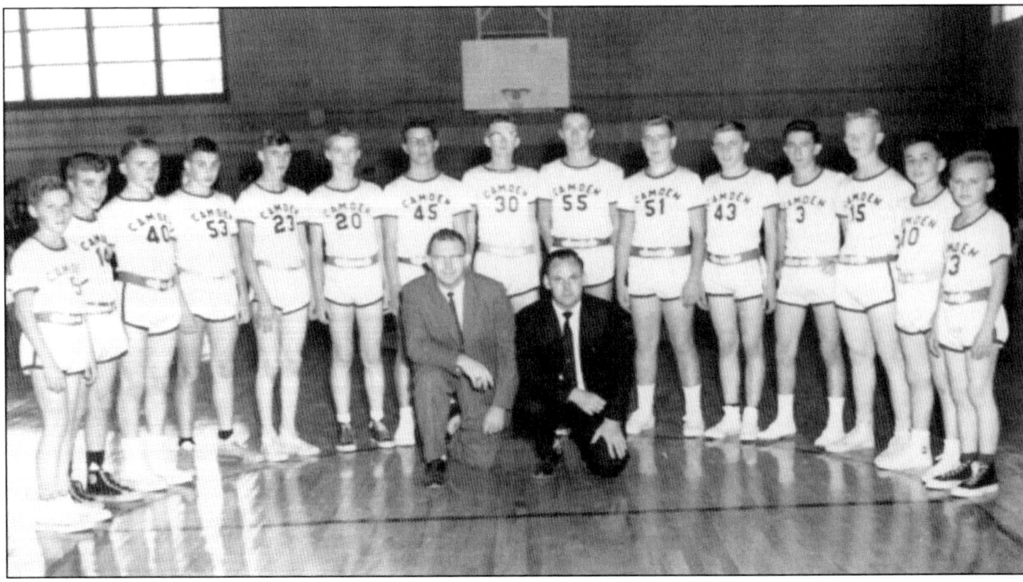

Kneeling in front of the Camden County junior varsity basketball team of 1958–1959 are coaches Bill Hooper and Dennis Basnight. The team members are, from left to right, Douglas McPherson, William Earl Brinkley, Jimmy West, Sonny Dozier, Lynn Howard Berry, Bobby Hurdle, Milford Jones, Jack Forehand, Alex Leary, Charles Walston, Eugene White, Phillip Leary, George Tarkington, Larry Lamb, and Ronnie Meiggs. (Courtesy of Anita Whitehurst.)

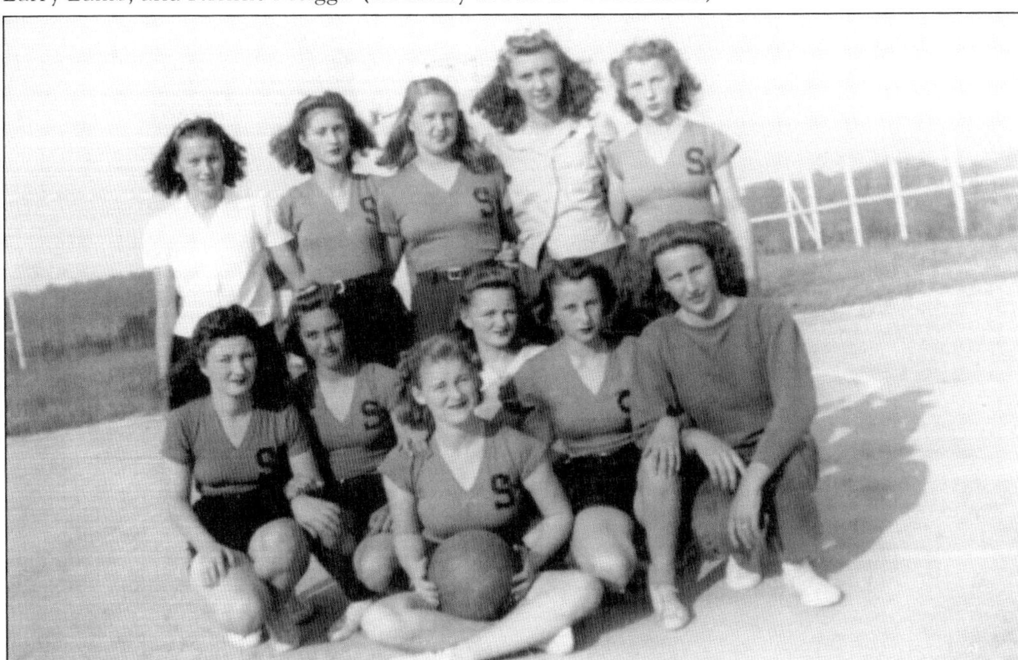

The Shiloh High School girls' basketball team in about 1943 is made up of, from left to right, (first row) Susie Bartlett; (second row) Alma Forbes, Lula Mae Becham, Susie Jones, Ida Mae Forbes, and Annie Ruth Berry; (third row) Doris Burgess, Mildred Kight, Ollie Mae Forbes, Doris Staples, and Eleanor Forbes. Since Shiloh High School had no gymnasium, all of the basketball games were played outside. (Courtesy of Anita Whitehurst.)

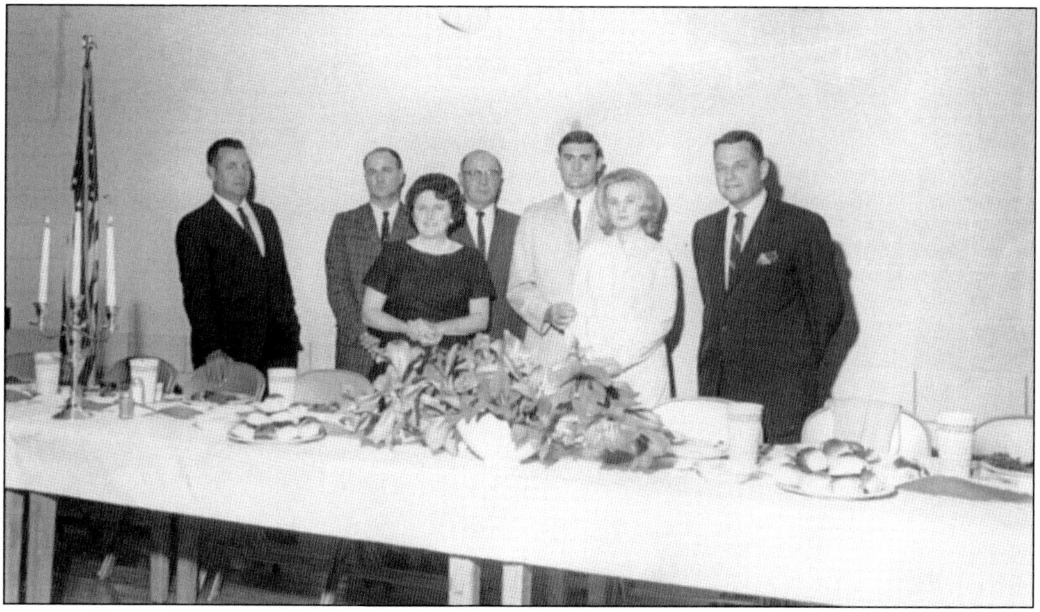

In 1965, citizens of Camden County gave a banquet at Grandy Primary School to honor Shelby Mansfield for his scholastic and football career while at North Carolina State University (NCSU). Earl Edwards, the NCSU football coach, and his staff were invited. From left to right are Bill Smaltz, Richard Mansfield, Rebecca Mansfield, Earl Edwards, Shelby, Linda Mansfield, and George Wood. (Courtesy of Linda Ann Mansfield.)

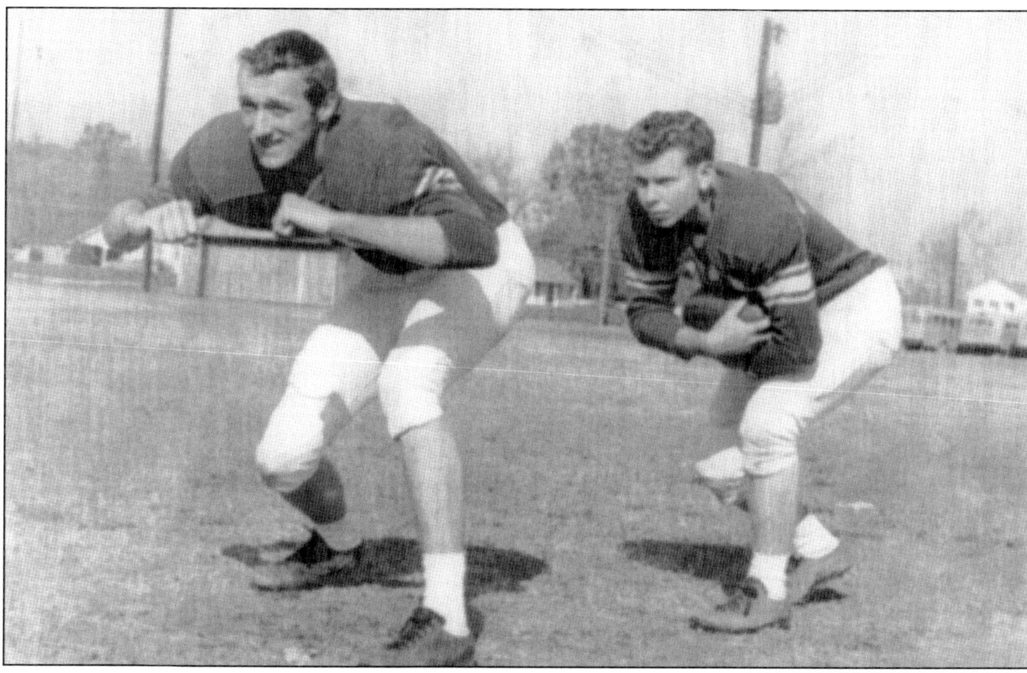

Alex Leary (left), who played end, and Garland Staples (right), fullback, are members of the 1960–1961 Camden County High School football team. After graduating from college, Leary returned to Camden County to teach and coach there for a few years. Leary always had a keen interest in history and is the present Camden County historian. (Courtesy of Alex Leary.)

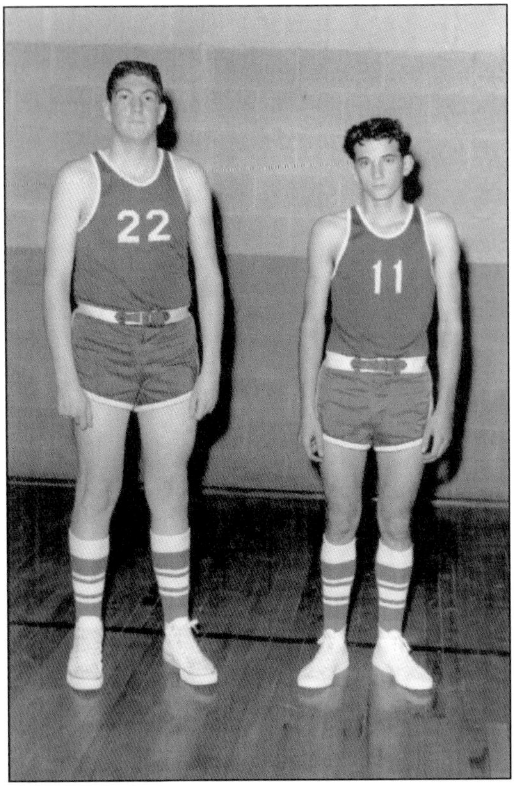

Pictured are Brian Forehand (left) and James Harrison, cocaptains of the 1961–1962 Camden County High School basketball team coached by Dennis Basnight. Camden County High School was a member of the Tidewater Conference, which also included Central, J.P. Knapp, Creswell, Columbia, Chowan, and Manteo High Schools. A top local historian, Forehand returned to Camden County in 1970 to teach and coach until he retired in 1997. (Courtesy of Brian Forehand.)

This picture of the seniors of the 1963 Camden County High School basketball team includes, from left to right, (first row) Joe Seymour, Chuck Brown, and Olin Leary; (second row) Harry McPherson, Brian Forehand, Robert Foster, and coach Dennis Basnight. Seymour was inducted into the National Softball Hall of Fame in 1986 with a career batting average of .620, more than 3,000 homers, and over 100 game MVP awards in the 1970s and 1980s. (Courtesy of Brian Forehand.)

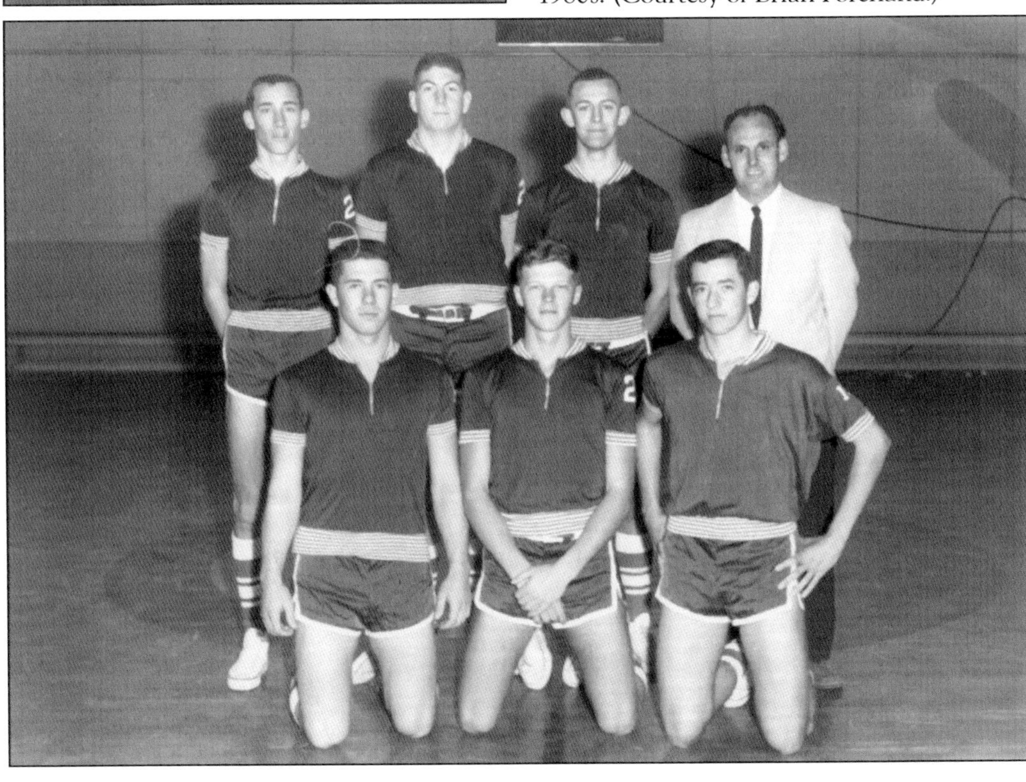

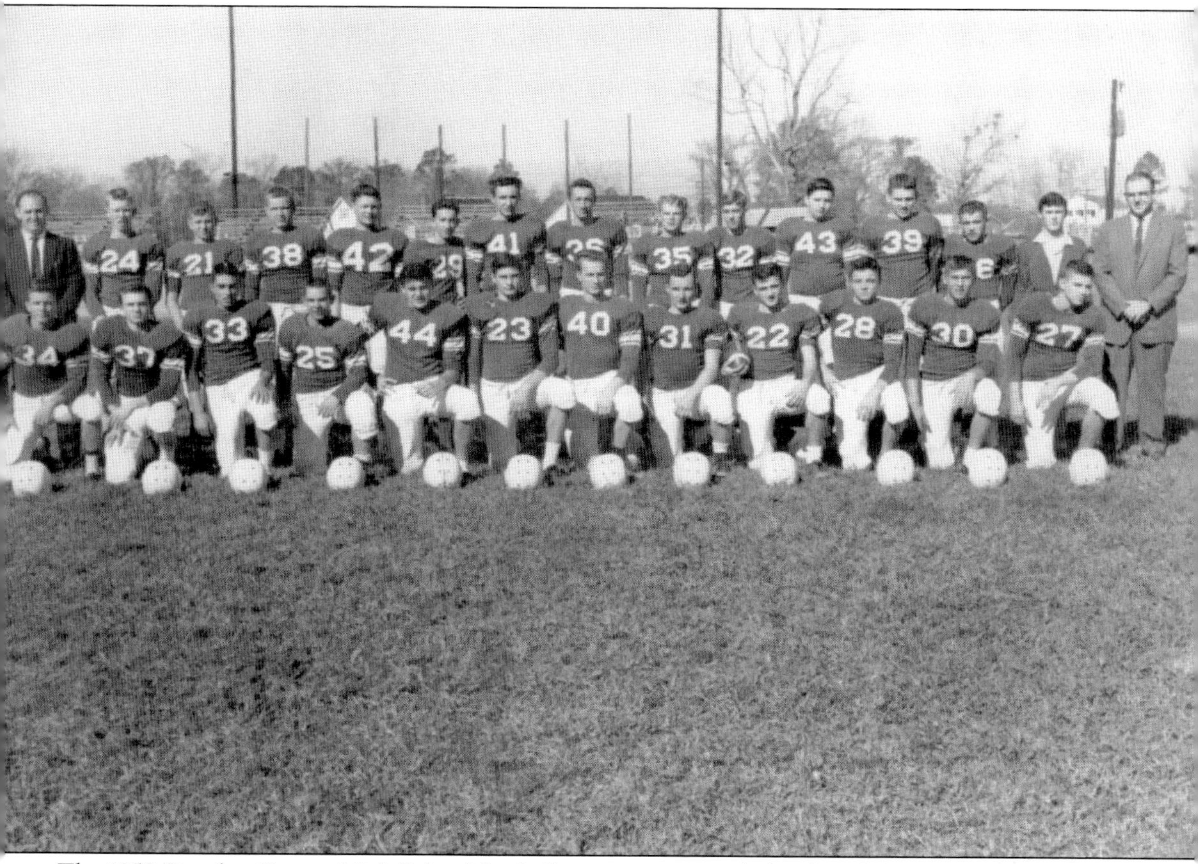

The 1958 Camden County High School football team pictures includes, from left to right, (first row) Arthur Forbes, Wilson Winslow, Billy Games, Billy Wilder, Claymon Sawyer, Shelby Mansfield, Billy Banks, Orville House, Richard Mansfield, Jimmy Seymour, Douglas Cartwright, and Ray Hollowell; (second row) coach Dennis Basnight, George Tarkington, Charles Williams, Charles Walston, Glenn White, Phillip Leary, Harry Coppersmith, Alex Leary, Staley Paul, Lynn Howard Berry, Billy Jones, Charlie Pierce, Russell Boseman, manager D.K. Duncan, and coach William Hooper. (Courtesy of Alex Leary.)

Consistent with our mission to preserve history on a local level, this book was printed in South Carolina on American-made paper and manufactured entirely in the United States. Products carrying the accredited Forest Stewardship Council (FSC) label are printed on 100 percent FSC-certified paper.

MADE IN THE USA